SPARTACUS

SPARTACUS

THE MYTH AND THE MAN

M.J. TROW

SUTTON PUBLISHING

First published in the United Kingdom in 2006 by
Sutton Publishing Limited · Phoenix Mill
Thrupp · Stroud · Gloucestershire · GL5 2BU

British Library Cataloguing in Publication Data
A catalogue record for this book is available from the British Library.

ISBN 0-7509-3907-9

Typeset in 11/14.5pt Sabon.
Typesetting and origination by
Sutton Publishing Limited.
Printed and bound in England by
J.H. Haynes & Co. Ltd, Sparkford.

Contents

For
Issur Danielovitch Demsky
– who brought Spartacus to life.

Acknowledgements

Many thanks to everyone who has helped in the production of this book: to my editor Jaqueline Mitchell and her team at Sutton; to my agent Andrew Lownie for his friendship and encouragement; to Professor Brent D. Shaw of the University of Pennsylvania for permission to quote extracts from his translations in *Spartacus and the Slave Wars* (Bedford/St Martin's, 2001); to all those who have allowed us to use their images; to Taliesin Trow, archaeologist and film buff; and as always to Carol Trow, whose own career as a writer is constantly being interrupted by mine!

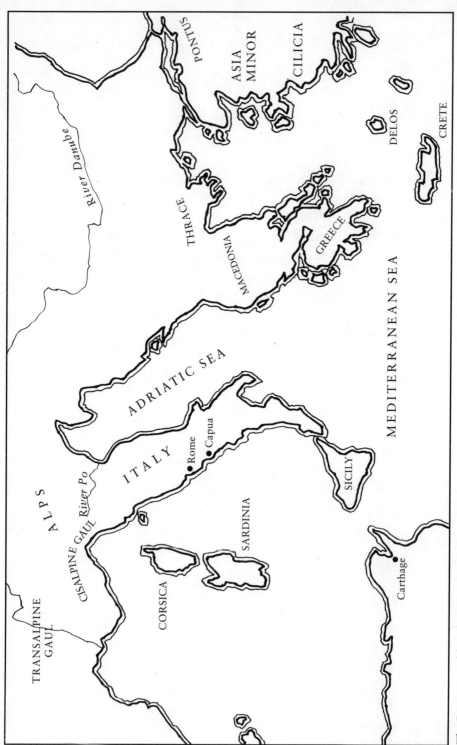

The Roman world at the time of Spartacus.

River Po

ADRIATIC SEA

PICENUM

ETRURIA

River Tiber

Rome

Garganus
Mts

APULIA

CAMPANIA

VIA APPIA

Capua

Forum
Annii

Brundisium

Vesuvius

Nola

Pompeii

Nares

Metapontum

Nuceria Lucania

Thurii

VIA ANNIA

MEDITERRANEAN

BRUTTIUM

SEA

LINE OF CRASSUS'
FORTIFICATIONS

RHEGIUM

STRAITS OF MESSINA

The Spartacus War, 73–71BC.

ONE

'I Am Spartacus'

The battle is over. From the bloody valley, a riderless horse breaks away, exhausted, its flanks flecked red and white. It is dawn; a new dawn, empty, bitter. The dead lie in heaps, weapons cold and still, like the men who used them. Faces are turning black in the already climbing heat. Wives lie for the last time with their husbands; babies cling with dead lips to the breasts of their mothers. There is a deep stillness here, the stillness of death. Eyes that see no more stare at the sky; hands still grip the hilts of swords.

High in the cloudless blue of another Campanian day, the crows wheel, scanning the field below, the corpses, torn and ripped in the crevices of the ravines.

From somewhere in this slaughterhouse comes a baby's cry. A new birth. A new beginning.

Two figures wander the dead, picking their way through the carnage. The taller of them, in his beautiful, white, muscled cuirass and his carefully curled hair, is Marcus Licinius Crassus, the richest man in Rome. This is his victory. These are his dead. His cold, dark eyes dart everywhere. He is looking for a body; among those thousands of bodies, he is looking for just one. He turns to the legatus at his elbow: 'Have we account of the numbers?'

'We have not made the final count, sir.'

Dead lie on top of dead. Legionary locked in battle with slave. Defender of Rome with the scum of the earth; the lowest, the worst. Men. Women. Children. Tall Gauls with auburn hair from across the far mountains; stocky Marsians from the Apennines; fierce fighters from distant Thrace.

On the slope of the hill a tribune gallops over corpses with a knot of cavalrymen at his heels. They rein in their horses as the fierce sun *burns the leather on their feet, the iron on their shoulders, the horsehair plumes on their heads. The horsemen fan out, joining others in a ring of steel around the defeated.*

They sit chained in huddled circles, exhausted, broken, caked in mud and blood. Old sweat has run its rivulets down their careworn faces. They barely move as they hear the tribune shout: 'I bring a message from Marcus Licinius Crassus, commander of the army of Italy. By command of his most worshipful Excellency, your lives are to be spared.'

Now the defeated move, lolling heads rise, backs square, each man searches the face of his comrade. What sort of trick is this? And what price? Each of them has heard the empty promises of Romans before.

'Slaves you were,' the tribune does not need to remind them, 'and slaves you remain. But the dreadful penalty of crucifixion has been set aside on the single condition that you identify the body or living person of the slave called Spartacus.'

The chains rattle for an instant as the words sink home. Then silence. For a moment no one stirs. Crassus waits, the haughty patrician, eyebrow arcing in anticipation, upper lip curling. He has been hunting this man and his rabble for months.

On the hillside a ragged slave struggles to his feet, bloody like the others; unbowed like the others. But before he can speak, another stands beside him and shouts, 'I am Spartacus!' Then another, on a further hillock, is also on his feet, shoulders broad, voice defiant: 'I am Spartacus!' And a third. And a fourth. And soon the whole cohort are on their feet, forcing their tired limbs into action once more and they roar with all the passion and the hatred of their desperate position, echoing and re-echoing around the hills of Campania: 'I am Spartacus!'

Those three words are among the most famous in film history. And in reality they were never spoken. At least, not in the way we hear them on the big screen. They are the invention of a fascinating collection of men whose task was to recreate a legend; to put flesh and blood and clothes on an idea.

'Spartacus was a real man,' wrote the actor/producer whose brainchild the film of *Spartacus* was, 'but if you look him up in the history books, you find only a short paragraph about him. Rome was ashamed; this man had almost destroyed them. They wanted to bury him. I was intrigued with the story of Spartacus the slave, dreaming of the death of slavery, driving into the armour of Rome the wedge that would eventually destroy her.'[1]

The actor/producer was Issur Danielovitch Demsky, the son of an immigrant Russian-Jewish ragman from Amsterdam, New York, who burst on to the Hollywood scene as Kirk Douglas. The chapter on 'The Wars of Spartacus' from his autobiography is almost as gripping as the film itself, and Douglas's account repays the telling here. If Douglas, who came from impoverished Eastern European peasant stock, was Spartacus, then surely Universal Studios and the whole edifice of 'Tinseltown' with its money, its opulence, its vulgarity and its odd streak of cruelty was the Republic of Rome.

In 1957 there was already a film of Spartacus' life in the offing. It was to star Yul Brynner, like Douglas a major Hollywood star. It was based on the novel *The Gladiators*, written by Arthur Koestler, a hands-on communist who wrote the book at the end of the Spanish Civil War, in which he had been spying on the Nationalist Forces under Francisco Franco. Douglas's version was to be developed from Howard Fast's book *Spartacus*, and the race was on. Fast's book, written as a novel in flashback in the aftermath of the slave revolt, saw the gladiator as a hero of the people. That was because Fast himself, the son of a New York factory worker, became a member of the American Communist Party in 1943 and virtually all his works, fiction and non-fiction, had a distinctly leftist basis. As Douglas tells it, having heard that *The Gladiators* had a vast budget of $5.5 million, he sent a telegram to Arthur Karim, head of the vast United Artists Studios – 'We are spending five million five hundred thousand and two dollars on Spartacus. Your move. Kirk.'[2]

'Film is a battleground,' wrote director Sam Fuller. 'Love, hate, action, death. In a word, emotion.'[3] Virtually all of this range of human experience came into play in the spring of 1958. Karim was persuaded to invest in Douglas's project and Brynner's United Artists version was consigned to the dustbin of history. But it would not be easy going. Howard Fast's screenplay was, in Douglas's words, 'a disaster, unusable . . . It was just characters spouting ideas; speeches on two legs.' Douglas turned instead to Dalton Trumbo, a screenplay writer with a reputation for speed. On an upright manual typewriter, his rate was an astonishing forty pages a day. Bringing in another writer to adapt an author's book was problematic in itself, but the situation was further complicated because of Fast's and Trumbo's political views. While they were both communists, they did not see eye to eye. According to biographer John Baxter, 'Fast thought Trumbo a cocktail party Communist,'[4] whereas Trumbo's view on Fast was that he was a fanatic. Writing under the pseudonym of 'Sam Johnson', Trumbo began the *Spartacus* script at breakneck speed, often writing on a tray while soaking in the bath with his pet parrot perched on his shoulder.

And the writing was not Douglas's only problem. Clearly, he had earmarked the role of the slave-turned-gladiator for himself and he wanted the celebrated Shakespearean actor and producer Laurence Olivier as his nemesis, the proconsul Marcus Licinius Crassus. Olivier was indeed interested, but he not only wanted to play Spartacus himself, he also wanted to direct! Douglas was chancing his arm by pitching the film to two other actors with egos almost as monstrous as Olivier's – Charles Laughton and Peter Ustinov. Laughton, asked to play the combative senator Gracchus, was not impressed. 'I glanced at the script,' he told Douglas, 'Really, a piece of shit.'[5] That, however, was a typical piece of Laughton theatricality. He needed the money and agreed to take the part. He was also an American citizen by this time and on hand in Hollywood. Ustinov agreed too, with considerable suggestions as to how the script – especially his role as Lentulus Batiatus the *lanista* – could be improved. In the event, both men did their best to steal the film – and almost succeeded.

Even the love interest in *Spartacus* ran into difficulties. A scattering of Hollywood lovelies had already turned down the role of the slave-gladiator's love Varinia, and the final choice was the beautiful German actress Sabina Bethumann. Unfortunately, it would be several weeks into filming before it became evident that she was not very good in the part. In the end the English actress Jean Simmons, who had already turned it down, agreed to accept the role.

Shooting on the film began at the end of January 1959, and Douglas soon had problems with his director, Anthony Mann. According to Douglas, it was Universal Studios who begged him to remove Mann on the grounds that he 'wasn't right for the movie'.[6] There seems to have been an undercurrent of conspiracy going on between Mann and Ustinov. 'You have to be careful,' Ustinov quipped at dinner parties, 'not to act too well'[7] in a Kirk Douglas movie.

Shooting had barely started and there were no directors. Douglas hired the virtually unknown 31-year-old Stanley Kubrick, who had directed the First World War drama *Paths of Glory*. If Mann had artistic differences with Douglas, Kubrick would often prove impossible. As Kubrick's biographer John Baxter tells it, the director was 'soon taking charge of any part of the film that wasn't nailed down'.[8] Kubrick himself was not impressed, either with Fast's novel or Trumbo's screenplay. 'It had everything,' he said, with his infuriating passionless stare, 'but a good story.'[9] Within days, Jean Simmons needed surgery and Douglas had to change his shooting schedule. The runaway slave Antoninus, played by Tony Curtis, also had to delay his scenes as a result of a tennis accident. As Douglas sums it up in *The Ragman's Son*: 'Jean Simmons had been out sick for over a month; Tony Curtis was in a wheelchair; I was in the middle of an epic movie, written by a blacklisted ex-convict, directed by a 29-year-old [*sic*]. I was months over schedule, 250 percent over budget.'[10]

The epic film, hugely popular from the 1920s to the present, reached its zenith in the 1960s. 'The epic appears,' wrote John Cary[11] of the film's antecedents, 'as the first literary genre in the cultural history of the world, the final stage of the arch folk tale and the tribal chronicle.' The epic film is 'a matter of language, not of

religious, patriotic or cultural fervour.'[12] What was new about this
film was that it was the first sword and sandal epic that did not have
an awestruck religious theme. Its central character pre-dates Christ
by two generations. Dalton Trumbo made 1,400 pages of rewrites
and Stanley Kubrick's first cut was an impossible six hours long.

Composer Alex North worked on the film's music. North, too,
had a leftist take on life and there are those who say he deliberately
wove strains of the Communist 'Internationale' into the various
themes. His problem, like that of any composer attempting to
recreate a Roman mood, is that we have virtually no idea what
Roman music sounded like:

> I strove for a barbaric quality, which was exemplified in the cold,
> brutal inhumanity of Crassus. There is also a simple, universal
> theme for the slaves, a liberation theme after their breakout from
> the gladiator school and typical period music when the slave army
> trains and prepares for battle, which uses an odd 5/8 metre, early
> Greek style, never written contemporarily.

The whole venture cost a staggering $12 million, then the most
expensive film Hollywood had ever produced. 'Who cares?' Douglas
famously asked. 'If *Spartacus* is a thrilling experience, twelve million
dollars is a drop in the bucket. If not, twelve dollars is too much.'

What was the result? Kubrick himself removed the sentimental
scenes of the slave army at play, with dancing children, cuddling old
couples and country crafts. Then the censors went to work. The film
first saw the light of day on 6 October 1960 and the trade preview
audiences were nauseated by the mutilations in the final battle
sequence. Pressure from the Catholic Legion of Decency ensured
that most of these were removed. Most famously, the seduction
scene between Olivier and Tony Curtis was removed. Douglas
wrote, 'It was very subtle; nothing explicit. The censors weren't
quite sure it was about homosexuality, but just in case, they wanted
it out . . . It was just another way Romans abused the slaves.'[13]

Not until 1994, when the 'director's cut' restoration by Jimmy
Harris appeared, would some of these scenes be reinstated.[14]

What is today regarded as a cinematic classic was received with less than exhilaration at the time, but an altogether more interesting question is how far Douglas *et al.* managed to get under the skin of a man whose factual details barely fill ten pages of history. George Macdonald Fraser encapsulates it well: 'Folk like Spartacus are not to be understood. He had a genius which enabled him to organize and hold together and transport a great slave army and its families and at the same time outgeneral and outfight the greatest power in the world in its own heartland; there has never been anything like him.'[15]

It was the columnist Hedda Hopper, maker and breaker of Hollywood careers, who left the most damning comment: 'It has acres of dead people, more blood and gore than you ever saw in your whole life . . . That story was sold to Universal from a book written by a Commie and the screenscript was written by a Commie, so don't go and see it.'[16]

Hopper was backed by thousands of members of the American Legion, the world's largest veterans' organisation, who protested loudly against 'the renewed invasion of American filmdom by Soviet-indoctrinated artists'.[17] To understand their attitude, we have to understand the America of the 1940s and '50s, and the role of the slave Spartacus in it.

In a carefully staged publicity stunt, at the end of the Second World War American GIs were photographed smiling, shaking hands with soldiers of the Red Army in a war-torn, newly beaten Germany, the pavements of Berlin ripped and crumbling beneath their feet. Within weeks, however, the old antipathy of capitalism versus communism, Capitol Hill versus the Kremlin, began to emerge. Within a year of the end of the war, on 5 March 1946, the former British prime minister and war hero Winston Churchill gave a speech in Fulton, Missouri. 'An iron curtain,' he said, 'has come down across Europe.' And the shock waves of that curtain's metal descent reverberated across the Atlantic.

Marxism, once a fashionable literary debating ground for American intellectuals, now became a threat. There were 'Reds under the bed' and everyone's virtue was in the spotlight. Spearheading the attack was the shady junior senator from

Wisconsin, Joseph McCarthy. Anxious to retain the Senate seat which he held by his fingernails, McCarthy launched into a communist witch-hunt in the spring of 1950, waving in his hand a list of fifty-seven officers of the State Department who were members of the American Communist Party. Much of the 'dirt' on these people had been fed to McCarthy by his friend, the rabid neo-Fascist transvestite J. Edgar Hoover of the Federal Bureau of Investigation.

'McCarthyism' struck a nerve across America. 'Attacking him [McCarthy] in this state,' wrote the *Boston Post*, 'is regarded as a certain method of committing suicide.'[18] Intellectuals like Arthur Miller were forced to take oblique sideswipes at him, as in Miller's play *The Crucible*, which dealt with *actual* witch-hunts in the Massachusetts of 1692. Over 30,000 books were removed from American libraries by McCarthy's staff on the grounds that they were written by 'communists, pro-communists, former communists and anti-anti communists'.[19] The House Un-American Activities Committee, the government instrument used to investigate those with unacceptable political beliefs, turned its spotlight on the motion picture industry, and the *Spartacus* screenwriter Dalton Trumbo was one of its early victims. Most of the Hollywood studios, fearing government pressure, had already passed the Waldorf Amendment in 1947, promising not to hire anyone with communist leanings. A host of stars including John Wayne, Ward Bond, Gary Cooper and Ronald Reagan testified before tribunals and named names. One of the names was Trumbo's.

He appeared before the Committee on 28 October 1947 along with nine others who collectively came to be known as the Hollywood Ten or the Unfriendly Ten. They all sought refuge under the First Amendment of the Constitution and refused to give answers in the face of the probing malevolence of their inquisitors; the result was contempt of court and ten months in jail. When Trumbo got out, he was blacklisted, but managed to eke out a living at $2,500 a script, using a variety of aliases. On the film of *Spartacus* he was 'Sam Johnson', meeting secretly at Kirk Douglas's house and receiving cheques under pseudonyms.

Even though McCarthy eventually overreached himself by attacking the then untouchable American army and infuriating President Dwight Eisenhower, the 'reds under the bed' panic persisted. The discredited McCarthy, an alcoholic homosexual, lost his political power base and died of cirrhosis of the liver in May 1957. Despite the fall of McCarthy, however, there was still a great deal of anti-communist hysteria in American public life.

According to Kubrick's biographer, the decision to use a blacklisted communist on *Spartacus* was a calculated one. In any case, the gaff was quickly blown. The McCarthyite Walter Winchell broadcast to the nation in March 1959 that not only was Trumbo writing the *Spartacus* screenplay, but he was being paid $50,000 to do it. Kirk Douglas, tired of all the hypocrisy and subterfuge, left a pass at the gates of Universal Studios in the name of Dalton Trumbo. 'The blacklist,' he wrote, 'was broken.'[20] In fact, it was technically broken by Jules Dassim, a Hollywood exile who wrote – and was openly credited for – the thriller *Rififi* in 1956; perhaps as a 'foreign' film this did not count.

James Dalton Trumbo first appeared in print in the 1930s, a defining decade in which the forces of Marxism and fascism were squaring up to each other for European, perhaps world, domination. After a series of articles, novels and screenplays, Trumbo joined the Communist Party in 1943. The House Un-American Activities Committee may have imprisoned him, but it did not break his spirit. Many years later, he wrote to a friend: 'Whatever else may be said of Communists and the goals they pursued . . . those who joined the Party were animated by a sincere desire to change the world and make it better . . . [they] were good people.'[21] He also spoke wisely when he said, 'The blacklist was a time of evil . . . it will do no good to search for villains or heroes or saints or devils because there were none; there were only victims.'

But if Trumbo's career was resurrected as a result of *Spartacus*, at the time he had to contend with the novel's author, Howard Fast. The novelist exploded at the work of another screenwriter even before he knew who it was. Fast's novel, with its long speeches and 'plonky' explanations of the Roman way of life was, according to Kubrick's biographer, 'a piece of Marxist historiography, contrasting the rival visions of mankind held by Spartacus, the unlettered immigrant slave, and therefore archetypal humanist; and his nemesis Crassus, the cultivated, decadent and ambitious Roman general and potential dictator . . .'[22] 'A time would come,' wrote Fast at the end of his novel in June 1951, 'when Rome would be torn down – not by slaves alone, but by slaves and serfs and peasants and by free barbarians who joined them.'

The tearing down of an all-powerful capitalist state was something American society could not condone, even in literature.

Fast spent three months in prison for pleading the First Amendment and *Spartacus* was published in 1951 under the auspices of his own publishing house, the Blue Heron Press. More of a committed 'revolutionary' than Trumbo, Fast had been instrumental in building a hospital in France for communist casualties of the Spanish Civil War. His prison term made him even more committed and he 'began more deeply than ever before to comprehend the full agony and hopelessness of the underclass', as he later recalled.[23]

Even Kirk Douglas found the man impossible. 'Howard was an incredible egomaniac, the only person who was always right. Everybody else was wrong,'[24] he recalled.

'Everybody else' included a large section of the American people. In the introduction to the 1996 reprint of *Spartacus*, Fast wrote:

The country was as close to a police state as it had ever been. J. Edgar Hoover . . . took on the role of a petty dictator. The fear of Hoover and his file on thousands of Liberals permeated the country. That fear and that persecution reached the publishers. Little, Brown and Company, at first so enthusiastic about the project, turned it down, as did seven others. Eventually, George Hecht of Doubleday, disgusted by the cowardice of his editorial board, suggested to Fast that he publish the book himself and promised to place an order for 600 copies.

In the event, it sold 40,000 in hardback and millions more after 'the terror' (Fast's words) was over. He wrote in the introduction to the film's souvenir brochure:

Here is the story of Spartacus, who led the great slave revolt against Rome. I wrote this novel because I considered it an important story for the times in which we live. Not in the mechanical sense of historical parallels, but because there is hope and strength to be taken from such a story about the age-old fight for freedom – and because Spartacus lived not for one time of man, but for all times of man. I wrote it to give hope and courage to those who would read it, and in the process of writing it, I gained hope and courage myself.[25]

'Not for one time of man, but for all times of man.' If Kirk Douglas turned Spartacus into a film because he was fascinated by him and if Trumbo and Fast had their own agenda, so too did the German revolutionaries Karl Liebknecht and Rosa Luxemburg. The guns had barely cooled along the shell-pocked trenches of the Western Front and Germany was in ruins. The Kaiser, Wilhelm II Hohenzollern, fled in a rather sedate motorcade to Holland and the new government was spearheaded first by Prince Max of Baden, then by the Socialist Democratic Party coalition of Friedrich Ebert. This was a provisional government which met on 25 November 1918 to discuss the creation of a national assembly and launch a new Germany. But democracy was new to the German people. Indeed, the notion of nationhood was new – 'Germany' was born in Bismarck's blood and iron of 1871 and it had just lost a crippling war. Its once proud army had been decimated by huge battlefield losses and the deadlier grip of influenza – the plague of the Spanish Lady. Its navy refused to sail against the British. Prices were rocketing. Armed men roamed the streets with rifles cocked and murder in their hearts. The focus of most of the violence, born out of the frustration and despair of defeat, was to be found in Munich, Bavaria, where a communist group had seized power under Kurt Eisner, and in the old Prussian capital of Berlin. By the end of 1918, machine-gun smoke drifted across the city, banners danced in the streets and heads were broken in running battles. A month later, a rapid series of revolts broke out, most of them orchestrated by a radical left-wing group who called themselves the Spartacus League. Its leaders were Liebknecht and Luxemburg.

Karl Liebknecht was the son of the co-founder of the Social Democratic Party (SDP) when that group was set up in 1891. A lawyer, originally from Leipzig, Liebknecht had become converted to Marxism at university and regularly defended clients accused of smuggling socialist propaganda into Russia, itself on the eve of revolution. In 1912 he was elected to the Reichstag, the German parliament, and grimly opposed the more 'liberal' elements in the SDP. Opposing Germany's entry into the Great War, Liebknecht and a handful of others formed the underground *Spartakusbund*, publishing their pacifist, socialist views in a series of Spartacus letters. Arrested for attempting to turn the conflict into a war of revolution, Liebknecht was conscripted into the army and served on the ghastly Eastern Front, burying the frozen dead in iron-hard clay because he refused to fight. The Spartacus League held its first open demonstration on the streets of Berlin on 1 May 1916 and Liebknecht and others were imprisoned, not to be released until Prince Max von Baden's political amnesty in October 1918.

Liebknecht's comrade Rosa Luxemburg was a stronger influence on the Spartacus League, however. 'She was undoubtedly a much stronger character than Liebknecht. She was the real "man" in the Spartacus Movement',[26] wrote the *New York Times* in January 1919.

A Jew from Zamosch in Poland, 'Red Rosa' was in pain for most of her life, hobbling on a deformed leg. Friend of exiled Russian revolutionaries, she found herself imprisoned in Warsaw for her outspoken advocacy of state overthrow. It was somehow natural that she and Liebknecht should join forces when they both left the too-moderate SDP and Luxemburg penned the 'Junius Pamphlet', which was the bible of the Spartacus League.

For all that 'Red Rosa' may have been on an intellectual par with the far more famous revolutionaries Lenin and Trotsky, Berlin was not Moscow and the German people not a mass of peasantry, downtrodden for centuries. It seems likely that the clashes in the Unter den Linden were spontaneous eruptions of fury and impotence, but they left Liebknecht and Luxemburg with a dilemma. They knew the timing for successful revolution was wrong, but they could not ignore the fact that it was *their* people on the streets and decided, probably against their better judgement, to back it. The real Spartacus probably faced a similar dilemma in the summer of 71 BC, when making the decision to fight or not.

When it was all over, the *New York Times* wrote, 'In choosing the name (Spartacists) the German leader (Liebknecht) forgot to take into consideration that similar as he thought the present situation to Roman times, the movement of the original Spartacus has attached to it besides the glory of the temporary victories of the oppressed, the stigma of ultimate defeat.'[27]

There was a deep irony in the contrast between the rhetoric of revolution and its debasing on the streets. The *Spartacus Manifesto*, quoted in the *New York Times* at the end of November 1918, railed that:

Europe has been ruined through the infamous international murder. Twelve million bodies cover the gruesome scenes of the imperialistic crime. The flower of youth and the best men of the peoples have been mowed down . . . Humanity is threatened with the most dreadful famine, a stoppage of the entire mechanism of production, plagues and degeneration.[28]

And Franz Schoenberner had his tongue only a *little* in his cheek when he described the street-fighting in Berlin – 'the masses hurrying for cover under machine-gun fire dutifully avoiding taking the short-cut over the lawn . . .' and 'at regular intervals, marked by flag signals, the civil war was stopped briefly every half-hour so that the traffic through Friedrichstrasse could proceed as usual.'[29]

Eccentric battleground or not, Berlin was a dangerous place in the winter of 1918/19 and Chancellor Ebert left town for the safer climes of Weimar. In his wake, he gave orders for General Gustav Noske, 'the bulldog of counter-revolution', to put the Spartacus rising down; in a sense, he was the Marcus Licinius Crassus of his day. This he did, but in *his* wake came the drunken, fascistic soldiery of the *Freikorps*, smashing socialists of all degrees and murdering both Liebknecht and Luxemburg. Like Spartacus himself, they died without trial for their crimes.

The official verdict ran like this. Both were arrested on 15 January 1919 by soldiers of General Walther von Lüttuitz's Horse Guards Division. An 'unknown assailant' had hit Liebknecht on the head from behind when the car taking him to prison developed engine trouble. He was shot while trying to escape. Luxemburg was attacked by an anti-socialist mob in the Eden Hotel and her *Freikorps* escort bundled her, unconscious, into a car. As it drove off, an unknown assailant (Berlin was clearly crawling with them) leapt on to the running boards and shot Luxemburg with his pistol. At the Landwehr Canal, a mob forced the car to stop and, screaming 'This is Rosa!', dragged her body away.

The reality was different. Liebknecht was held in a room at the Eden Hotel under guard by Captain Waldemar Pabst. He was rifle-butted twice in the head and his pleas for a bandage were ignored. In the car, allegedly en route to prison, he was rifle-butted again and shot several times. At the mortuary, the doctor wrote 'an unknown man found dead in the Freigarten'. As for Luxemburg, it was arranged that, as a Jew, she should die by the hands of a mob, but the mob could not be mustered at the last minute and Otto Runge of the *Freikorps* smashed her skull with the butt of his carbine on the way out of the hotel. She had probably already been sexually assaulted and was taken away in a car to be bludgeoned and shot in the head by Lieutenant Kurt Vogel. Her battered and bleeding body was thrown into the canal at the Liechtenstein Bridge; it would not be found until May.

Why did Karl Liebknecht and Rosa Luxemburg take the slave's name for their ill-judged revolution of 1919? The answer lies in a wild-bearded German Jew whose cranky visions of a Utopian future were born out of the bitter experiences of Britain's Industrial Revolution. Karl Liebknecht's father had known Karl Marx, and his son had read the great man's works at university.

Marx's *Communist Manifesto* burst upon an already revolutionary Europe in 1848, with its message of class exploitation and its incitement to class war. If the downtrodden peasantry of the Proletariat had everything to win by revolution and nothing to lose but their chains, then Spartacus was the embodiment of them. He 'is the most splendid fellow in the whole of ancient history', Marx wrote in a letter to his friend and co-conspirator Friedrich Engels. 'Great general . . . noble character, genuine representative of the ancient proletariat.'[30] Marx retained his high opinion of Spartacus throughout his life. On 1 April 1865 Jenny Marx, the philosopher's eldest daughter, gave him a questionnaire about his likes and dislikes. He listed his heroes as Spartacus and Kepler. We are not concerned with the sixteenth-century German astronomer who had captured Marx's admiration, but four years earlier, in the above-quoted letter to Engels, he added: 'For recreation in the evenings, I have been reading Appian's *Roman Civil Wars* in the original Greek text. A very valuable book . . . Spartacus emerges as one of the best characters in the whole of ancient history. A great general (unlike Garibaldi).'[31]

Leaving aside Marx's giant disregard for the realities of Roman *realpolitik*, Spartacus' place as folk-hero and class warrior was assured for all time. His great generalship cannot be doubted, though it will be analysed in this book. His noble character is actually a blank page – we cannot hope, with the biased material available, to do more than outline it. His role as proletarian superman is highly suspect, if only because Marx imputed to him nineteenth-century ideas set in a rapidly changing capitalist world that thumped to the rhythm of machines that Spartacus could not have imagined in his wildest dreams.

Until the collapse of the Berlin Wall and the 'evil empire' that was Soviet Russia, East German school history books wrote of Spartacus' rebellion as the defining event in ancient history. He was the first of the people's heroes and a messiah for the revolutions to come.

Kirk Douglas, Dalton Trumbo, Howard Fast, Karl Liebknecht, Rosa Luxemburg, Karl Marx – they all took the name of Spartacus to various degrees in vain. They took the sparse historical records of the time and wove their own wonderful tapestries. Douglas was Spartacus on the big screen, with arty 'Thracian' haircut and bright-blue eyes. Trumbo conjured him in the steam of his bath, hacking away at an upright typewriter. Fast used him to spout Marxist propaganda at a time when he was in prison for being a Marxist. Karl Liebknecht and 'Red Rosa' carried him as an icon of simple strength and dignity when a shattered and demoralised Germany needed such things. Karl Marx found in him a model of a class hero of the type he himself longed to be.

In reality, he was Spartacus, not for all time, but for his own time. And it is time we tried to find him.

TWO

The Man from Thrace

The rising of the gladiators and their devastation of Italy, which is generally known as the war of Spartacus, began as follows . . .[1]

The words of Lucius Mestrius Plutarchus, better known to us as Plutarch, take us back to the spring or summer of 73 BC. Spartacus' most detailed biographer in the ancient world, Plutarch was a cultured Greek from Chaeronea in Boeotia (central Greece), although he may have travelled extensively in Egypt. He lectured in philosophy in the reign of the Emperor Domitian and was fascinated by the links between his own culture and that of Rome. A prolific writer of over 200 books, his work is didactic and moralistic and his pronouncements on Spartacus can be found in sections 8 to 11 of the biography of Crassus which appears in his *Lives*, a collection of twenty-three pairs of famous Greeks and Romans. Plutarch is concerned to point up Crassus' strengths and weaknesses as a moral yardstick for his readers. He was writing about 180 years after the events he is describing, with all the problems that that time-gap engenders.

Unbeknown to Plutarch or the man he was writing about, the world was turning that summer of 73 BC. Chinese mathematicians were already using negative numbers in their equations and the Greek philosopher Poseidonius was correlating the shifts of the seas with the cycle of the moon when Spartacus was a baby. The Roman general Lucius Licinius Lucullus, who would be brought back from the east to cope with the Spartacus rising, brought cherry trees from Persia to plant in his villa near Rome while master craftsmen made glass window-panes for him to view them. In Spain, glass-blowing was accomplished for the first time and the Chinese historian Sima

Qian wrote a careful description of a device that floated on air and is clearly a parachute.

'[Spartacus] was a Thracian from the nomadic tribes,' wrote Plutarch, 'and not only had a great spirit and great physical strength, but was, much more than one would expect from his condition [status] most intelligent and cultured, being more like a Greek than a Thracian.'

The whole question of Spartacus' origins is shrouded in mystery. The original Greek of Plutarch is usually read as *ton nomadikon genous*, meaning 'of the nomadic peoples'. If it should actually read *ton Maidikon genous*, then it specifies Spartacus' tribe – the Maidi.

Thrace or Thracia was the Roman name for the area that now roughly corresponds with the country of Bulgaria, extending to the river Danube to the north (then called the Istros), the Black Sea coast to the east and the great kingdom of Macedonia to the south. Nearly two centuries after Spartacus, the most philosophic of the emperors, Marcus Aurelius, stood on the banks of the Danube looking north at the head of his army and 'the most beautiful figure in history',[2] as Matthew Arnold called him, contemplated the meaning of life:

> Look back at the phases of your own growth: childhood, boyhood, youth, age: each change itself a kind of death. Was this so frightening? Or take the lives you lived under your grandfather and then your mother and then your father; trace the numerous differences and changes and discontinuances there were in those days and ask yourself 'Were they so frightening?'[3]

Our problem is that we have no written record at all of most of the phases of Spartacus' life. His birth and childhood are total blanks and we know virtually nothing about his youth. The fact that there was a settlement called Spartakos in Thrace perhaps indicates that he came from there, rather in the way that Owen Wister's fictional cowboy is referred to as 'The Virginian' or Christ is sometimes called 'The Galilean'. On the other hand, if Plutarch is right about the man belonging to a nomadic tribe, how far did he have a permanent home anyway? Spartacus springs fully formed on to the vast Roman stage; a slave, but an intelligent one. We know from many sources that he was trained as a gladiator, so he was probably under thirty; men older than that would be too slow on the turns and poor value for money. We know he was acknowledged as leader by upwards of 70,000 runaways, slaves and freemen, and it is unlikely that a man of under twenty would have commanded such respect. Logic dictates, then, that Spartacus was born between 100 and 90 BC. If it was 100 BC, then he shared a birth year with the greatest Roman general of them all – Julius Caesar. Again, if Plutarch is right that Spartacus was 'more like a Greek' it is likely that he was born in the south, where Greco-Macedonian influence would have been at its strongest.

Spartacus' country is described in Homer's *Iliad*, the epic story of the ten-year war between the Trojans and the Greeks which was, in all probability, a series of wars over several centuries, given an additional divine twist by the intervention of the Greek gods. 'It is in my mind,' said Zeus, 'to cause the great war with Troy.' Homer believed that Thrace extended along the coast of the Aegean and that it was bounded by various rivers, the Hebrus and the Nestus, the Strymon and the Axios. That was in the thirteenth century BC and by the time of Herodotus (the fifth century BC) the area had either grown or his description was more accurate than that of Homer. The northern frontier, he said, was the Istros, the Danube. Herodotus, 'the father of history', was using data provided by the geographers of his day, men like the squint-eyed Strabo who was himself a Thracian from Pontus on the Black Sea.

To Herodotus the Thracians were barbarians, but the term 'barbarian' was used widely to mean anything from the literal 'bearded ones' to those who had no written command of Greek. Its use therefore tells us almost nothing about Thracian civilisation. As a racial group, the Thracians disappeared in the seventh century AD as waves of nomadic conquerors swept from the east. The area became a patchwork of warring factions holding loose allegiance to the Eastern Christian Empire's capital of Byzantium (later known as Constantinople). The fall of that city to the warring Ottoman Turks of Mehmed II in 1453 eclipsed a unique way of life and created 'Turkey in Europe', a hybrid world that was Muslim in all important political and legal aspects.

It was not until the Enlightenment that ancient Thrace emerged from the rubble of history when travellers like Count L. Marsigli sailed down the river Yantra from the Danube, finding archaeological remains and artefacts as he went. Subsequent historians, archaeologists and numismatists were hampered in their investigations by the fact that the Thracians had no written language. Most of these scholars were all too ready to follow Herodotus, ignoring Homer's assertion that Thracian civilisation was as accomplished as that of their allies, the Trojans.

It was in the fields of spoken language traditions and religion that most progress was made in the study of Thrace and these studies resulted in a new word being coined for such studies – Thraceology. The heartlands of Thrace were indeed in modern Bulgaria, but its outlying areas reached north of the Danube to the foothills of the Carpathians and perhaps beyond. There are few recognisable stages of Thracian development. Almost nothing is known about neolithic Thrace, but there are archaeological traces of a society there at the end of the Bronze Age, notably the Vulchitrun treasure in northern Bulgaria. Between the end of the second millennium BC and the sixth century BC, evidence is lacking, but impressive tombs have been found which suggest that Thracians could rival their more 'civilised' Greek neighbours to the south. The entrance chamber to a tomb at Kazanluk, dating from the late fourth or early third century BC, shows a painted frieze of a battle scene which would not have looked out of place on a wall in Roman Pompeii 400 years later. Silverwork from Letnitsa proves conclusively that the Thracian metalsmiths were masters of their trade, showing appliqué or bas-relief warriors, mounted and in shirts of mail from the mid-fourth century BC.

It is in the third stage of Thracian development, between the sixth and third centuries, that we see marked political and social development taking place. Tribal names emerge, fighting each other and allying in an ever shifting power struggle. Forty major tribes have been identified, mostly from the writings of Greek scholars of this period. The Getai, worshipping their god Zalmoxis, believed in immortality and lived north of the Danube in the Carpathians; the Triballi held out alone against the greatest general in history – Alexander the Great. Some came from the hot, dry plains – the Moesi and Odrysae; others from the mountains – the Dii, the Bessi, the Thynii and the Odomanti. The historian Herodotus believed the Thracians were the most numerous race on earth after the Indians, and ethno-archaeologists today have little trouble accepting the figure of one million of them. In this third stage of their development, the Odrysae emerge as the most powerful group. It was in the third century that a serious crisis developed in Thrace, largely due to Celtic invasions that shaped the country's future and especially its religion. Decentralisation took place at an alarming speed after the collapse of the regime of Decebalus, king of Dacia, north of the Danube.

The diaspora that resulted from this collapse is difficult to chart because it is almost impossible to find evidence of something that is uniquely Thracian in other parts of the then known world. The Thracians were the chameleons of the ancient world. Under Greek influence, they adopted Greek armour and civilian clothes, probably coining Greek words too. Later, under Roman colonisation, they had no trouble adapting to that way of life. Spartacus lived in the era when the Macedonian and Greek influence of Philip and his astonishing son, Alexander, were giving way to that of an ever expanding Rome.

The link between the Latinised 'Spartacus' and the Greek 'Sparadakos' was probably made for the first time by the historian Joshua Whatmough in the 1930s. A coin from the fifth century BC in Thrace bears the name Sparadakos. He was a son of Teres, one of the powerful Odryssian kings of Thrace, which makes him a prince. Many historians today accept the view that Sparadakos was a common name in Thrace, but those are the only two of which records have been found.

'They say,' wrote Plutarch, 'that when [Spartacus] was first taken to Rome to be sold, a snake was seen coiled round his head while he was asleep . . . this sign meant that he would have a great and terrible power which would end in misfortune.'⁴

The religious influences which worked on men like Spartacus were many and complicated. It is particularly difficult to unravel them because the Greeks gave Thracian deities the names of their own pantheon of gods, unable to accept perhaps that there could be any other terminology. By the time of Spartacus, Roman names had eclipsed those of the Greeks, and this patchwork of classical religious influences overlays important Celtic traditions.

One of the most original Thracian gods, of whom over 3,000 images have been found in the areas where we know the Thracians lived, is the Horseman. The Greeks called him Hero, but the Thracians seem to have no name for him – or perhaps many. He is often shown in mail or other types of armour, as though he is a warrior, and is often brandishing a spear, though whether this refers to battle or the hunt is uncertain. He is sometimes shown with a second figure hovering in the air behind him, with dogs or lions snapping at his stirrupless heels. Sometimes he has three heads.

The three-headed or at least three-faced god occurs in pre-Aryan temples as far east as India and as long ago as 2,000 years before Spartacus. There are enough depictions of the Horseman with the sun and the moon to link him with both these cults in ancient mythology. To emphasise that he was all things to all men, the Horseman occurs in a temple at Lozen as Apollo, with a cloak, long curly Greek hair and a lyre. South of the Danube he is shown as Pluto, god of the Underworld, with a long robe, beard and cornucopia. Around the Black Sea settlement of Odessa he was called Darzalus.

The Horseman is central to Thracian mythology because the Thracians were, pre-eminently, the horse people. Homer may have been right in his belief that the mounted horsemen of the Odrysae, one of the largest and most successful of the Thracian tribes, outnumbered the cavalry of the whole of Greece. Thracians domesticated the horse before the Greeks and it is highly likely that the centaur legend was born of the Greeks' first sight of this mounted warrior race. To the Thracian, the horse was a symbol of both the sun and the darkness of the underworld. It also had a clear social position reflected in most societies, ancient and modern. The horse raised a man high above the clay from which he came. It made him far more swift and mobile than a running man, and the money spent on harnesses and other equestrian equipment throughout antiquity is evidence of the prestige of horse ownership. The Odrysae fought entirely as cavalry; lesser tribes fought for them on foot.

The horse also held a special place in Celtic mythology. At least two British tribes in Spartacus' time were linked with the animal – the Epidii of Kintyre in Scotland and the Iceni, the East Anglian warriors who fought for Boudicca. The horse brought energy and speed and oversaw, with patient eyes and a courageous heart, the whole mysterious cycle of birth, death and the afterlife. It is likely that in some parts of Thrace the Horseman evolved into the horse-goddess Epona, the only Celtic deity to be worshipped in Rome and whose feast day dovetailed with the Saturnalia in December. The animal was associated with the power of procreation and fertility, underscored by the Celtic ceremony of Beltane, the time of mating, in May.

But there are other symbols in art and archaeology associated with the Horseman. Near him is often carved a stylised tree, heavily in leaf. The Thracians built their temples in groves, an acknowledgement of the almost universal notion of the tree of life. But groves and tree stands were especially sacred in Celtic mythology, for the trees themselves had souls.

Often the Horseman is aiming his spear at a boar, an animal no doubt common enough all over Thrace in Spartacus' time. In the mythology of ancient Greece and throughout Asia Minor, the boar is symbolic of life and death, featuring in numerous stories about the Greek gods. In the Celtic tradition, the boar is a symbol of power. He is the very spirit of the warrior and, as such, Celtic tribesmen wore his bronze likeness on their helmets. Even the ever superstitious Roman legions borrowed the badge for their legionary standards.

What of the snake coiling around the head of Spartacus as he slept? The animal has been associated with some of the most famous names in antiquity – Asclepius, the doctor who became a god; Nero, the deranged emperor; Hannibal, one of the greatest generals of all who drove marauding Rome back to her own gates. In Greek and some Thracian depictions, the snake is often shown twined around the branches of the tree of life – and as 'that old Serpent, Satan', he appears as Adam and Eve's downfall in the Garden of Eden. The snake was a symbol of rebirth, shedding its skin each spring, and was linked therefore, not with misfortune, as Plutarch believed, but with immortality. In western Celtic mythology, the snake inevitably became focused on one of the few native British snakes, the adder.

'I have been a Serpent,' wrote Taliesin, the bard of Rheged in the sixth century, 'I am love; I have been an Adder of the Mountain; I have been a Serpent in the River.'[5]

The snake was, above all, the symbol of fertility, with the phallic shape of its head and sinuous movements. It is a common emblem in Celtic art, most notably on the extraordinary Gundestrup cauldron, discovered by archaeologists in Denmark's peat bogs, but probably originating in Thrace in the century before Spartacus' birth.

Three women are often depicted with the Horseman in Thracian art. Who they are is not clear, but they may be connected with a confused and ancient tradition in Thracian mythology that a three-headed dragon once ruled the earth and held captive all its women and its waters. It was the Horseman who killed it and set free its captives, so that the women became his wives – three of them because of his three faces and also because three is a sacred number in Celtic mythology. The fourth woman in the Horseman's life, and a prominent figure in Thracian art and archaeology, is the Great Mother of the Gods: the Horseman's mother.·

To the Thracians, as with virtually every other ancient civilisation, the Great Mother was the earth goddess, heaven and hell, progenitor of the human race. Towards the end of the Bronze Age, the Mother is often depicted as two females – they may be mother and daughter, representing the endless cycle of procreation and life. Herodotus wrote of the Thracian goddess Artemis, goddess of the hunt, Mistress of the Animals, whom the Romans called Diana. Some Thracian tribes may have called her Bendis and in various depictions she carries a bow and quiver or a spear and twigs. Socrates witnessed her ceremonies: 'I went down to Piraeus [the harbour of Athens] yesterday . . . to honour the goddess and to see how they were going to arrange the procession as this was being held for the first time. The procession of the local citizens was very nice, but that of the Thracians was no less beautiful.'⁶

The Bendideia festival was held in the Greek month of Thargelion (May to June) and during it sows were sacrificed, the corn sprinkled with their blood to ensure the success of the next year's harvest.

It is now that the Greek influence begins to show itself in Thracian mythology as the ever expansionist reigns of Philip and his son Alexander saw invasions from the south. Herodotus, curiously ignoring the Horseman entirely, emphasises the importance in the Thracian pantheon of Artemis, Ares and Dionysius.

Ares was the Greek god of war and a society as naturally pugnacious as the Thracians must have had such a deity. The Scythians (an eastern enclave of Thracians) worshipped a sword (the *akinakes*) which may have been an early form of the *thrax* carried by Spartacus in the arena. Its blade was daubed with the blood of men slain in battle and sacrifices of men and animals were made in front of the enemy as much to terrify them as to appease the gods. In 29 BC when Marcus Licinius Crassus' troops invaded Moesia (south-western Thrace) the Thracians butchered a horse in the open ground between their armies and promised to offer the entrails of the Romans to their god in a similar way. Crassus' grandfather had seen it all before – Spartacus himself had crucified a man in full view of his legions in the spring of 71 BC across the fortifications at Rhegium. Such sacrifices were not merely a grisly device to frighten the enemy; they also took the form of religious sacrifices. The rebel's contemporary, the historian Livy, recorded that the Thracians hacked off their opponents' heads and waved them in the air on their spear-points, a grim custom they may have inherited from the Celts. Crassus' head would one day be similarly displayed.

In purely Greek, as opposed to Thracian, mythology, Thrace itself features widely. It was the home of Boreas, the North Wind, son of Eos, the goddess of the dawn, who was wild and tempestuous. He had blown through his great conch shell and destroyed the Persian battle fleet at Artemisium in 480 BC. Like Artemis, Boreas was worshipped in Athens with his own festival. Orpheus was believed to have been a Thracian singer; the son of Calliope, the muse of poetry. His wife Eurydice died as a result of a snake bite and Orpheus sang and played no more. He risked his own life by entering the Underworld, chaining Charon the ferryman and the terrible three-headed dog Cerberus. Hades and Persephone, king and queen of the Underworld, granted permission for Eurydice to follow Orpheus as long as he did not look back as he left. Unable to resist, as the lovers reached the light, Orpheus glanced behind him and Eurydice sank back into the shadows. It was his fate in turn to be torn apart by the frenzied maenads, the female worshippers of Dionysius. Only his head was left in one piece, floating down a river, still calling for his Eurydice. And it is this story that brings us directly to Spartacus.

Plutarch's description of the man as being 'most intelligent and cultured, being more like a Greek than a Thracian' is given substance by a later comment – 'his wife, who came from the same tribe . . . was a prophetess subject to possession by the frenzy of Dionysius'.

Dionysius was believed to be the son of Zeus, king and father of the gods, and Semele, a princess of Thebes. She stupidly urged her great lover to show himself in all his splendour and in the lightning flashing from his brow she was burned to death, giving birth prematurely to Dionysius. He became the beautiful, bearded evocation of vegetation, wine and ecstasy, able to transform himself into a bull. He is often portrayed in Greek art with vine leaves twined in his ringletted hair and a lynx skin draped over his shoulders. In some aspects of Greco-Thracian culture he appears as a male form of Artemis, the mother goddess we have discussed already.

There is a great deal of evidence that Dionysius was originally a Thracian god, originating in Asia Minor and crossing the Bosphorus into northern Bulgaria. Many Greeks believed the Thracians to be appalling drunkards, so the association made perfect sense. He is first mentioned by Homer as meeting Lycurgus, who seems to have been a Thracian king. Although this is pure legend, it probably represents the arrival of the cult of Dionysius in Thrace and its co-existence with older faiths over a period of several centuries.

Over time, it is likely that Dionysius took on a more important aspect in Thracian religion than he did in Greek. His sanctuaries were built on high ground, on mountain tops where the sun's rays touched first at dawn, and archaeologist Ivan Marazov conjectures that Dionysius *was* the sun god, Apollo, in Thrace. Interestingly, at one of Dionysius' temples, the priests were chosen exclusively from the Bessi tribe. Plutarch does not tell us (because he probably did not know) which of the 'nomadic tribes' Spartacus hailed from, but if he is right about his Greekness and his translation does not in fact refer to the Maidi, the Bessi are likely candidates as they were the nearest tribe to the Greek frontier.

The Thracian, as opposed to the Greek, manifestation of Dionysius is linked strongly with prophecy, which has echoes in the snake episode and its enormous importance for Spartacus' wife. By the time of the slave revolts, the cult of Dionysius had developed into one of personal salvation, but the drunken debauchery and riotous behaviour, especially of its female adherents, caused alarm.

'Lifted' as Dionysius was from Cretan, Phrygian and Lydian mythology, he became all things to all men and the Greeks held numerous festivals in his honour. In the Agrionia, held in Boeotia, boys were burned as sacrifices. This was replaced on Chios and Lesbos by flagellation, but death was probably still the end result. In Attica, two festivals were held – Lenaea or wine-press in December and Anthesteria in February, when the last of the old vintage was drunk. In a festival held at the sanctuary of Lenoeon in early March, orgies took place in torrents of red wine on the slopes of Mount Cithaeron.

Plutarch's description of Spartacus' unnamed wife makes it clear that she was a maenad, a devotee of Dionysius, accustomed to imbibing in the orgiastic festivals of the god. A whole host of lesser deities were believed to roll and gambol in Dionysius' retinue – the monkey-faced, goat-footed satyrs, renowned for their sexual excesses and the drunken, bold, staggering *sileni*, often riding on a donkey. The great god Pan sauntered there too, and the centaurs we have already met, metamorphoses of the mounted warriors, the Thracians themselves.

The Romans, always more strait-laced than the Greeks, demoted Dionysius to Bacchus, a figure of fun. Even so, the cult refused to lie down and 100 years before Spartacus the Senate outlawed the more excessive forms of worship of the god. This ruthless suppression has a peculiar resonance with the fate of Spartacus, not just because of the cruelty with which the cult was destroyed, but because its devotees were believed to be a secret, underground organisation popular with the mob, the unpredictable 'many-headed monster' that civilised Rome feared most. It occurred at a time when the first serious slave revolts broke out in Sicily and it cannot be coincidence that Plutarch links Spartacus, through his wife, with a cult that Roman society considered dangerous and out of control.

Livy positively bristles with disgust when describing their activities:

> when they [the maenads] were heated with wine, and all sense of modesty had been extinguished by the darkness of the night and the commingling of males with females, tender youths with elders, then debaucheries of every kind commenced: each had pleasures at hand to satisfy the lust to which he was most inclined . . . Much was ventured by guile, more by violence, which was kept secret, because the cries of those calling for help amid the debauchery and murder could not be heard through the howling and the crash of drums and cymbals.[7]

No doubt the extent of the debauchery was exaggerated – the early Christians were held to be guilty of similar excesses – but the result was a witch-hunt. The cult's priests were placed under house arrest and the army was posted as nightwatchmen to disperse would-be revellers. The Senate wanted names – as the House Un-American Activities Committee did two millennia later – and got them. Livy estimates that over 7,000 people were implicated. Those who had merely been initiated and chanted the priestly directions were imprisoned; those who had lied, murdered, or taken part in a whole variety of sex acts were executed. These ritualistic killings ran into thousands and can be seen in a variety of ways – the Senate controlling the mob; Roman religion establishing its parameters over the wilder excesses of Greco-Thracian mythology; and even the will to stamp out what was seen as over familiarity between freeman and slave.

The cult was far from extinct. It re-emerged in the years after Spartacus' death in the clash at the end of the Republic between Octavian (the future Emperor Augustus) and Marcus Antonius (Shakespeare's Mark Anthony) in which the latter's opponents equated him with the drunken, priapic god of lust and debauchery because of his infatuation with Cleopatra of Egypt.

In Pompeii, the city so famously preserved under the choking volcanic ash of Vesuvius's eruption in AD 79, there are a number of mosaics of Dionysius and the House of Mysteries is an extraordinary testament to the cult's importance. In what seems to be a narrative of a young girl being initiated into the cult, the walls of several rooms in the opulent villa are bright red with scenes of sex and flagellation. Typically, the windows of the house are on the inside of the building, facing the atrium or courtyard, so that nosy neighbours or inquisitive passers-by could not see in. Experts date these dazzling paintings to the middle of the first century BC, within twenty years of the war of Spartacus.

What does all this tell us about Spartacus the man? The bare facts are that he was a slave who became a gladiator who became a rebel. Of his origins we know almost nothing, but Plutarch at least allows us to speculate. If he was more cultured and more like a Greek than the chronicler expected, and if his wife was a priestess of Dionysius, then surely Spartacus was initially a freeman, not, as Fast and Trumbo speculated, born into slavery. The only problem is that we have no idea what his status was. And the following pronouncement by Appian does not help: 'Spartacus, a Thracian whom the Romans had imprisoned and then sold to be trained as a gladiator, had once fought as a soldier for the Roman army.'[8]

This is not the only interpretation of a difficult Latin passage, but in the light of Spartacus' later ability to defeat Roman armies, it makes perfect sense. Why a free Thracian should have joined the army is unclear, but the military life has always had an appeal for certain types of men and we do not know whether or not Spartacus was already married. Various Greek and Roman writers may well have been exaggerating when they described the Thracians as murderous, drunken louts. They painted a similar picture of the Celts of Gaul and Britannia in a later period. Thucydides wrote: 'For the Thracian race, like all the most bloodthirsty barbarians, are always particularly bloodthirsty when everything is going their way.'[9]

Strabo records how the Thracians loved to get drunk and to sing their war songs. Like the dreaded 'Ça Ira' of Napoleon's Old Guard 2,000 years later, the Thracian battle cry known to the Greeks as the 'titanismos' (the cry of the Titans) struck terror into the hearts of their enemies. Spartacus would have been steeped in the warlike traditions of his people.

Nearly 500 years after Spartacus' death, the writer Flavius Vegetius Renatus penned his *Epitome Institutiones Rei Militaris*, a military handbook still widely read in the fifteenth century. Although the book considerably post-dates Spartacus, Vegetius drew on the works of a number of earlier military experts, including Gaius Julius Caesar, who was of course an exact contemporary of the rebellious slave. Vegetius describes a typical recruit thus:

> a young soldier who is chosen for the work of Mars should have alert eyes and should hold his head upright. The recruit should be broad-chested with powerful shoulders and brawny arms. His fingers should be long rather than short. He should not be pot-bellied or have a fat bottom. His calves and feet should not be flabby; instead they should be made entirely of tough sinew . . . Fishermen, bird-catchers, sweet-makers, weavers and all those who do the kind of job that women normally do should be kept away from the army. On the other hand, smiths, carpenters, butchers and hunters of deer and wild boar are the most suitable . . .[10]

We cannot of course make too many assumptions about Spartacus – that he was a butcher or hunter rather than a sweet-maker – but we know from Plutarch that he was extraordinarily tough and ideal material for the army. We know from archaeological excavations at various sites in Bulgaria that most adult male Thracians were large, powerfully built men. Eyewitness accounts of them by the smaller, swarthy Greeks and Romans to the south and west comment on their fair skin, sandy hair and grey or blue eyes. In Spartacus' day Thrace was a client kingdom of Rome, and the Thracian ruler held his position only with Rome's acquiescence. Thracians had made superb mercenaries in the armies of Alexander; now they made equally vital contributions to the forces of the Roman Republic. It is likely that Thracian sons were held captive in Rome to ensure continued loyalty and subservience. But men with ambition – or men made desperate by the endless, cruel lottery of the harvest – would look to ever expanding Rome as their salvation. Again, as is so often the case with Spartacus, the brevity of ancient writers' comments throws up more questions than answers. If Appian is right about his army career, then this again points to his being a freeman. Slaves were not legally allowed to enlist and if caught, risked execution or at least any of the variety of appalling punishments the Roman army routinely dished out.[11]

Appian of Alexandria is the second most detailed ancient historian on Spartacus. He practised as a lawyer in Rome in the reign of Domitian, which makes him a contemporary of Plutarch, although it is likely that the two men used different sources. It was in the reign of Antoninus Pius (AD 136–61) that Appian wrote his monumental 24-volume *History of Rome*, but it is clear from other literary sources that he did not, as a foreigner, always fully understand his material. The section of the work that deals with Spartacus is *The Civil Wars*, which covers the period from the Gracchi (second century BC) to the Emperor Augustus (died AD 14). By Spartacus' day, there was a lack of enthusiasm among Romans and Italians in general for enlisting in the army – ironic at a time of huge Roman expansion – and increasingly the Senate looked elsewhere for its recruits. One titled Roman went so far as to cut off the thumbs of his two sons rather than have them undergo the expected military service of a citizen; he was sold into slavery by the emperor.[12]

There were, according to the Emperor Trajan a century after Spartacus, three categories of recruits. First, in terms of preference, came the *voluntarii*, the volunteers. These are the men in the peak of physical condition described by Vegetius above and they may have joined for any number of reasons. The local authorities in Thrace or the legionary tribunes would probably have made the army life appear as glorious and welcoming as possible, exactly as 'the bringer', the recruiting sergeant, was doing in European armies 1,900 years later. They glossed over the back-breaking training, the night marches in driving rain, the moving of tons of earth to build ramparts and fortifications, the ceaseless sting of the centurions' vine-sticks across backs and faces. They probably focused on food, wine, comradeship, adventure and excitement – the attractions that have drawn men to the military throughout history. Pay may have been an incentive, too. The first accurate records we have come from Polybius, the Greek historian who wrote a great deal on military matters in the second century BC. A centurion (commanding eighty men) received four obols, an infantryman three obols and a cavalryman (always better paid because of the need to feed his horse) one drachma a day. By Caesar's time, the infantryman of the legions received 225 silver denarii (pennies) a year, but this represents a huge salary increase by Caesar and was probably half that when various legions were sent out against Spartacus himself.

Such figures are meaningless on their own, but the attraction of army life was that this money was regular and not dependent on the seasons. Skilled men in important cities such as Rome and Capua could earn more, but there might be weeks or months between work projects and then, times could be very lean indeed.

The second type of recruit for the army was the *lectus*, the conscript. We have no accurate information of how conscription was carried out, but a system of conscription known as *dilectus* was used in times of crisis. The Emperor Augustus used this method twice in quick succession after severe losses to his legions in Pannonia

(Hungary) in AD 6 and in the Teutoburger Forest in Germany three years later. Despite the eruption of the so-called Social War fifteen years before the Spartacus Revolt, there seems to have been no *dilectus* in the period, although, as we shall see, a number of consuls recruited slaves illegally into their armies to make up numbers.

The third category of recruit was the *vicarius*, the substitute. Such men were presumably paid to take another's place, but evidence on them is very sketchy and it is unlikely there were many who could be induced to take up this proxy employment. Soldiers *could* make money (as could gladiators), as is evidenced by the fact that they were uniquely allowed to make wills during their father's lifetime. We have various stele (grave-markers) from the end of the Republic showing the statues of some soldiers. A poor man cannot afford a marker; there is no known grave for Spartacus. The downside was that service was normally for twenty-five years and the likelihood of surviving for that long was not very high.

Of the three categories, it is likely that Spartacus was a volunteer, which, if correct, makes the assumption that his income as a civilian was at least poor and probably erratic. If he came from a rural area of Thrace, as is likely in that towns of the Roman type did not exist, he would have been preferable to the officers as a tough 'outlaw' type accustomed to hard physical labour, perhaps as a shepherd or herdsman. The only major city in Thrace was Σeuthopolis, in the central area midway between the Istros and the Hebrus. Minor settlements built by the Greeks existed in the south, but in so far as Spartacus had a home, it was probably a collection of small, native huts.

We cannot know whether Spartacus joined a regular legion or an auxiliary unit (*auxilia*). By AD 180 there were three full legions stationed in or near Thrace, but by that time Thrace was fully a part of the Roman Empire, whose Danubian frontiers had to be protected against the lawless Getae tribe, despite their apparent destruction under the Emperor Trajan eighty years earlier. Only one legion, the legio Macedonica, from its name at least, serving a Thracian frontier and possibly taking recruits from there, existed in Spartacus' time. Regular legions were better paid and regarded as the elite of the army, but the *auxilia* were every bit as important, reflecting the highly cosmopolitan nature of the Roman army. Units like these often served as cavalry (*ala*) and a local regiment – I Ala Thracia (the First Thracian Cavalry) – were serving in Roman Britain at the time of Boudicca's rebellion in AD 60. The fact that Thracians were famous cavalrymen, and that the only possible pictorial depiction of Spartacus shows him mounted, perhaps indicates that he was indeed a cavalryman. The depiction is a much-worn fresco on the portico of a house in Pompeii. It probably shows a gladiatorial display, with mounted gladiators and the musical accompaniment of a horn player. 'Spartaks' is written in Oscan, the older, pre-Roman language of southern and central Italy, and is inscribed backwards, as Oscan was written in the Arabic style, from right to left. The figure can be dated to somewhere between 100 and 70 BC. Pompeii was 33 miles from Capua, where Spartacus was trained as a gladiator, and it seems at least a probability that this was intended as a portrait of him. Spartacus' clear understanding of Roman legionary tactics and his extraordinary success against successive Roman armies also suggests that he was able to get inside the heads of the infantry – always the backbone of Roman military strength.

Whether infantryman or cavalryman, it is likely that Spartacus would have been given his Romanised name at this time; Sparadakos became Latinised. Like the Nazis centuries later, the Romans were sticklers for paperwork and the bureaucracy of both army and Republic was formidable; the tragedy is that so little of it has survived. In the first century an Egyptian recruit called Apion joined the much less prestigious Roman navy and wrote home to tell his family that he was now Antonius Maximus. No doubt this was all part of the psychological process by which his earlier life ceased to exist and now he was bound in every sense to Rome. Sparadakos was no longer a Thracian; Spartacus was a soldier of Rome. We know that the *cornicularii*, regimental clerks, kept careful records of the new recruits on papyrus. Avidius Arrianus, clerk of the Cohors III Ituraeorum, lists six men joining his unit in the winter of AD 103. Caius Longianus Priscus was twenty-two with a scar on his left eyebrow; Marcus Antonius Valens was the same age with a scar on the right side of his forehead. The oldest man was twenty-five, the youngest twenty. It is likely that there was a similar laconic entry on Spartacus the Thracian that has long since crumbled to dust.

Spartacus would now have undergone the *probatio*, the inspection for beginners, and it was at this point that his status would need to be established. The Romans placed great store by the rights of citizenship and a law of Octavian in 41 BC clarified the legal position of those who already held citizenship in another state, as Spartacus may have done in Thrace. Roman citizens always took precedence in the legions, although non-citizens could win the coveted status by their 25-year service. The issue of citizenship was a thorny one because the withdrawal of the privilege was seen as a root cause of the Social War which only finished shortly before Spartacus' likely date of enlistment. There was also a medical examination, although relative disabilities such as flat feet and poor eyesight or hearing were not necessarily grounds for refusal. The ideal description by Vegetius above was by no means always adhered to. The army needed clerks, doctors, engineers and cooks as well as fighters. If Appian is correct about Spartacus serving with the army, then he clearly passed this stage and was given the *signaculum*, a lead tablet worn around the neck in a leather pouch which was the Roman equivalent of dog tags. At this stage, he would have sworn an oath to serve Rome with the utmost courage and zeal. Then he would be sent to join his unit.

Virtually nothing is known of the next phase of Spartacus' life. Only Appian, writing nearly three centuries after Spartacus and unfamiliar with some aspects of the Republic, contends that he was actually in the army at all. He certainly gives no details of where Spartacus served or where he was recruited. One logical possibility is Macedonia, since it stood on the southern frontier of Thrace and had been formally annexed to Rome after the overwhelming defeat of its king, Perseus, at Pydna in 168 BC. If he had to travel to join his unit, Spartacus would have been given the *viaticum* (travelling expenses), which consisted of three gold coins amounting to a symbolic 75 denarii. This was the exact equivalent of the 'bounty' given to recruits to the British Army in the nineteenth century, and like them, the recruits of Spartacus' day would find this money magically disappearing in various trumped-up 'expenses'.

If it is assumed that Spartacus joined an auxiliary infantry unit, he would have found himself, probably for the first time, in a formal, close-knit environment that was replicated all over the Roman world and would remain essentially unchanged for three centuries. Auxiliary barracks were normally smaller versions of the huge legionary depots dotted around the Mediterranean.

The army did not have huge permanent defensive fortresses until much later. Essentially, the barracks in which Spartacus would have lived would be an extension of the marching camp, a geometric creation in the form of a square or rectangle, where such a unit would pass the winter. Spartacus joined the army at a time of rapid expansion and forts like these provided the holding unit for a specific number of men with enough storage for all the supplies they would need. Only on campaign itself would the legions erect makeshift camps on the line of march and no one liked being under canvas.[13] As the Republic faded to the Empire, these camps became larger and more permanent, huts replacing tents and tiled roofs replacing thatch. Earthworks were strengthened, walls raised and stone replaced wood. The camp where Spartacus found himself was probably one in transition.

No doubt it was built on a riverbank or at least near a water supply and of the 'playing card' design – a rectangle with rounded corners. Intersecting it were the two major roads: the central bisecting thoroughfare called via principalis (main street) and at right angles to it via praetoria (the general's street) which led from the porta praetoria, the camp's main gate and the one through which Spartacus would first have entered. Other streets went off these, always at right angles, like the *via decumana* (pay street). The buildings were invariably the same, although as in the gladiatorial schools that Spartacus would join later, each camp probably had its slight variations.

The camp headquarters was the *principia*, the heart of the legion or auxiliary unit, with a large frontage, courtyard behind and various offices in a square formation. The one at Lambaesis in North Africa has survived largely intact and is a massive stone edifice with a colonnade across its front and a large barracks square for parades and drill. Behind the *principia* was a basilica, a hall with a raised dais at each end – one for the tribunes and senior officers and the other a shrine (*aedes*) where the legion's sacred standards were housed. In a cellar below there were usually vaults where valuables were kept, and soldiers like Spartacus could lodge their pay for safekeeping with the *signiferi*, the standard-bearers who doubled as pay clerks.

The *praetorum*, the commander's house, was probably a place Spartacus never visited. Whereas other ranks were not officially permitted to marry, senior officers lived with their wives, children and a whole retinue of civilians, freedmen and slaves. Within the strict hierarchy of the legion, the *tribunus laticlavius*, nominally the general's second in command, was of senatorial rank back home and required a large house that befitted his status. The *praefectus castrorum* (camp commander) had a large building too, and the *primi ordines*, centurions of the elite first cohort, had quarters only a little less lavish. They all outranked Spartacus of course, and he would have had to learn Latin quickly to cope at all.

Spartacus would have lived in the barracks, the most numerous buildings in any camp. Each room was built to house a century (company) of eighty men, or in the cavalry a *turma* (troop) of a similar number. Within this, men were subdivided into *contubernia* (squads) of eight housed in two rooms, presumably four to a room. Beds were possibly wooden bunks to save space, but none has survived the ravages of time. It is likely that most of these rooms had small windows if any, so internal lights were provided by tallow and oil lamps. Centurions seem to have had more rooms and storage space at the ends of the blocks.

Spartacus would probably be unused to living like this, cheek by jowl with others in a dark, confined space. He would certainly be unused to the other camp buildings. Essential to any fighting unit was the *valetudinarium*, the camp hospital. A particularly large one at the legionary base at Inchtuthil in Scotland was 300 feet by 200 feet, divided into 64 wards. Military historian Adrian Goldsworthy has estimated that such a structure could accommodate up to a 10 per cent injury or sickness rate. Clearly beyond that, as in epidemics or major battles, the ill and wounded had to lie where the orderlies placed them, in the barracks or courtyards depending on the weather.

We have no idea of the state of Thracian personal hygiene, so we cannot know whether Spartacus was a frequent visitor to the bathhouse or not. The bathhouse was as much a sports centre as a place to wash. We do not know if temporary camps ran to the elegant hot and cold rooms of the more established Roman baths, or if rough soldiers had time to worry about strigil work: scraping off sweat with curved sticks or tweezing out body hair, as their social superiors at home in Rome did. The grooming artefacts from Pompeii and Herculaneum in Campania, where Spartacus would launch his revolt, are cruel iron curves that still look surprisingly sharp in their museum cases today.

Other buildings with which Spartacus would have been familiar were workshops (*fabricae*) where armourers, smiths, fletchers and leather-workers toiled to provide and maintain the all-important battle gear of the legions. The *horrea* were the granaries housing all the food and wine the legion required. Their floors were built on stilts above ground level to keep out rats and they had ventilation slits at regular intervals to prevent the food from getting stale or catching fire.

What kind of life would Spartacus, the tyro, or new recruit, have had? Clearly, many hours of a soldier's life were given over to training. It was the routine, the monotonous drill of the Roman units that gave them their edge in battle. While a whole variety of 'barbarian' enemies relied on talismanic chants and warpaint, hurling themselves at the Romans in an orgy of noise and bravado, the legions themselves practised tirelessly, grouping and regrouping on the battlefield in an eerie silence and responding to the instinctive commands learned on the drill field. We shall look at the army in action later, but Spartacus would have learned his basic sword skills here, not in the arena. He carried the short, straight-bladed stabbing sword, the *gladius*, with its double edge and heavy pommel and a smaller version, the *pugio*, at his belt. In his day, legionaries and auxiliaries also carried two spears. The first was the small-headed *pilum* or javelin, intended for throwing. Such weapons could be recovered, from body or ground, as the cohorts moved forward. The second was the heavier, broad-bladed *hasta*, intended for stabbing. Completing the weaponry was the shield or *scutum*, primarily a defensive object, a rectangle of several layers of wood covered in leather and with bronze fittings. It was curved to protect the carrier and fitted over the left arm with a series of straps. The shield was used to batter enemies aside, the heavy central boss doing a great deal of damage in its own right.

A surviving duty roster from the Legio III Cyrenacia, stationed in Egypt late in the first century AD, gives us all kinds of information about the sort of work Spartacus might be expected to do that did not involve fighting. The century listed in this roster, which ought to have contained eighty men, in fact only had forty, which must have been the case quite often in times of illness, epidemic or battle-loss. Nine legionaries were *immunes*, exempt from duty, either because they had specialised skills which took them elsewhere, or else they bribed the centurion into avoiding work; coming the 'old soldier' was well established even 2,000 years ago. In the Cyrenacia, Caius Julius Valens was involved in area training on 1 October; the next day in the tower (presumably lookout duty); on the 3rd, drainage boots [?]; the next day working in the armoury; then attending the bathhouse; and finally acting as an orderly to a senior officer. Soldiers guarded gates and supervised camp markets; they polished or mended boots, were seconded to other centuries and dug latrines. Much of it was unglamorous and back-breaking,

We do not know if Spartacus fought a campaign during his time with the army, but in view of the ease with which he later dispatched Roman armies that ought to have beaten him out of hand, it seems likely that he did. And there is one campaign that fits the bill.

Risings against Roman influence and indirect rule were not unusual in Thrace. If we believe in nationalistic traits, this might have more than a little bearing on Spartacus' own career in Capua in the summer of 73 BC. In Roman-ruled Macedonia in 149 BC, a

Thracian named Andriscus led a force lent to him by his king, Teres, although the rising was soon crushed. Forty years later the Scordisci (a mix of Celts, Thracians and Illyrians) defeated and killed the Roman governor. With them were the Maidi, possibly Spartacus' own people, and this lends a fascinating colour to the rebel-gladiator's story. The year was 119 BC, about twenty years before Spartacus' birth; it is not impossible that his grandfather or even his father was involved in this anti-Roman struggle. By 107 BC, this rebelliousness was punished harshly by Marcus Minucius Rufus, who increased Rome's stranglehold on the whole of southern Thrace.

Probably the most serious rising took place when Spartacus was a boy, perhaps nine or ten years old. Throughout 91 BC a whole series of attacks were made on the rule of the Macedonian governor, Sentius. The only campaign in which Spartacus could have fought, however, was that of Appius Claudius Pulcher (the handsome) in the winter of 77 to 76 BC. There is of course no hard evidence at all for this, but the particular tribe that Pulcher was fighting were the Maidi, Spartacus' own tribe. From what little we can glean from the man's personality in his own revolt three years later, he did stand out as principled, if not quite as exemplary as Karl Marx suggested. Did he desert from the Roman army because he was caught in the hopelessly compromising position of having to march through his own village and look his family in the face before duty demanded that he cut them down? The Roman campaign was a success, but it led to the death of Pulcher and it may have been the deciding factor in turning Spartacus into Rome's greatest enemy.

Desertion was a common and constant problem for the Roman army. Punishment was both cruel and arbitrary, totally at the whim of superior officers. It was usual for deserters to be brought back and beaten, execution only taking place after two or even three attempts. Significantly, Gnaeus Domitius Corbilo, one of the most brilliant generals of the early years of the Empire, decapitated men after their first attempted escape.

The inference, taken solely from Appian, is that Spartacus ran from the army and probably simply went home. Was it now that he met the anonymous woman he would marry? Soldiers were frequently allowed to bend the rules and have wives and even children in camp, but it seems more feasible that the women from Spartacus' own tribe joined him while he was on the run. Again, Appian raises more questions than answers. He simply says: 'Spartacus, the Thracian whom the Romans had imprisoned and then sent to be trained as a gladiator, had once fought as a soldier for the Roman army.'

There is no mention of desertion or the life of an outlaw in the hills of Thrace, possible though these things are. On the other hand, why should Spartacus be a prisoner of Rome if he had not offended in some way?

Where he was operating, exactly how and for how long, is unknown. That he lived from banditry is highly likely and the survival skills he learned here would make him, one day soon, a formidable enemy. If he was in Thrace, would his unit have been allowed to go looking for him and would they actually bother? The fact is, he was clearly caught and luckily his general was not Corbilo.

There is little evidence in the Roman record about deserters brought back to their units. They were disgruntled men, already unhappy with aspects of army life, who had been physically punished and were back in the same old routine. Was it that Spartacus would not conform? And did this lead to his imprisonment, rather than his return to the standards? Again, questions. Again, no certain answers. 'Rome was ashamed,' Kirk Douglas reminds us, '. . . they wanted to bury him.'

If Spartacus was not fit for the legions, he would be sold to be trained as a gladiator, to fight for the delight of the mob in the arena. And the odds were that he would die there.

THREE

Men for Bread and Circuses

Decimus Junius Brutus died two centuries before the war of Spartacus. A brilliant general, consul and proconsul, he won the appellation Callaicus after he defeated the Callaici tribe in Galicia as part of the ongoing conquests of the Roman Republic.

For us, Brutus' death is more important than his life and achievements, because it provides the first recorded instance of the gladiatorial displays in which men like Spartacus were expected to give their lives. In his will, Brutus left a large sum of money for his sons to stage a *munus*, in which six of Brutus' slaves would fight in pairs to the death in honour of the great man. On the ninth day after the proconsul's passing, in accordance with ancient rites and with due solemnity, three more men died in the sand of Rome's cattle market, the Forum Boarium; no doubt the family of the proconsul approved.

Munus means 'obligation', and the idea probably came from the much older civilisation of the Etruscans, a highly advanced people who occupied central Italy when Rome was a ramshackle cluster of wooden huts on the slopes of one of its seven hills. Like many ancient peoples, the Etruscans slaughtered prisoners taken in battle to accompany their own heroes to the afterlife. Some doubt is cast today on this Etruscan link, because no archaeological evidence has been found to back it up. It is more likely that the practice had its origins among the Oscan-Lucanian peoples, who lived in central/southern Italy in the fourth century BC. One of the oldest depictions of a gladiatorial duel was found in the necropolis at Laghetto. Both men are wounded and appear to be going for the kill. Alexander the Great often ordered such butchery during his epic invasion of the Persian Empire of Darius, and Homer wrote in his *Iliad* that the legendary warrior Achilles, whose anger was terrifying, burned a dozen sons of the Trojan nobility when his friend Patroclus was killed. At some point, unrecorded, an element of choice crept into the ritual votive offerings, so that by the time of Brutus' death, some of the sacrificial lambs survived.

The purpose of *munera* was to ensure that the deceased's will was carried out. Family members, friends and slaves would witness the event – any failure here would result in angering a dead man's ghost. The other factor was the one that led to the escalation of gladiatorial shows in the later Republic and Empire – the need to impress. This seems a deep-rooted human desire – however lowly a man's life has been, his relatives like to give him a good send-off. In Victorian England, thousands of widows got themselves into serious debt paying for their husband's funerals. The sons of Decimus Brutus were honouring not only their father, but a long line of distinguished Romans who had, long before, overthrown the last tyrannical king of Rome, Tarquinius Superbus.

It is in this context that Roman officialdom took on the mantle of providing blood sports as a permanent institution. The Carthaginian historian Quintus Tertillianus, writing in the 190s BC, explains the situation:

> What was offered to appease the dead was counted as a funeral rite . . . It is called a *munus* from being a service due . . . The ancients thought that by this sort of spectacle they rendered a service to the dead, after they had tempered it with a more cultured form of cruelty. For of old, in the belief that the souls of the dead are propitiated with human blood, they used at funerals to sacrifice captives or slaves of poor quality. Afterwards it seemed good to obscure their impiety by making it a pleasure. So after the persons procured had been trained in such arms . . . their training was to learn to be killed! – they then did them to death on the appointed funeral day at the tombs. So they found comfort for death in murder.[1]

The religious ritual associated with gladiatorial contests never quite vanished. As a Christian, Tertillianus was appalled by the apparently insatiable bloodlust of the crowd, especially at a time when Christians were convenient sacrificial lambs in the arena. Older religions saw things differently. Nicholas of Damascus, a Greek historian born some ten years after the Spartacus War, traced the Etruscan origins of the games, pointing out that when a gladiator died in the arena, he was dragged through a gate representing death – the Porta Libitinensis, named for the goddess of burial – by a slave carrying the hammer and wearing the mask of Charun, the death-demon. The Etruscan concept of an underworld was adapted by the Greeks and duly handed on to the Romans. At the moment of death, the soul was grabbed by evil genii led by Charun. A second group led by Vanth represented benevolent spirits, so that the soul was the prize for which Charun and Vanth struggled in a personification of the age-old struggle between good and evil. Because of the way in which gladiators were regarded in the Republic and Empire, there was no such contest in the case of their deaths. Their evil souls were hauled to Hell.[2]

By 174 BC, when Titus Quinctius Flaminius died, the *munera* had become much more lavish and audiences extended beyond the families of those concerned. Flaminius was one of the dazzling generals the Republic produced that made Rome the master of the Mediterranean world by Spartacus' time. His funeral games lasted for three days and there were seventy-four gladiatorial combats. Not only was this the first time that the clash of iron took priority over eating and drinking, but it took place not at the time of the general's death, but at the midwinter solstice of Saturnalia (21–25 December) to allow audiences to enjoy it.

Saturn was the Roman god of the harvest, a former king of Italy in the mythic golden age which most Romans assumed had once existed. His name was derived from the old Latin/Etruscan words for a sower and gorging, in other words, abundance. His festival was technically on 17 December – schools were closed, shops shut, the law courts did not operate and the army took its rest around its legionary eagles kept in Saturn's Temple near the Capitol. His marble statue was wrapped in woollen bands to prevent him leaving the city, but at the Saturnalia these ties were cut. Slaves could talk to their masters as equals and the world became topsy-turvy. The traditions of the mischievous spirit of Twelfth Night and the Lord of Misrule had their origins in the Saturnalia. A more sinister tradition links Saturn with the Greek god Kronos, who ate his children rather as the Romans devoured theirs in the sand of the arena.

Today, most people associate gladiatorial spectacle with the Coliseum with its dazzling architecture and labyrinth of underground tunnels. In fact, this was not built until the reign of Vespasian, two generations after Spartacus, and the arena in which he fought was a much less lavish platform. The Forum Boarium was a perfect Roman setting for slaughter because the cattle pens could be dismantled quickly and the proximity of shops and houses meant a virtually instant audience for the contests. Upper windowsills were hired out to the wealthy, but the mob elbowed each other to get a vantage point as close to the blood as possible.

By the time of Spartacus' birth, the central Forum in Rome had replaced the cattle market as the most popular of the killing venues. It was in many ways the heart of the city and the heart of the Republic, so staging gladiatorial fights here gave them a singular prominence in the minds of the people. The much larger Circus Maximus nearby had already housed chariot races for decades, and the Circus has its share of spills and thrills in which there were few rules and in which men sometimes died.

The earliest known arenas with elliptical seating to provide a clear view of the action were built in Campania to the south of Rome, where Spartacus himself would be trained for the entertainment of the crowd. The largest was probably in Capua, where Lentulus Batiatus taught Spartacus the moves of his last duel, but the smallest building at Pompeii is better chronicled. Built around 80 BC when Spartacus may still have been a serving soldier, it was dug into the ground with earth ramparts and steps leading to an auditorium. At its greatest extent its seating capacity was an astonishing 20,000: a third of the size of the Millennium Stadium in Cardiff, Wales, but enormous in the context of the population figures of Spartacus' time.

Pompeii does not feature directly in the story of Spartacus at all, but its proximity to the man's revolt cannot be ignored. We have already noted the House of Mysteries with its erotic, Dionysius-inspired wall paintings. Its amphitheatre has a particular resonance because it dates from Spartacus' time and may have links with the enigmatic wall graffito of the mounted warrior Spartaks in the House of the Sacerdos (priest) Amandus.

Built into the embankment that flanked the town's walls, the amphitheatre was funded by Caius Quinctius Valeus and Marcus Porcius, the *duoviri quinquennali*, a rough equivalent of a joint mayoralty. Such buildings were called *spectacular*, 'amphitheatrum' being a later term. The parapet which surrounded the arena itself was brightly painted and served as a barrier for the safety of the crowd. Unlike the larger building at Capua, there were no underground chambers here, but there are holding pens at each end of the arena which were the 'green rooms' of the gladiators before they made their entrance and probably housed the animal cages.

Most arenas were still relatively flimsy timber contraptions, and accidents were not uncommon. In the reign of the emperor Tiberius, overcrowding of the kind still seen in today's football grounds led to disaster. The historian Tacitus may have exaggerated numbers (50,000 killed) in his graphic account, but that in no way detracts from the horrors he describes:

> The packed structure collapsed, subsiding both inwards and outwards . . . overwhelming a huge crowd of spectators . . . Those killed at the outset . . . at least escaped torture, as far as their violent deaths permitted. More pitiable where those, mangled but not yet dead, who knew their wives and children lay there too. In daytime they could see them and at night they heard their screams and moans . . . The Senate decreed that in future no one with a capital of less than four hundred sesterces should exhibit a gladiatorial show and no amphitheatre should be constructed except on ground of proved solidity.[3]

How much the stagers of the games understood the mass psychology of their audiences is debatable, but they were clearly aware of it, and the issue is crucial to an understanding of the men who bred, trained, fought and ultimately defeated Spartacus. The Roman bloodlust is widely acknowledged and discussed, but it is an infinitely complex phenomenon. To those who staged the games, it could be hugely rewarding, although expenses, too, were huge. Responsibility for staging gladiatorial shows fell to the *aediles*, the officials who were at first secular officers in the Temples of Ceres, the goddess of the corn. In 367 BC, their number was increased to four and the role embraced the whole public life of the city. They maintained and built public buildings, like the Forum Boarium itself; they cleaned the streets; they checked the weights and measures of the street traders; and they organised the games.

It was the games that made or broke an *aedile*. Successful games earned enormous popularity and the likelihood of greater promotion, perhaps to proconsul or consul. Unsuccessful games meant that they had to be restaged, at personal cost and probably to the detriment of a man's future. Above all, the games were public. A man could put up with stumbling in goose droppings along the Via Appia and could tolerate being 'ripped off' by a shady slave-leader in the Forum, as long as he had a good seat in the arena and could enjoy the spectacle of death.

An *aedile* had only twelve months in office (ten in Spartacus' era) and he had to make his mark. Adapting the numerous Roman festivals and inventing new ones gave huge opportunities. Vows were made to any one of the panoply of gods, to mark the end of a drought, the sight of a shooting star or the birth of a great man's son. The older festivals of Saturnalia and Lupercalia (14 February) were fixed in the year's calendar, but by the time of Spartacus, there were nearly 100 days, almost a third of the year, given over to holy days on which various festivals took place.

In Greco-Roman mythology, the mysterious figure of Evander, the son of the prophetess nymph Carmente and the god Hermes, whom the Romans called Mercury, was the instigator of important celebrations whose actual origins were lost in time. The oldest of his events was the Ludus Consuales, essentially a horse race held in August in honour of the corn god Consus. The god's altar was buried and excavated annually so that by Spartacus' time, men worshipping him whispered to the grass growing over his shrine their innermost secrets. All horses and donkeys in Rome were given the day off and were led through the streets garlanded with flowers. By the fourth century BC the horse races had developed into chariot events where *quadrigas* competed against each other and the *essedarii* drove in the colours of their owners, not unlike modern jockeys.

Most spectacular of all the festivals organised by the *aediles* was the Ludi Maximi, the Great Games, held in honour of Jupiter, the father of the gods. Only the people of Rome as a body could worship Jupiter – individuals were too unworthy. Chariot races moved from the open fields of the Campus Martius to the purpose-built Circus Maximus for this event and gladiatorial contests too became the norm.

The Ludi Apollinares, named for Apollo, the most beautiful of the gods whose chariot was the sun, were held by the *aediles* in memory of the moment when the Carthaginian general, Hannibal, abandoned his siege of Rome in the spring of 212 BC. Everyone wore laurels in their hair as a mark of victory, watched plays and listened to music, as well as crowding into the arena.

The Ludi Megalenses were held in April, although they did not become a regular fixture until the reign of Claudius, two generations after Spartacus. They honoured Cybele, whose meteorite temple stood on the Palatine Hill. She was the mother of the gods and originally her temple was tended by eunuch priests. The Ludi Plebii – literally, the People's Games – marked the gathering of the grape harvest in November and the participants inevitably sampled a high percentage of the crop. The Ludi Floralia, sacred to the goddess of flowers, was another erratic festival which many *aediles* were probably anxious to ignore. Flora was a Sabine deity from the tribe beyond the Apennines, and since the rape of the Sabine women was one of the more shameful and spectacular examples of ancient bloodlust the festival's content was not to the taste of respectable Roman society. No doubt the *plebii* loved it, however.

At a stroke, then, the *aediles* and later the emperors whose unbounded generosity made the games possible, managed to appeal to traditionalists who expected the religious festivals to be observed as well as giving the crowd what they wanted. It is Lord Byron whose line still impresses most – 'Butchered to make a Roman holiday',[4] although the throwaway line from the Roman poet Juvenal has better stood the test of time. Emperors, he said mockingly, ruled through 'panem et circenses'[5] – bread and circuses.

Understanding how Rome's games worked provides a deeper understanding of the men to whom Spartacus was a pawn. There was a deep paradox in Roman society. It was at once the most advanced and the most cruel of the ancient civilisations and it took a long time before the Romans themselves began to realise just how brutal their society was. The Roman writer Seneca exposed the viciousness of the people who gave the world straight roads, a common language, European law and the best military organisation in the ancient period.

By chance I attended a midday exhibition . . . an exhibition at which men's eyes have respite from the slaughter of their fellow-men. But it was quite the reverse . . . the men have no defensive armour. They are exposed to blows at all points and no one ever strikes in vain . . . what is the need of defensive armour or skill? All these mean delaying death. In the morning they threw men to the lions and the bears; at noon, they threw them to the spectators . . . The outcome of every fight is death and the means are fire and sword . . . In the morning they cried 'Kill him! Lash him! Burn him! Why does he meet the sword in so cowardly a way? Why does he strike so feebly? Why doesn't he die game? Whip him to meet his wounds! Let them receive blow for blow, with chests bare and exposed to the stroke!' And when the games stop for the intermission, they announce; 'A little throat-cutting in the meantime, so that there may still be something going on'![6]

Seneca was disgusted with himself, but even more disgusted with his fellow man: 'I mean that I came home more greedy, more ambitious, more voluptuous and even more cruel and inhuman – because I have been among human beings.'

But the younger Seneca was decidedly untypical of his times. Born in Spain in the generation after Spartacus, the man became a revered Stoic philosopher and adviser to Nero, whose excesses in and out of the arena were infamous. Along with many others of whom the petulant emperor was insanely jealous, Seneca was forced to commit suicide, having outlived his usefulness.

Men of Seneca's generation had seen the games grow in size and number under the unbelievable cruelty of the earlier emperors. Claudius reputedly had a string of the trident- and net-carrying gladiators, the *retiarii*, butchered so that he could watch their faces as their throats were slit. Caligula, almost certainly deranged, matched dwarfs against women and cripples to see who would last longest in the bloody sand. But even in Spartacus' time, the shedding of blood in cruel ways for entertainment was an established part of the Roman scene.

The Romans did not stand alone in their practices, however; this kind of cruelty was the norm in ancient civilisations. Certainly, violent death was a daily occurrence in the days of Spartacus, despite the Romans' claim that they had established law and safety – the famous Pax Romana. The virtues of manhood and courage were prized above all others in the Roman world. Ritual slaughter in the arena whetted the appetite for warfare and the seasoned men to carry out the tough duty of the rulers of the Mediterranean world. An inscription on a wall at Minternae, north of Rome, celebrates the fact that Publius Baebus Justus had ten bears killed in the sand with the greatest cruelty.

The problem with providing ever more cruel and spectacular blood sports for the entertainment of the Roman mob was that it led to a vicious circle. The more blood the *aediles* and the gladiators provided, the more the mob seemed to need. Caligula virtually bankrupted himself staging gladiatorial shows, especially the more bizarre matches against wild beasts. For man versus man, he trebled the prize money on offer and in AD 38, the money – and the spectacle – ran out. The man who had already declared himself a god was jeered by a crowd disappointed by mangy lions and paunchy, unfit gladiators. He had the complainants dragged to the anterooms of the arena in the Forum and their tongues cut out so that they could jeer no more. Then he forced them to face starving animals, attracted by the blood gushing from the jeerers' mouths. Miranda Twiss, who cites this event in her book on evil,[7] says 'The Roman people were stunned.' I suspect that just as many of them joined their mad emperor in applauding as, one by one, the jeerers went down under the slashing claws and closing jaws of the lions. Blood begat blood – and successful *aediles* could at least claim they could only stage so many contests in their year in office. Under the longer-reigning emperors, this could not be an excuse.

'Bread and circuses' were precisely what the great unwashed demanded. The mob was a dangerous and unruly element in Roman society. It was fickle and could turn its allegiance and its mood on a sesterci. Brave indeed was the *aedile* or emperor who did not give the mob what it wanted.

In a sense, Spartacus fitted into that group of gladiators who were virtually *noxii*; that is, condemned criminals. The man had deserted from the Roman army and lived as a renegade and thief in the mountains of Thrace. All the care and training lavished on him at Capua by the *lanista* Lentulus Batiatus could not disguise the fact that he was actually on the equivalent of modern America's Death Row; the only issue was exactly where and when he would die – *how* was fairly obvious.

Gladiators were at the bottom of the social order. Both Seneca and the poet Juvenal equate them with male prostitutes and it is at least possible that some of them provided such services for wealthy bisexual Romans. They are specifically mentioned as undesirables in several ancient texts: in the town of Mercato Saraceno, the only three categories denied burial in the new cemetery were suicides, prostitutes and pimps, and gladiators. 'A hungry people,' warned Tacitus, 'does not listen to reason'[8] and in the reign of Augustus, forty years after Spartacus, foreigners and gladiators were banished from Rome in an attempt to solve the famine caused by a grain shortage.

One of the obvious reasons that gladiators were detested was that most of them had started off as slaves, who had an almost sub-human status in Roman society. Another reason was that gladiators were potentially very dangerous. The Spartacus rising aside, there were several insurrections in the decades before the birth of Christ when gladiators featured prominently. When rebellion threatened in 63 BC, gladiator troupes were billeted in Capua and other towns in Campania to act as crowd control. When Julius Caesar crossed the Rubicon fourteen years later, precipitating a war with his rival Pompey the Great, his 500 gladiators at Capua were dispersed and kept under guard in various villas throughout the provinces. When Caesar was murdered by republican conspirators in the March of 44 BC, Brutus and the rest responsible had gladiators standing by in the Theatre of Pompey ready to move against senators who tried to support their overambitious target. Such men were dangerous and they had to be watched.

Nowhere, however, is the hypocrisy of the Romans more apparent than in their ambivalent attitudes to gladiators. They were sex objects, not just for men, but women too, and it is possible to see in the leering females in the crowd of the arena the 'ladettes' of our own time who drool over male strippers at hen nights. Howard Fast[9] hints at all kinds of longings in the women who arrive at Lentulus Batiatus' training school, anxious to watch the gladiators going through their paces. At a lower level, the graffiti at Pompeii is often of a sexual nature, reflecting street girls' fascination for men whose oiled muscles flexed before them in the hot sand of the town's amphitheatre. Antigonus of Nicaea, born three generations after Spartacus, was said to be 'erotic and fond of gladiators'.[10] The graffiti is euphemistic by today's standards – Celadus the Thracian was 'suspirium et dues puellarum'[11] (the darling of the girls who sighed for him). Crescens the Retiarius was 'dominus et medicum puparum nocturnarum' (master and healer to the dolls by night). The poet Juvenal, writing a series of satirical odes in the first century, was particularly scathing about women, especially those who set their caps at gladiators:

What was the youthful charm that Eppia found so enchanting?
What did she see worth while being labelled 'The Gladiatress'?
This dear boy had begun to shave a long time ago, and one arm

Wounded, gave hope of retirement; besides he was frightfully ugly.

Scarred by his helmet, a wart on his nose and his eyes always running.

Gladiators, though, look better than any Adonis;

This is what she preferred to children, country and sister. This to her husband. The sword is what they dote on, these women.[12]

The clever Juvenal is punning in the last line. *Gladius* was the technical word for the short, double-edged sword carried by gladiators and soldiers alike, but it was also used in the sexually euphemistic sense of a weapon whose shape spoke for itself.

The sexual prowess of the gladiators was legendary and crossed the gender barrier too. Female gladiators were a novelty and almost certainly held the same position as mud-wrestlers do for modern male audiences. Juvenal wrote in AD 116:

And what about female athletes, with their purple robes and wrestling in mud? Not to mention our lady swordsmen . . . But then, what modesty can be looked for in some Helmeted hoyden, a renegade from her sex,

Who thrives on masculine violence – yet would not prefer

To *be* a man, since the pleasure is so much less?

Hark how she snorts at each positive thrust, bowed down by the weight of her Helmet;

See the big coarse leggings wrapped round her ample buttocks . . .[13]

A bas-relief stone slab from London seems to show female gladiators in action. Armoured like the men, they face each other armed with swords and shields, their helmets on the ground to show their obviously female hair. Their stage names are inscribed in Greek letters under their feet – Amazonia and Achilia.

If men like Juvenal, cynical and bitter though he was (perhaps because of the failure of his own military career), disapproved of the sexually ambiguous status of the gladiators, others resented the fact that such 'scum' occasionally floated to the surface. Contrary to myth and commonly held belief, gladiators did not always fight to the death. Those who won enough fights and impressed the crowd, and *aedile* or emperor, might eventually earn their freedom and receive the *rudis*, the wooden sword which was a symbol of liberty. Such men were held in contempt by the affluent classes of Rome, but a tiny minority were able to gain respectability, at least on a local level. In Ancyra (today's Ankara) a gladiator was given the much-coveted right of citizenship of seven towns across what is now Turkey and Greece. In the reign of Claudius, Curtius Rufus, almost certainly the son of a gladiator, was given a general's triumph and the proconsulship of an African province, despite his unfortunate origins.

Long after Spartacus, an apogee of violence was reached in the reign of the emperor Comodus.[14] Earlier emperors such as Caligula and Hadrian had occasionally ventured into the arena, rather as the English king Charles II rode horses to victory at Newmarket near Cambridge. At six foot two, Charles was hardly of jockey build, yet his wins were frequent. No doubt the gladiators facing their emperors were told to ease off in these contests in which the outcome could be in no doubt. The unstable Comodus, however, identified with the mighty Hercules and claimed to have killed 12,000 men in the arena. He certainly fought hundreds of times, and prided himself on his left-handed swordplay. 'Comodus arranged to kill a man now and then,' wrote the historian Dio Cassius, 'and in making close passes with others, as if trying to clip off a bit of their hair, he sliced off the noses of some, the ears of others . . . but in public he refrained from using steel and shedding human blood.'[15]

Most of the actual killing took place in his private apartments in the gladiatorial school of Rome.

Much of the information that has survived in the documentary and artistic record on the gladiator comes from the decades and even centuries after Spartacus. The irony is that we do not know whether the man ever actually fought in the arena; but we know he was trained to do so and we know how.

FOUR

Thrax

'A man called Lentulus Batiatus,' wrote Plutarch, 'had an establishment for gladiators at Capua. Most of them were Gauls and Thracians.'[1] We have no record of how Spartacus reached Capua, but there would seem to be only two possibilities. The first is that he was taken, no doubt chained or roped together with other slaves, through the Roman province of Macedonia and then by ship across the Adriatic to Italy's east coast and finally across country again. Interestingly, both the recent epic film depictions of gladiators[2] show would-be gladiators carried on a wagon, presumably to protect potentially valuable merchandise from incurring wear and tear. Kirk Douglas's *Spartacus* has Batiatus travelling in person to recruit likely lads, but since this scene is wrongly set in Libya, we cannot know how accurate it was. More likely, Spartacus was bought in Italy itself, perhaps at the seaport of Brindisium, a place to which the rebel would return. Plutarch contends that he was sold in Rome, but whether he means the city itself or somewhere within its sphere of influence is unknown.

His other likely route was by sea all the way from the Thracian coast on the Pontus Euxinus (the Black Sea) or the Sea of Marmara and on through the Aegean. Piracy was an ongoing problem in the Mediterranean and the Cilicians made a fortune out of it; it may be that the land route was safer.

Capua today has lost the status it had in Spartacus' time. Santa Maria Cápua Vetere is a rather unprepossessing place with suburbs full of petrol stations, run-down housing and small shops. Around 70 BC it was the second city of Italy, with a long Etruscan and Samnite history and, according to archaeological evidence, a bronze-manufacturing industry. The amphitheatre whose remains still stand today, partly concreted over, dates from the first century AD, but it was almost certainly built on the site of an earlier construction, the one in which Spartacus may have fought.

Unlike Pompeii, with its solid arena on the ground, this one has a hollow, vaulted floor, like the more famous Coliseum in Rome itself. Holes in it have been patched with planking and railway sleepers, and toughened glass lets the visitor peer down into the murky recesses. There are the usual gates, the entry of life and the exit of death, and a huge carved tablet proclaiming that this place was built in the reign of the divine Augustus. It is probably the underground tunnels that Spartacus would have been most familiar with: the damp, dripping darkness where the gladiators waited to take their turn in the sand above, the holes that let in sunlight and the snarling, terrified, caged beasts.

There is no sign of the *ludus gladiatorus*, Batiatus' school of gladiators, and we have to turn to the preserved remains at Pompeii, 40 miles away, for a glimpse of the world into which Spartacus had been sold. It was not until AD 62 that the Pompeii school became a permanent barracks for gladiators, but its size and structure reflected a style of training that evolved little (except in excess) over five centuries. Between 1766 and 1769, excavations were carried out in the area to the rear of the amphitheatre. Built in the second century BC, it was a large rectangular building with walkways, originally intended as an area for theatregoers to wander during the long intervals in plays. An earthquake at unlucky Pompeii in AD 62 obviously led to major rebuilding and reassignment of some public buildings, because the *quadriporticus* then became the gladiatorial school, the rectangular area the fighters' training ground. A sundial at its centre regulated the day's practice sessions. It is not known where the men lived and trained in the days of Spartacus. Spartacus would once again have been a tyro, a novice, as he had been three or four years earlier in the army camp, and he would have received savage treatment from those around him. He would have understood his fellow Thracians (although we have no accurate knowledge of the variety of Thracian dialects), and may have talked to them in the few minutes of leisure afforded each day. The Gauls were a different prospect – tall, auburn-haired men with long limbs and an alien language. If Spartacus was a typical Thracian, he would have not looked unlike these men, and the casual Italian looking at them in the arena would not have been able to tell them apart. The rebellion that was to follow would throw up a leader among the Gauls – Crixus. Tyros were the lowest of the low, the dross from which a tiny handful of great gladiators could be picked, by the random chance of luck and the drawing of lots. They were also expendable – tyros were often maimed and killed in practice bouts or became victims of experienced professionals in exhibitions in the arena itself. If Spartacus did in fact serve with the army, then he would have a marked advantage over most of his fellow tyros – he would already have a certain expertise with the *gladius*, the short, double-edged sword carried by legionaries and the *pugio*, the dagger. As we shall see, however, the majority of slaves in this period were actually prisoners of war, so a tough, violent regime was probably a way of life for most of them.

In Kirk Douglas's film, Spartacus undergoes an initiation at Capua in which his hair is cut with a distinctive scalp lock on top of the cranium and he is branded with a red-hot iron on the sole of the foot. The haircut seems to have been the invention of a Hollywood stylist. Most of the contemporary depictions of gladiators show them helmeted; only the net-carrying *retiarus* fought bareheaded. The topknot was actually a Thracian distinction, although it seems to have been reserved for the aristocracy and may well have ceased to be fashionable by Spartacus' time. Branding was not carried out routinely on slaves, except those who escaped, in which case the red-hot iron was stamped on their foreheads. Certainly, the Thracian would have to swear an oath common to all gladiators – 'Uri, vincere, verberari, ferroque necari' (to be burned with fire, bound in chains, beaten with rods and killed with iron).[3] This was not so much a spoken contract with Batiatus as a recognition of the daily realities of life at Capua.

From now on – and this may have occurred some time in the year 74 BC – Spartacus was one of the *familia gladiatorae*. He belonged to Batiatus and his life was in the *lanista*'s hands. We have no knowledge of this man, but Spartacus' escape bid indicates that he was hard and ran a tight ship. The word *lanista* is an old Etruscan variant of the Latin *lanius*, a butcher, and by the first century AD it had the colloquial construction of an agitator or barrack-room lawyer. Such men were equated with pimps and procurers because they carried out similar functions – receiving money for other people's enjoyment of their property's bodies. One enterprising *lanista* styled himself 'negotiator familiae gladiatoriae' (business manager of gladiator troupes)[4] in the hope that the euphemism would fool somebody. It is most likely that Batiatus would have been an ex-gladiator himself, a survivor of the arena whose success and prize money had enabled him to open the school at Capua.[5] As such, his choice of Spartacus as a tyro would have been based on the man's physique and potential as a crowd-pleaser. And now the Thracian would have found himself standing in the arena of the school at Capua, in a hostile, alien environment he would probably only partially understand.

With him, in the hot sand of a baking Campanian day or under a lowering sky spitting rain, were a motley assortment of slaves and freemen from the local area, as well as foreigners like himself. Most bizarre of all were the volunteers, men who had deliberately opted for this way of life, ruled by fire, rods and the agony of sharp iron. Spartacus may have noticed that these men were not shackled, that Batiatus talked and joked with them, even though they had just taken the same pledge that he had.

Perhaps Batiatus inspected his new charges, ordering them, with prods from whips and canes, to strip to their waists. The Gauls wore light, loose leggings of dyed wool, an unusual sight in the Mediterranean world, and leather shoes. They would not keep these for long. Gladiators fought barefoot; probably so that they had a better grip in the sand when that grip might mean the difference between life and death. Batiatus would have walked along the rows, whip in hand, double-checking his selection. He wrenched open mouths to test the toughness of enamel on teeth, he tapped pectorals, biceps and buttocks. His charges stood in their *subligculi*, the triangular cloth pulled up between the legs which was the Roman version of underwear. Batiatus was already weighing up who was best equipped to take the trident, the *gladius*, the curved, murderous sword called the *thrax*. He was actually selecting men to die, but they would do it when and how he told them, and it had to be done in style.

Spartacus would have noticed that there were troops everywhere; not the legionaries, the cream of the army he had run from, but auxiliaries like him, tough men who may have been less reliable in the field, but heavily armed and no doubt inventive in their cruelty. They were posted at every doorway, every gate on every high point, watching the doomed tyros arrive.[6] Gladiators were *infamis*, the disgraced, and they could not be trusted. Suicide was not uncommon among them. The bizarre example related in AD 393 by the consul and orator Quintus Aurelius Symmachus came from four centuries later, but is still strongly relevant. Twenty-nine Saxon slaves had been trained for the arena, possibly in Egypt, but they had other ideas. In a letter to his brother Flavius, Symmachus wrote 'The first day of the gladiatorial games had barely begun when these twenty nine Saxons managed to strangle themselves without even having the rope to accomplish the task.'

He does not tell us how this mass suicide was possible, but he writes the dead men off with a highly pertinent response: 'I will not, therefore, trouble myself with this gang of slaves, worse than Spartacus himself.'[7]

Spartacus and the other tyros would have been escorted to their cells, slightly smaller than those of nineteenth-century British prison accommodation. These rooms were dark and damp – no point wasting fine accommodation on men whose survival rate was alarmingly low. The examples at Pompeii have tiny windows and a single door and they are built in the rectangle of stonework around the practice ground. No doubt cool and even refreshing in summer, they must have been grim in the Campanian winter months. At ten to fifteen metres square, these cells probably housed two or three men. The longer-serving gladiators, especially the most successful *primus pallus*, had better quarters, probably with two or three rooms, almost certainly on the second storey of the barracks. These men were the stars of the arena, the crowd-pullers, and it is unlikely that Spartacus ever reached their dizzy heights. Elsewhere in the Capua school Batiatus would have his own comfortable quarters, with couches and an atrium to welcome fashionable guests, 'slumming' by inspecting the gladiators. At Pompeii a stable was discovered, complete with the skeleton of a horse and stable-boy. Communal rooms included the kitchen and dining room and various storerooms. The cell walls of the tyros at Capua, like those at Pompeii, would have been covered with graffiti carved by the men themselves. Deprived as they were of sharp implements, because of the risk of violence or self-mutilation, we do not know how the inhabitants made these inscriptions; perhaps with bones thrown out with the kitchen slops. Some of these carvings show the names of women, probably prostitutes like those laid on by Batiatus. Their exact status remains a mystery, but in Howard Fast's imagination, the gladiators were allotted different women at the whim of the *lanista* and Batiatus indulges himself in a voyeuristic sideline, complete with schoolboy giggles, peering into the gladiators' cells. In fiction, the British slave girl Varinia meets Spartacus in this way. Since we know from Plutarch that the Thracian was already married and that his wife was sold with him (actually an unusual situation) the reality was altogether more domestic.

Little evidence has survived of the way of life of prostitutes in the late Republican period. Slave women generally are less well chronicled than the men, which is true, of course, of Roman society in general. Where they are mentioned it is on memorial tablets and in the wills of great men, who sometimes owned several thousand slaves of both sexes, working at a huge range of tasks on their many estates.

In common with the household chores expected – spinning, weaving, cooking, sewing and general domesticity – sexual favours came with the territory. It is likely that some women were bought specifically for the purpose and that most wives accepted this situation. The great general Scipio Africanus had a favourite girl whom his wife set free on the man's death. Marcus Porcius Cato, called Censor, came from peasant stock in Tusculum over a century before Spartacus' time. After the death of his wife, one of his slaves became his constant bedroom companion and he charged his male slaves a going rate to have sex with his female slaves. We do not know whether the girls at Capua were slaves belonging to the school, the property of Batiatus, or whether they were bought in from a local brothel. Again, evidence on this is limited. Women worked in inns as waitresses and 'barmaids' and as actresses, sometimes naked and performing sex acts on stage. Several examples of graffiti at Pompeii refer to such girls, often scurrilously commenting on their availability. Some could be had for the cost of a loaf of bread or two asses; the highest amount in the inscriptions is sixteen asses.[8] Some prostitutes – probably, ironically, free women who had no protection from a pimp or owner – offered their services on street corners. The very word fornicate comes from 'fornix', an arch.

More complex relationships than casual couplings can only be guessed at. Marriages were probably entered into by the gladiators at Capua, especially among the more select because of their reputations as sex gods. Whether the *amatrix* who wrote the following message on papyrus was a slave-prostitute, we cannot know:

> At the command of a proud man, *myrmillo*,
> Among the net-fighters, alas, you are gone,
> Gripping in strong hands a sword, your sole weapon
> And me you have left in my anguish alone.[9]

In Roman law, slave marriages were called *contubernium*, literally 'tent-companion', and the same word used for an eight-man platoon in the legions; they were regarded as a mere cohabitation with no legal status. We know that children were sometimes born of these liaisons (there was, of course, no effective contraception in ancient Rome)[10] and, oddly, many people believed that one way to avoid pregnancy was for the prostitute to wriggle her hips. In the barracks at Pompeii, archaeologists have uncovered the body of a child, together with a richly jewelled female who may or may not have been the baby's mother and may or may not have been the wife of a gladiator. In Smyrna, in Asia Minor, every gladiator contributed to the funeral expenses of the daughter of one of their number.

None of this, of course, helps us with the central question of Spartacus' unnamed wife. Did she work in the kitchens and service other gladiators? Or was she allowed to live with Spartacus in his cell? We simply have no idea.

At Capua, as in all gladiatorial schools, training included careful attention to diet. Gladiators were known as 'hordearii', 'barleymen', because of what they were given to eat. The soup, lentils and peas probably included, would be prepared in the kitchens and served up in earthenware pots with wooden ladles. Dr Fabian Kanz of the University of Vienna's Chemistry Department recently carried out research on the skeletons of a number of gladiators' bones found at Ephesus in modern Turkey that date from the second century AD. Typically, the cemetery is outside the city, well away from the graves of respectable society. Hidden under an olive grove, the stele (grave-markers) give us a great deal of information about the life of Spartacus' successors, still training for death 200 years after his rebellion. It is clear from the damage to various bones that these men died violently. Chemical analysis carried out by Kanz shows that the bones have a high strontium and a low zinc content, implying that the diet of men like Spartacus would have been virtually vegetarian. Dr Karl Grosschmidt, also of the University of Vienna, believes this diet gave gladiators a layer of subcutaneous fat which might have given added protection. In the vicious cut and thrust of the arena, it might make the difference between life and death. Various depictions of gladiators in mosaic art show very strong men, but whether this is an attempt to depict their musculature or their flab is not clear. Dieticians today know that a diet of pulses provides long-lasting energy and possibly acts as a brain food, increasing the speed of reflexes.

Just as important as the diet for Spartacus and his fellow gladiators was the work of the *medici*, the doctors at Capua. Research by Grosschmidt at Ephesus has found that the medical care here was excellent. Fractures had healed, bones had been reset. Digital X-ray techniques provide clear evidence that physiotherapy was regularly administered, and at Capua Batiatus would have had *unctores* (anointers) who acted as masseurs on aching muscles and torn ligaments. Such men sold bottles of gladiator sweat to ageing ladies hoping to stave off wrinkles. As few gladiators lived much beyond thirty, they may have had some reason to hope!

Testimony to the time and money invested in medical support for the gladiators is the fact that one of the most respected doctors of antiquity, Galen of Pergamum, started his career in the gladiatorial school in Pergamum. The son of a Greek architect, Galen was trained in medicine after his father had a dream that this was the boy's true calling. In AD 157 he was working at the gladiatorial school, but as a deeply religious man he found it painful to heal men only to see them die. Five years later, therefore, he moved to Rome, where he eventually became personal physician to the emperor Marcus Aurelius and passed into medical legend. Galen claimed, no doubt with some justification, that he cut mortality substantially during his time at the school.

Confusingly for us, the *doctor* in a gladiatorial school like Capua was more important than the *medici*. The *doctor* was the trainer, like Batiatus an ex-gladiator, and we have the names of some of them who served at Capua. These men were specialists in one or more of the highly technical fight routines of the arena and they also acted like referees of modern rugby matches at the games themselves, shouting out rules of engagement and separating fighters whose show had become sloppy. Unlike modern referees, they carried whips or burning torches to prod the overcautious into action.

We have no detailed evidence of the moves taught to the gladiators. As an ex-legionary, Spartacus would have been familiar with throwing the *pilum*, the javelin, but this was not a skill required in the arena. He would also have been accustomed to the *hasta*, the stabbing spear and in this context, the thrusting work of the net-men, the *retiarii*, with their three-pronged trident would have the familiarity of the battlefield. It is likely that the swordplay of the legionary was fairly basic, because the strength of the Roman infantry lay in its tight formations and rigid discipline. There was no room for flashy individual skills against the phalanxes of Macedonia or the cohorts from Carthage.

It is likely that all tyros were taught first to use a wooden sword. Sharp iron weapons caused accidents and were another incitement to murder or suicide. There was an irony here; the really successful gladiators, if they survived to 'retirement' in their thirties, were given the *rudis* (literally, a stick), a wooden sword that was the symbol of their freedom. The tyros would have spent several hours a day for several weeks hacking at a wooden post, the *palus*, which was the height of a man and driven deep into the ground. Some schools, perhaps Batiatus' at Capua, padded this with straw and sacking, stuffing a shield and helmet into the dummy to add reality. Mindless hacking like this would not impress an audience who had paid good money to see blood, so the next phase would be the cuts.

There is great debate about the use of real weapons in the practice field while Batiatus and his *doctori* looked on from the cool of the colonnade, but at some point, Spartacus would have been given a sharp sword to use and the *doctor* would have explained exactly where and how to cut. Recent research by archaeologist Steve Tuck of the University of Miami seems to have missed the point about gladiatorial displays. His contention is that most gladiatorial bouts were to display weapon skills, not fights to the death. He bases his assumption on artistic depictions of gladiatorial contests and on medieval and Renaissance fencing manuals. Both sources are highly suspect. Many Roman depictions, says Tuck, show gladiators with shields on the ground, as though they have deliberately thrown them away in order to grapple with their opponents and so bring the contest to an end in a sort of honourable draw. This ignores the likelihood that wounded gladiators who were finished might well have discarded their useless shields prior to raising the index finger of their left hand to signify the fact that they conceded the bout. It is also possible that a great deal of artistic licence was employed in the depiction of gladiators. In only a slightly different context, Harriet Beecher Stowe, who wrote so convincingly of slavery in *Uncle Tom's Cabin* in 1852, had never actually seen a slave or a plantation in her life. Renaissance fight manuals are not reliable sources for information about gladiators. By the time they were published the Christian ethic had helped transform the public attitude to fighting and perhaps toned down their bloodlust. We have already seen how nauseated Seneca was by the slaughter of the arena as early as the second century. Swordsmen in medieval and Renaissance Europe used their skills as a pure art form. Tournaments were mere *practice* for warfare, not the real thing. The assertion by Steve Tuck that gladiatorial displays may have been aimed at showing off weapon skills rather than fights to the death ignores the bloodlust we know was the *raison d'être* of the Roman mob. Crowds would not pay to see men *playing* when they could have reality. Men like Batiatus knew this, but they also knew that the crowd wanted spectacle. Modern fencing is a fascinating sport to take part in, but as a spectacle it is surprisingly dull – the moves are too fast and the audience feels cheated. Theatricality and showmanship were essential, but they were not, as Tuck contends, ends in themselves; merely the prelude to a kill.

There were a number of types of gladiator and we have no record of which speciality Spartacus adopted at Capua. Least likely was the sagittarius, the archer. Teams of these men shot at each other across the arena and an extra frisson must have been provided by these men as their curved, composite bows and iron barbed arrows were likely to inflict at least potential damage on the roaring crowd. Both the emperors Caligula and Comodus joined in with these sports, though usually from the relative safety of the imperial podium. The *essedarius* was a charioteer, often involved in the re-creation of historic Roman victories or fights against wild animals. It is probable that these did not make an appearance until after Claudius' invasion of Britain in AD 43, although the Celtic war chariot had been remarked on by Julius Caesar two generations earlier. Both the poet Martial (Marcus Valerius Martialis) and the satirist Petronius Arbiter ('the expert') refer to a female charioteer performing in the arena. This may be an oblique reference to Boudicca, the warrior queen of the Iceni who challenged Roman authority in AD 61. The more spectacular shows of the Empire re-staged in a stylised, theatrical way actual victories won by Roman armies, rather as Buffalo Bill Cody's Wild West Show depicted Indian battles in the early 1900s.

The mounted gladiators were the *eques*, the horsemen. They wore visored helmets and *manica* (defences made of overlapping plates) to protect both their thighs and their right arms. They carried lances and the *parma equestris*, a round shield similar to that used by auxiliary cavalry. The enigmatic graffito from the house of Sacerdos Amandus in Pompeii showing a mounted warrior called Spartaks conforms exactly to this type, and the possibility of its being the Spartacus of legend is too tantalising to overlook.

The least likely of all is the *paegniarius*, the equivalent of a warm-up comedian put on stage to get the audience primed for the star of a variety show. Men like this came closest to Steven Tuck's interpretation of gladiator as showman. They fought with wooden swords in a mimicry of the *real* entertainment which was to follow, and their gyrations were accompanied by a band playing lutes, cymbals and tubas. Under the deranged Comodus even this playful element of the games turned nasty. He had all the crippled slaves in Rome rounded up and ordered that serpents' tails be tied around their stumps before beating them all to death with a club. It is not recorded that any of them were armed with anything other than a certain resignation.

The *hoplomachus* and the *provocator* (challenger) were merely variants of one of the four most common types of gladiator and it is surely here we will find Spartacus' niche. The *retiarius*, the net fighter, is a particularly interesting variant, though it is unlikely that Spartacus was in this category. Such is the influence of Kirk Douglas's *Spartacus* that we almost expect these men to be Nubians, tall, athletic black men like Woody Strode, but in fact they were regarded as the most lightweight of gladiators in their day and had the air of effeminacy about them. They were the only regular exhibitors in the arena whose heads were bare and faces exposed, and this may have been a factor in the public perception of them. The fact that these men's faces were on display also made them the favourites of the ladies, be they respectable matrons or tarts from the town – perhaps that is why other men despised them. But there was another factor. With the six-foot reach of his trident and the even longer play of his net, the *retiarius* kept some distance from his opponent and did not have to grapple in the dust of the arena as the other fighters did.

The trident was a nod in the direction of the mythological origin of the games. It was carried by Neptune, god of the sea, and the net was used to catch the fish-gladiator called *myrmillo*. The weapon had three iron prongs with which the gladiator could hamstring an opponent by pinning his foot to the ground. A lucky hit could pierce the visor of his helmet and slice through his skull. An interesting set of wounds has been found on one of the gladiator's skulls at Ephesus, which clearly corresponds to a trident thrust. The interpretation given by Dr Karl Grosschmidt is that this is a *retiarius* killed by his own weapon, snatched from him by a victorious opponent. This is of course possible, but most victorious gladiators kill with their own weapons. Even the victorious *retiarius* used his *pugio* (dagger) to dispatch his victim. Another possibility is that the dead man had lost his helmet in the bout or (most unusually) that this was the result of a *retiarius* versus *retiarius* contest.

The net itself (reticulum) was nine foot nine inches in diameter and had weights attached to make it more effective as a weapon. An opponent could be blinded by the weights or trapped in the net as he struggled to hold his footing on the hot sand. The net was secured to the *retiarius*'s broad belt (*balteus*) with ropes so that he could snatch it up again if his opponent wrenched it from his grip. Likewise, if an opponent held him fast, the *retiarius* could cut himself free with his dagger.

Traditionally, the *retiarius* had the poorest cell at schools like Capua. The ever cynical Juvenal is very disparaging of such men:

The games! Go there for the ultimate scandal,
Looking at Gracchus who fights, but not with the arms of a
                                             swordsman.
Not with a dagger or shield (he hates and despises such weapons),
Nor does a helmet hide his face. What he holds is a trident,

What he hurls is a net, and he misses, of course, and we see him
Look up at the seats, then run for his life, all around the arena,
Easy for all to know and identify. Look at his tunic,
Golden cord and fringe, and that queer conspicuous arm guard![11]

Like all gladiators, the *retiarius* wore fabric padding on both legs
and on his net arm (the left, most often facing his opponent). The
arm guard that Juvenal sneers at was a *galerus*, a bronze shoulder
defence with a high flange to protect the gladiator's head from a
sword slash. Three of these have been found in the gladiatorial
school at Pompeii, decorated with sea symbols such as crabs and
anchors; the head of Hercules; and the palm leaf wreath of victory.
One carries the inscription RET SECUND (Retiarius, second rank).

The usual enemy of the *retiarius* was the *secutor* (pursuer), and it
is possible that Spartacus was trained as one of these. These men
wore smooth rounded helmets, hinged at the front so that only their
eyes were visible. The least aerated of all gladiatorial headgear, the
secutor's headpiece allowed for a frontal approach only. Remarkable
reconstructions have been carried out on all gladiatorial armour and
equipment by experimental archaeologist Dr Marcus Junkelmann.
He has proved from archaeological finds that the *secutor*'s helmet
gave a very restricted field of vision and that its wearer may even
have had difficulty hearing the barked commands of the *doctori*.
Unlike the *retiarius*, the *secutor* carried a straight-bladed *gladius* and
a curved, rectangular shield which was a smaller and lighter version
of the *scutum* carried by the regular army. Pitted against the *retiarius*
as he usually was, the *secutor* could block the flailing net with his
shield, then close in to dispatch his opponent by stabbing him after
batting his trident aside. The armour on his right arm and the
bronze greaves on his legs made him slower, so that in that
particular contest, two distinctive fighting styles were on display.
Ornate examples of greaves have been excavated at Pompeii,
decorated with cupids and winged victory. Bronze rings on the lower
calf section held the leather cross-straps in place.

The *myrmillo* was similarly equipped, except that the huge
metallic crest on his helmet was fashioned to resemble the dorsal fin

of a fish, from which the name is derived in the original Greek.[12] Very elaborate forms of these helmets have survived, including one fitted with individual scales of silver and gold that shimmered and dazzled in the Capuan/Pompeian sunshine. The *myrmillo* too carried a *gladius* and *scutum* and only one greave, almost certainly on the left leg (the one presented to his opponent during bouts), although both were padded with fabric tied at regular intervals. In practice, such wadding must have resembled modern cricket pads, but allowing mobility at elbows and knees.

Most spectacular of all the gladiators was the *thrax*, the Thracian. It is tempting to assume that Spartacus was equipped and trained as one of these, if only because of his own origins. Most of those who appeared in the arena wore equipment symbolic at least of the many nations Rome had beaten in the field in the long wars of conquest. The Thracian took his name not merely from the country, but from the vicious curved sword he carried in the arena. There is some debate as to how these swords were used, which depends on the way the curve went. It is most likely that the sword was held so that the curve went upwards, as with light cavalry sabres used in later centuries. It is possible, however, that it curved downwards, rather like the Gurkha knife, and that the tip and blade edge were used to rip and slash accordingly. The Thracian's right arm was padded with the usual *manica* and it is not known whether overlapping metal plates were added by Spartacus' time; they certainly were later. The shield which Spartacus may have carried was a *parma*, a half-size rectangle made in the same way as the *scutum* – layers of wood glued together like modern plywood and edged and bossed with bronze. The huge helmet was not unlike that of the *myrmillo*, but had a distinctive griffin crest with provision for horsehair and feather plumes, reflecting the Macedonian influence in Spartacus' homeland.[13] More lightly armed than the *myrmillo* or the *secutor*, the *thrax* was expected to be faster, using nimble footwork and parrying blows with sword and shield.[14] Altogether, when Spartacus the Thracian faced an opponent, he stood up in perhaps 20 pounds of equipment, the griffin emblem of the dreadful goddess Nemesis looming over his visored face.

We do not know if Spartacus ever fought for his life in the arena. The scenario imagined by Howard Fast, that titled Romans travelling through Capua demanded a show to the death from Batiatus, is entirely possible. Equally, Spartacus may have faced opponents in any one of the games staged by wealthy Capuan officials or the *munus* of a great man, now long forgotten. Certainly, an enterprising businessman like Batiatus would have his eye on the main chance. The *lanista* was despised, but he had his definite place in society and he could earn a fortune. Details would be worked out in advance, prices agreed. If there was a fight to the death, the senior *doctor* would salute the *aedile* or *editor* with the famous phrase, 'Ave, morituri te salutant' (Hail: those about to die salute you) and the bout would commence. Clashes between gladiators, especially the *primi palus* who were well known and had their *amatores* following, were clashes of titans, like heavyweight boxing championships today. In Capua, in Pompeii, but above all in Rome itself, the crowd was entertained by dwarfs, musicians, mock fights and the slaughter of criminals before these main bouts took place. In the case of the more spectacular games, where whole days were involved, these contests might take place after dark and the gladiators would whirl and parry in the flicker of torchlight. The man who had lost his weapons or dropped, exhausted, with a serious wound, raised his left index finger to signal it was over. As the crowd roared 'Habet! Hoc Habet!' (Got him! He's had it!) the victor turned to the *aedile* or the *editor* for the signal. More argument rages about this than about any other aspect of gladiator lore. Technically the decision to end a fighter's life or grant him the *missus* (literally 'let go') lay with the holder of the games, but a sensible *aedile*, *editor* and even, in later years, emperor, would be wise to follow the wishes of the crowd. For many years, historians have made the assumption that the thumb upward was the symbol for the *missus*, life (in which context it is still regarded as a positive gesture) and the thumb downwards meant death. Today, most historians have veered to the exact opposite, that the thumb upwards meant kill by using the weapon, and a thumb tucked into the palm of the hand meant life. There is yet another school of thought which suggests that the gesture is actually the right hand brought smartly back to the throat, signifying death. Whatever the reality, the *aedile* would wave a cloth if the *missus* was granted; for death, the signal was a flat sweep of the hand.

Just as the actual fighting in the arena had its traditional, stereotypical elements, so the killing of the defeated gladiator was highly ritualised. Several of the bones at Ephesus show sword cuts on the vertebrae below the skull and on the clavicles and ribs. In other words, the sword (or in the case of the *retiarius*, the dagger) was driven downwards, either at the nape of the neck or alongside the neck. Either way, the target was probably the heart. The more spectacular throat-cutting was no doubt sometimes employed, but it might not cause death without a second or third blow, which may have caused aesthetic upset. Several artistic interpretations of gladiators show a victim kneeling in resolution, hugging the legs of the man about to kill him. The significance of this is now lost. It was probably not a piece of body language associated with begging for mercy, for the winning gladiator was in fact the wrong man to ask. It probably had more to do with a brotherly gesture born of the confraternity of those trained to die. All gladiators were encouraged to die silently with the stoicism expected of men born to the sword. Modern research has proven that most amphitheatres' acoustics were such that sound carried outwards and up, so that even the poor and women sitting 'in the gods' could hear every grunt and groan. The *doctori* would then supervise the litter-bearer slaves as they carried the dead gladiator through the gate of death. Here, his body would be laid out in the *spoliarium*, stripped of its armour and equipment, and arrangements would be made for burial. In the arena, the winner received his payment – in coin – and trotted around the ground in the equivalent of a lap of honour.

But at Capua, some time in 73 BC, something had gone wrong. Any attempt at explaining gladiator psychology quickly runs into difficulty. The fact that some men *volunteered* for this work speaks volumes for its positive side – winnings were huge for non-slaves who did not have to hand them over to the *lanista*. There was the thrill of the chase, the excitement of battle, the chance to preen and there was always an admiring entourage of ladies. We know that some gladiators took their profession of arms seriously. Two generations after Spartacus, a *myrmillo* complained that his time was being wasted, not to mention his talent, when the emperor Tiberius reduced the number of games to cut the crippling expense. Even for slaves like Spartacus, the advantages of regular food, good training and 'free' women must have had their attractions.

Clearly, from archaeological evidence, we know that life for gladiators at Pompeii in the generation after Spartacus was good. Not only was there the Schola armaturarum, the building in which gladiatorial weapons were housed on public display, but the House of the Gladiators was a sort of hostel for the fighters. It and the amphitheatre where they fought are across town from the gladiator school itself, implying that the gladiators could come and go with a reasonable degree of freedom. The presence of the jewelled female body in the school itself may mean that visitors from the town were commonplace.

The downside was that the *familia gladiatorae* was not really a family at all. How could a man truly bond with a man who he may have to kill tomorrow? How could he be a friend to a man who will kill him? We have seen already that suicide was not uncommon; a Germanic gladiator killed himself by ramming a toilet sponge down his throat and choking on it.

Plutarch implies that what happened at Capua was over-zealousness on the part of Batiatus' regime. 'They [the gladiators] had done nothing wrong, but, simply because of the cruelty of their owner, were kept in close confinement until the time came for them to engage in combat.'[15]

The implication, perhaps, is that not all schools treated their tyros in this way. It is well brought out by Fast and Douglas – the silent system, the merciless provoking of Spartacus, the selling of the slave woman he had come to love. The only problem is that this is fiction and we cannot know what the real facts were. 'Two hundred of them planned to escape,' says Plutarch, 'but their plan was betrayed and only seventy eight, who realised this, managed to act in time and get away, armed with choppers and spits which they seized from some cookhouse.'[16]

Appian already has Spartacus at the heart of the rising and breakout: 'Spartacus . . . persuaded about seventy of his fellows to risk their lives for freedom rather than for exhibition as a spectacle. With them, he overpowered their guards and escaped.'

It is easy to see Spartacus as a subversive, bent on overthrowing the system. It is much more likely that the uprising was a spontaneous loss of temper by one or more gladiators in which others joined. The speed and surprise of the attack generated its success. Fighting one-to-one, the agility and individual skill of the gladiators, even armed with kitchen implements, must have told against the second-rate auxiliaries posted to guard the Capua school.

They swarmed away across the arena training ground, snatching weapons from the guards they dispatched and smashed their way through the gates and grilles. Perhaps they ransacked the comfortable home of Lentulus Batiatus; perhaps they killed him – his name disappears entirely from the record after this. Perhaps they took the kitchen slaves, the *medici*, perhaps even the odd *doctor* with them; we cannot know. Little archaeology seems to have been unearthed at Capua, but a dig is in progress near the amphitheatre. If Capua was the second city in Italy in Spartacus' day, it would have had a town garrison, city gates, walls and ramparts. All these defences would have had to be tackled to break out and we have no details of how – or exactly when – this was accomplished.

But one thing is certain – the slave called Spartacus was free.

FIVE

In the Shadow of Vesuvius

The chronology of Spartacus' escape from the school in Capua is confused. According to the two most detailed sources, Plutarch and Appian, it appears that the first problem for the fugitives was a shortage of weapons. Appian says that they stole wooden clubs and daggers from travellers on the roads; Plutarch contends that they came across a wagonload of gladiatorial weapons which were bound for another city, presumably Rome, and liberated its contents. All this is perplexing because if the breakout had been thorough, the fugitives would surely have had weapons of their own. There were, according to all sources, almost seventy of them and the gladiatorial weapons – swords, and tridents – from the school, as well, surely, as *some* of the weapons of the guards they overcame, should have sufficed.

The confusion probably arises from the fact that the seventy had as yet no leader – although Appian contends that Spartacus was behind the breakout – and no clear aims. Plutarch says that a force from Capua was sent out to bring the slaves to heel and that they were defeated: 'In this engagement, they got hold of proper arms and gladly took them in exchange for their own gladiatorial equipment which they threw away, as being barbarous and dishonourable weapons to use.'[1]

This makes little sense. Gladiatorial weapons were only dishonourable if we take the more 'liberal' attitude of certain educated Romans, like Plutarch himself, to whom the whole notion of death for entertainment was distasteful. If the gladiators threw their own weapons away, it was because the swords, daggers, javelins and shields of the Capua troops were far more serviceable for the kind of fighting they would now have to face.

We have no information about this, the first of many clashes between what was to become the army of Spartacus and the forces of authority. Written sources are infuriatingly vague about town garrisons, focusing largely on the legions and their work in war. In the absence of anything resembling a modern police force, the local garrison would be expected to maintain law and order. A city like Capua, second largest in Italy and with a potentially dangerous underclass – the gladiators – should have had large numbers of soldiers. How the runaways defeated them we do not know, but they carried out raids in nearby villages, no doubt helping themselves to supplies, and made for a hill, possibly Vesuvius, 30 miles to the south-east.

Although Plutarch rather lamely calls the rebels' destination a 'hill', Appian is more certain and suggests that they were heading for Mount Vesuvius itself. Taking refuge on such a commanding landmark would make perfect sense. The view from Vesuvius was and is spectacular, and any approaching army would be visible at least a day's march away. The summit today is 1,821 feet above sea level, rising majestically over the Bay of Naples out of the black, volcanic soil which makes Campania so fertile. Poplars and pine trees clothe the foothills and lizards scuttle among the rosemary growing wild among the orange and lemon trees. Vesuvius is the only active volcano left in Europe, spectacularly erupting in AD 79 and burying the towns of Pompeii and Herculaneum in, respectively, a thick, choking layer of ash and a terrifying molten river of lava. It is this that has preserved in such macabre fashion the life of an ordinary Roman town in the late first century, a snapshot in time. Much of what we know about Roman urban civilisation comes from the finds made here. The volcano has erupted at least 100 time since AD 79, most destructively in December 1631 when an estimated 3,000 people died. Vesuvius was also erupting in March 1944 as Allied troops swarmed north through the country to knock Italy out of the Second World War.

We have no idea of the geological state of Vesuvius in 73 BC. Plutarch tells us that 'the top of the hill' [presumably where the smouldering crater is today] was covered with wild vines, and

Spartacus was to make good use of these in the clash that was to come. The commentator Sallust also refers to the place as a mountain and even a brief visit to the region makes it obvious there are several nearby to choose from. Any of them might be a contender for the first stronghold of the runaways, although they may not have wanted to have their movements watched by an enemy on higher ground, so perhaps it was Vesuvius.

Gaius Sallustus Crispus ought to be the best source for the war of Spartacus. He was thirteen when it broke out and living not far away at Amiternum in the Sabine country north-east of Rome. He began writing late in life, perhaps in 42 BC, and like many Roman historians was a moraliser, disgusted by the political corruption that characterised the late Republic. His *Histories*, written a few years later, contain five books, but most of these are lost and the remaining fragments are composed in an archaic, obscure and oblique style with a terseness copied much later by the more famous Tacitus.

The historical sources do not agree about the details of the first clash between Spartacus and Rome. According to Appian 'the first man the Romans sent out against Spartacus was Varinius Glaber', whereas Plutarch contends that it was 'the praetor Clodius, with 3,000 soldiers'. A more careful reading of the Latin text, however, confirms that 'Clodius' was actually Gaius Claudius Glaber. Appian hits the nail on the head when he writes that Glaber 'did not command the regular citizen army of legions, but rather whatever forces [he] could hastily conscript on the spot, since the Romans did not yet consider this a real war, but rather the raids and the predations of bandits'.[2]

To see why Glaber and his motley 3,000 did not take Spartacus seriously, we have to understand the nature of slave revolts – and of slavery – in the Republic at this time.

'In all social systems,' wrote the American Senator James H. Hammond in March 1858, 'there must be a class to do the menial duties, to perform the drudgery of life. Such a class you must have, or you would not have that other class which leads to progress, civilization and refinement . . . It constitutes the very mudsills of society and of political government . . .'[3]

The 'peculiar institution' that was slavery in nineteenth-century America might seem a far cry from the world of ancient Rome, but in fact it was a modern survival of a system that had been in operation somewhere in the world probably since the dawn of human history. Thus, when the French writer Victor Hugo reflected on the trial and execution of the fanatical abolitionist John Brown in December 1859, he wrote: 'The death of Brown is more than Cain killing Abel; it is Washington slaying Spartacus.'[4]

What was it that the slave-owning classes, from Marcus Licinius Crassus to Senator James H. Hammond, were afraid of?

'This momentous question,' wrote the slave-owner Thomas Jefferson, 'like a fire-bell in the night, awakened me and filled me with terror . . . We have a wolf by the ears and we can neither hold him, nor safely let him go. Justice is in one scale, and self-preservation in the other.'[5]

'As long as the slave remains ignorant,' observed the social reformer Harriet Martineau on her visit to America in the 1830s, 'docile and contented, he is taken good care of, humoured and spoken of with contemptuous, compassionate kindness. But from the moment he exhibits the attributes of a rational human being . . . the most deadly hatred springs up . . . It is a very old truth that we hate those whom we have injured.'[6]

'This is an age,' wrote Harriet Beecher Stowe in *Uncle Tom's Cabin*, 'when nations are trembling and convulsed. A mighty influence is abroad, surging and heaving the world, as with an earthquake . . . Every nation that carries in its bosom great and unredressed injustice has in it the elements of this last convulsion.'[7]

The reality of the unthinkable – the slave revolt, the wolf escaping from the ear-grip of its master – is borne out by the cold, almost psychopathic testimony of the slave rebel Nat Turner at his trial in Virginia in 1831:

Armed with a hatchet and accompanied by Will, I entered my master's chamber; it being dark, I could not give him a death-blow. The hatchet glanced from his head, he sprang from the bed and called his wife; it was his last word. Will laid him dead with a blow of his ax and Mrs Travis shared the same fate, as she lay in bed. The murder of his family, five in number, was the work of a moment. Not one of them awoke. There was a little infant sleeping in a cradle. That was forgotten until we had left the house and gone some distance . . . Henry and Will returned and killed it. It was my object to carry terror and destruction wherever we went.[8]

In the Roman world, slavery went hand in hand with the successes and growth of the state, echoing Senator Hammond's point of view above. In Spartacus' time it was actually a relatively new phenomenon, at least in scale, developing out of the changing economy of the latifundia in the third and second centuries BC. Every ancient civilisation had slaves, whether they were members of its own lower classes or captured prisoners of war. Ironically, it was the rapid expansion of the Roman state in the years of the Republic that led to the massive increase in slavery, because a great deal of hard, physical work was needed to carry out this expansion. As Karl Marx would write centuries later, wealth in Rome was concentrated in the hands of a very few families – his 'bourgeoisie' – whose major ambition seemed to be to acquire land.

Most of their territory, the wheatlands and olive and vine groves of the latifundia (the wide fields) lay in the hinterland of Rome, Campania and Lucania and the island of Sicily to the south. Unlike European slavery of the sixteenth century onwards, which brought Africans and shipped them around the world to distant colonies, Roman slavery was on Rome's doorstep; in fact, the sheer number of slaves in the capital itself caused many a patrician to check his door-bolts and watch his back.

Slaves came from all over the Roman world and because of the speed of this expansion, many of them, like Spartacus, were first-generation slaves. They were not the sons and grandsons of slaves, to whom the back-breaking toil and the lash were a way of life; they had known freedom and they resented its loss. The Romans arrogantly referred to all slaves as 'Syrians', regardless of their origins, a kind of racial stereotyping similar to the way white Americans in the nineteenth century called black slaves 'Sambo' and 'Boy'. Certainly, large numbers did come from the eastern shores of the Mediterranean, from Syria itself, from Cilicia, Egypt, Asia and Bithynia-Pontus. Still others were brought in chains from the steppelands north of the Black Sea, bringing Dacians from the Carpathians and Thracians like Spartacus from further south. They were brought from the North African coast, from Mauretania, Numidia and Cyrene now that the long struggle against Hannibal's Carthage was over. They came down the Rhone to Arelate and Massilia on what is today the southern coast of France, flaxen-haired Germans from the dark forests and tall, auburn Gauls like Spartacus' lieutenant, Crixus, from further west.

We have no accurate figures of slavery in this period,[9] but it is likely that most slaves came from the eastern Mediterranean – hence the pejorative label 'Syrian'. Many of these were provided for the Roman markets by the pirates of Cilicia, at once an economic help to the Roman state and a potential rival; Spartacus would seek to make use of them during his two and a half year campaign. The fact that the 'Syrians' probably shared a cultural, religious and linguistic heritage created a certain stability among them (a stability not always visible in the army of Spartacus), but it also created a potential headache for the slave-owning authorities. Native culture must be stamped out, subservience drilled in. Freedom was a memory. Outside Rome, the Aegean island of Delos was the largest centre of the slave trade, acting as a great holding camp for the Cilicians as they dumped one cargo ashore before sailing off on another raid to capture more slaves. Interestingly, in the context of Spartacus, Thrace was the busiest throughway of the slaves.

The importance of the slave trade is evident from the extraordinary range of talents required of slaves and the uses to which they were put. Most of the men who joined Spartacus on the vine-covered foothills of Vesuvius were agricultural workers from the latifundia, but even here there was divergence. From Campania and Etruria, further north, came the crop-growers, the exact equivalent of the field hands in nineteenth-century America. They sowed seed from their rough baskets, tended the vine and the olive and harvested corn on rich men's villa estates. Such men could not always be trusted and were herded into *ergastula*, prison pens which were sometimes underground, like the subterranean cells of the tyro gladiators. Further south, in Lucania, Bruttium and Sicilia, the economy was mixed. Cultivators of crops worked along the *pastores*, shepherds, cow- and swineherds who followed their flocks and herds. By definition, these men could not be penned in as their crop-growing colleagues were, so they were monitored by a trustee known as magister pecoris, the herd-master. The herdsmen were not only free to wander the hills of their master's estates, but they carried weapons to see off rustlers. No doubt many such men made their way to Vesuvius as news of the gladiators' breakout spread.

Much of what we know about slaves in the days of the Republic comes from Marcus Porcius Cato, called the Censor, but today almost universally known as Cato the Elder to distinguish him from his equally prolific great-grandson. Plutarch explains how the elder Cato obtained his slaves:

Cato purchased a great many slaves out of the captives taken in war, but chiefly bought up the young ones who, like whelps and colts, were still capable of being reared and trained . . . When at home, a slave had to be either at work or asleep. Indeed, Cato greatly favoured the sleepy ones, accounting them more docile than those who were wakeful . . . afterwards, when he grew richer and gave feasts for his friends and colleagues in office, as soon as dinner was over, he used to go with a leather thong and flog those who had been at all remiss in preparing or serving it, he always contrived too, that his slaves should have some discussion and difference among themselves, always suspecting and fearing harmony among them. Those who were thought to have committed an offence worthy of death he had judged by the entire body of slaves and put to death if convicted.[10]

Like Senator Hammond two millennia later, Cato knew he had a wolf by the ears. And the very harmony he feared among his slaves was about to be made starkly terrifying in 73 BC by Spartacus.

Again, Cato tells us a great deal of the minutiae of treating slaves on the estates of the latifundia. The field hands were to be given four *modii* (measures) of wheat in the winter months, four and a half in the summer. Shepherds received three, which, oddly, is the same amount given to the overseer and his wife. The chained slaves received four pounds of bread in winter, five when they started work on the vineyard 'until there begin to be figs [in late summer], then go back to four pounds'.[11]

Wine was more carefully issued. Its properties were known to be dangerous and few landowning Romans took the Bacchanalian cult of Dionysius lightly. In the fourth month they were given a half-*sextarius* a day, which amounted to two and a half *congii*. This doubled in months five, six, seven and eight, and in the remaining months of the year an amphora full was the allotted ration. On special religious occasions, such as Saturnalia in December or the Compitalia, a party held at the nearest cross-roads, each man got three and a half *congii*. For the chained slaves 'it is not too much if they drink ten amphorae of wine apiece in a year'.[12]

Cato recommended that slave luxuries should include dropped olives, fish pickle and vinegar. They were to receive one *sextarius* a month of olive oil and a single *modius* of salt for the year.

His slaves wore simple, lightweight clothing – a tunic which weighed three and a half pounds and a new cloak every other year. Ever the businessman, Cato insisted that the old cloaks be returned for making patchworks; this of course was the man who charged his male slaves a fee to have sex with his females.

'Slaves,' wrote Varro, 'should be neither cowed nor high-spirited.' Varro was Marcus Terentius Varro, born at Reate in the Sabian territory, north-east of Rome. As a soldier, and before he became the prolific writer of about 630 volumes on all aspects of Roman life, he fought with Pompey in Spain and may conceivably have been with him in the mopping-up operations against Spartacus in 71 BC. He instructed: 'They ought to have men over them who know how to read and write and have some little education, who are dependable and older than the hands . . . [the foremen and overseers] are not to be allowed to control their men with whips rather than words, if only you can achieve the same result.'

Like Cato, he warned slave-owners to 'avoid having too many slaves of the same nation', but for a different reason: 'for this is a fertile source of domestic quarrels'.

Herdsmen, said Varro, 'should be of a sturdy sort, swift, nimble, with supple limbs, men who can not only follow the herd, but can also protect it from beasts and robbers, who can lift loads to the back of pack animals, who can dash out and who can hurl the javelin . . .'[13]

Such men were joining Spartacus on Vesuvius daily.

Slave markets like Delos and Rome, where Spartacus may have been sold, were able to provide an extraordinary range of specialist labour, not just the bulky field hands and the nimble shepherds. The *lecticarii* were the litter-bearers, carrying their masters and mistresses above the mud and ooze of Roman streets where the excellent water supply systems did not reach. Such men needed to be strong and of a uniform size to avoid 'slippage'; they were usually bought in teams. The *mangones*, the slave dealers, were experts at hyperbole; 'mangonicare' came to mean 'to make something appear what it is not'. Dalton Trumbo's excellent screenplay in the mouth of Lentulus Batiatus and its equally excellent delivery by Peter Ustinov is a superb recreation of men like this: 'Did you ever see such shoulders?' he asks of the smallest actor on the Universal lot.

Before being bought and driven out on the long, dusty roads to country estates like those of Cato or Varro, slaves stood on the *catasta*, a revolving stage which showed them to prospective buyers from every angle. The newly arrived had their left foot whitened with *gypsatum* (chalk) to show they were fresh on the market and around their necks hung the *titulus*, a placard which listed their nationality, skills and any negative qualities.

Much sought after were the 'soft' boys sold as cooks, cupbearers and bath attendants. Tony Curtis's Antoninus in the Douglas film represents this type. Good looks were important. Powerful Romans wanted beautiful people around them and that included their slaves, although the odd slave buyer with a particularly perverse sense of humour might buy a dwarf, an idiot *morionus*, whose animal antics would amuse his guests. Marcus Valerius Martialis, the poet Martial, records in the century after Spartacus one slave 'with pointed head and long ears, which move like a donkey's'.[14]

Oddly, in a hierarchical society that watched its back and its slaves equally carefully, it was intelligence that was most highly prized in a slave, but this is not as paradoxical as it seems. Intelligent slaves – the Graeculi (Greek-like) who became the architects, engineers, teachers and musicians of the late Republic and Empire – could fetch huge sums on the *catasta*. One *grammaticus* (scholar) was bought for 700,000 sesterces, a vast sum for the time. That lack of paradox lies in the fact that clever slaves saw – as perhaps Spartacus did not – that it was not possible to beat the system. Such men at the lower end of the spectrum might become *villici*, foremen on the country estates – the literate leaders of whom Varro approved. At the other end, some Graeculi were able to buy their freedom and even become the confidants of emperors. The case of Narcissus makes the point. Originally a Greek slave of the emperor Claudius, he served as Praepositus Ab Epistulus, head of the Secretariat. He amassed a fortune estimated at 400 million sesterces, more than that of Marcus Crassus, Spartacus' nemesis, and made himself indispensable to the future emperor Vespasian. Such was his power and Claudius' faith in him, that when General Aulus Plautius' troops were on the point of rioting and refusing to cross the Oceania Britannia (the English Channel) to invade Britain, Narcissus arrived with chests of gold and long-forgotten jokes about 'Io, Saturnalia!' He got the legions laughing and – more importantly – marching to begin what would be the conquest of Britain in the years that followed. Such heights involved great falls, however. Enmeshed in politics as Narcissus inevitably was as Claudius' right-hand man, he was obliged to play the Roman and kill himself on the orders of the dead emperor's homicidal wife, Agrippina.

The point is that slaves like this had no need to risk their lives fighting for freedom; the poachers simply became gamekeepers and kept their mouths shut.

Slaves were a status symbol for the Romans. Stories of individuals owning up to 20,000 are apocryphal, but several hundred was not unusual. A poor man might be expected to own three; only the destitute had none at all. Being consigned to the country estate staff, known as *familia rustica*, was regarded as a step down or even a punishment by the *familia urbana*, the town slaves. These were supervised on behalf of a master like Marcus Crassus by the procurator, whose main function was to organise the household finances. The specialised tasks of the household were more cosmopolitan than the basics of their rural counterparts. The amanuensis was the letter-writing secretary, his work carried by the *tabellarii*, who dashed and dodged through Rome's teeming streets carrying the post. The *archemagirus* was the head cook, supervising his staff in the kitchen; the *dispensator* kept the books, assisted by accountants called *sumptuarii* or *arcarii*. Such specialists were known in the slave and slave-owning world as *ordinarii* (literally, the regulars) and cost proportionately far more than the general workers, the *vulgares* or *qualesquales* (basket-carriers).

The relationships between slave and master varied enormously, although they are at the heart of the story of Spartacus. Technically, all slaves, whether prisoners of war, musicians, teachers, bath attendants, field hands or gladiators were legally *res* (things or objects). Some masters treated them as such and these men probably did not sleep easy in their beds. Others knew it was better to have their slaves on their side, cracking jokes with then, allowing them free time, to be spent with their women and children, feeding them well, letting them enjoy the festivals and games. Pliny told of the murder of a freedman called Larcius Macedo by his slaves while he was bathing. We can well imagine that freedmen were regarded with hostility by those still in servitude – *they* had managed to get out. Liberals like Seneca reminded their readers that slaves had feelings too, but in the Republic, masters had absolute rights over them and Roman justice was inexorable; death was painful and slow.

A transfer to the *familia rustica* was the mildest punishment. Worse was the *ergastulum*, prison with hard labour and a whole series of mutilations, which put death in the arena into a certain perspective. The *eculeus* was a type of rack, mentioned by Cicero and designed to rip arms and thighs from sockets. Flogging of varying degrees of severity was regularly carried out on slaves, from the *ferula*, a leather strap through the *scutica*, a whip of parchment which literally produced paper cuts, to the ox-hide flagellum with its bone or iron tips along three or five 'tails'. Runaways (like Spartacus himself) were branded on the forehead with a white-hot iron bearing the letters FUG for 'fugitives'. Thieves were branded FUR for *furfurus*, the Latin for thief being interchangeable with the word for slave. Liars had the initials KAL burned into their skin, for 'Kalumniator', bearer of false witness, the unusual use of the letter 'K' (very rare in the Roman period) serving to underline the despicable nature of the crime. Certain thieves had a hand hacked off at the wrist; with the other, they could still work. Execution methods included crucifixion, the punishment meted out by Crassus to the survivors of Spartacus' army along the Appian Way. The condemned slave was made to wear a *furca*, a wooden yoke, and his wrists were tied to his thighs, not unlike the irons used in modern American penitentiaries. As the victim hobbled to the place of execution, he was beaten from behind by the *carnifices* (executioners) with rods and canes. Then he was nailed to a crossbeam and left to die in agony. Until the days of the Empire, a master, acting as judge in the case of his own slaves, had the right to consign a culprit to be mauled to death in the arena by wild beasts. Or they could be burned to death in the appalling *tunica molesta*, a cloak soaked in pitch and set alight.

Given this state of affairs and the fact that free Romans were outnumbered by their slaves, it is perhaps surprising that risings like that of Spartacus happened so rarely. The Spartacus War is generally regarded as the defining proletarian movement of ancient history, but it was in reality the last of three such incidents. To understand it, it is necessary to investigate the first two.

Sixty years before Spartacus, Sicily exploded in an orgy of slave violence. Despite the relatively small size of the island – about 200 miles east to west – there appear to have been two separate slave risings, although the second was almost certainly sparked by the first. Ironically the First Slave War, as it is often called, is better chronicled than that of Spartacus. Most prolific among the writers was Diodorus Siculus. The Sicilian was a contemporary of Spartacus and it is infuriating that he did not write at length on him. Siculus' interest of course was Sicily, where Spartacus planned to land in the spring of 71 BC. He was born in Agyrion, Sicilia in the 90s BC and settled in Rome where he wrote – in Greek – a 40-book world history called Bibliothêkê (the library). Only fifteen of these volumes have survived and the section on the Sicilian slave war exists in fragmentary quotations only. Two versions of the 135–132 BC slave rising exists; the first copied by the Byzantine scholar Photios, Patriarch of Constantinople in the ninth century, and the second collected by the Byzantine emperor Constantine Porphyrogennetos (905–59). This book relies more heavily on the second, because it is a fuller version than that of Photios.

'Never,' wrote Siculus/Constantine, 'had there been such a great uprising of slaves as then arose . . . Because of it, cities fell into terrible disasters and countless men and women, along with their children, experienced the gravest misfortunes.'[15]

The first of Siculus' versions assures his readers that the Sicilians had been prosperous and happy, translating their economic success into the purchase of slaves. These people were branded and tattooed, the majority of men used as herdsmen, especially in the west of the island where the topography of the area lent itself to pastoral agriculture. 'The masters were arrogant and harsh in their treatment of the slaves,' wrote Siculus/Photios, and they were forced to a life of semi-banditry in order to survive. 'The result was that every place in Sicily was filled with murder.' Siculus was almost certainly using the works of an earlier historian and a contemporary of these events, the Stoic philosopher Posidonius. His 52-volume work chronicling the history of the Mediterranean world is very fragmentary, but, unusually for an ancient historian, he was fascinated by economic and social causation and something of this comes through in the two Siculus versions.

The versions then divide on the methodology of the rising, just as Plutarch and Appian do for Spartacus. The Photios version talks of slaves in Sicily meeting in small groups and discussing revolt, the stuff of conspiracy. The Constantine version was that 'without any communication between themselves, tens of thousands of slaves joined forces to kill their masters'.

Slave risings were not new. Livy records outbreaks of violence in the towns of Setia and Praeneste, north-east of Rome, in 198 BC. These occurred in the aftermath of the protracted war with Carthage and the slaves around Setia were Carthaginian prisoners of war, men used to military discipline and handy with the sword. Waiting until most Romans were preoccupied with the games held in the town, they struck swiftly and took the town. Only the defection of two slaves to the authorities and the swift military intervention of the praetor Lucius Cornelius Lentulus drove the slaves out. Their survivors put up a similar resistance – the Roman sources call them conspiracies – around neighbouring Praeneste. Lentulus allegedly executed 500 slaves while crushing this rising. What is interesting is the panic that this engendered in Rome, exactly as it would with Spartacus over a century later: 'Therefore,' wrote Livy, 'night watches were maintained throughout the neighbourhoods of the city and the lower-ranking magistrates were ordered to patrol them, while the triumvirs [mayors] in charge of the underground prisons were ordered to maintain a more vigilant guard over them.'[16]

A letter was circulated to the effect that 'prisoners of war should be bound with leg irons of not less than ten pounds weight . . .'.

Two years later another slave revolt took place in Etruria, south of Rome, and a legion was dispatched under the praetor Manius Acilius Glabrio. Livy wrote: 'Some of the slaves who were the leaders of the conspiracy Glabrio ordered to be crucified after they had been whipped. Others he returned to their masters.'[17]

Thirteen years later, and probably as part of the Bacchanalian conspiracies we have already discussed, the praetor Lucius Postumius condemned 7,000 bandit herdsmen to death in Apulia, in mid-Italy, south of Mount Garganus.

But these earlier eruptions paled into insignificance in comparison with events in Sicily in 135 BC. The herdsmen slaves, with time on their hands, and weapons in them, preyed on lonely travellers on the roads, then took to night burglaries, creating a terrifying crime wave, with all its strange echoes of Mafia activity that would re-emerge nineteen centuries later.

'They brandished clubs, spears and imposing herdsmen's staffs,' wrote Siculus/Constantine, 'and their bodies were covered in the hides of wolves and wild boars . . . Following close on the heels of each man was a pack of fierce dogs, while a regular diet of milk and raw meat made the bodies and minds of the men themselves thoroughly savage.'

Siculus/Constantine expresses himself in a way that would resonate with both pro- and anti-slavery lobbies in nineteenth-century America: 'Not only in the public realm of power should those in superior position treat those who are humble and lowly with consideration. Just as arrogance and brutal treatment in states leads to social upheaval and civil strife among the freeborn citizens, in the same way maltreatment produces plots against the masters by the slaves within the household.'

Chief among the arrogant slave owners was Damophilos, from Enna in the centre of the island. Master of many slaves, especially, Siculus tells us, handsome boys, he rode around his considerable estates in a gilded chariot and entertained guests with 'finely chased silver vessels and purple-dyed coverings'. Spartan Romans, of whom Siculus was probably one, regarded the soft lifestyles of the Egyptians and the Persians as decadent. Damophilos was more decadent than that. Even the most reasonable request from his slaves, for the basics of food and clothing, would lead to excessive punishment. And Damophilos' wife, Megallis, vied with her husband in brutality.

The focus of the first Sicilian uprising was a slave called Eunus, who belonged to Damophilos' neighbour, Antigenes. Eunus hailed from the city of Apamea, and the reason the slaves flocked to him for a solution to their problems was that he was a seer.

'The slave was a magician,' wrote Siculus/Photios, 'and a wonder-worker who claimed that he was able to predict future events from messages sent to him by the gods while he was asleep.'

Siculus/Photios is clearly unimpressed. The man was a charlatan, using a hollowed-out shell contraption to breathe flames from his mouth as evidence of his power. He had a following because many of his predictions came true – 'quite by chance of course', says Siculus/Photios. Antigenes used Eunus' powers of prophecy as party entertainment. The slave had told his master to his face that he would one day be king of Sicily and Antigenes' friends, lounging in their togas on his couches, drinking his heavy Sicilian wine, laughingly offered the slave titbits if he promised to be kind to them after his coronation.

It is difficult to know the source of this first version's cynicism. Does it come from Siculus, because this was just silly slave talk and not to be compared with the 'real' religion of the Roman panoply of gods? Or is this the addition of the Christian Photios, convinced that all men were in darkness who did not know the only genuine wonder-worker, Jesus Christ? One thing is certain: the slaves took Eunus seriously and the sleeping prophecy has strange echoes in the incident of Spartacus and his wife, who saw a serpent coiling round his head.

Eunus' advice was to strike and quickly. An estimated 400 slaves swore oaths and made religious sacrifices in the middle of the night. Then they launched an attack on Enna itself. Photios describes it:

Breaking into the houses in the city, the rebel slaves instituted a general slaughter, not even sparing the suckling infants among the inhabitants. Tearing them from their mothers' breasts, they dashed the infants to the ground. One cannot actually say in words what they did to the women themselves – and with their husbands looking on – what terrible acts of outrage and utter lewdness were committed on them.

The Sicilian slave owners had let go of the ears of the wolf.

Both versions of the Siculus manuscript make the point that the slaves' actions were rooted in justice. Many of those who had, however jestingly, offered Eunus a cup of wine or a bowl of grapes at Antigenes' dinner parties, were spared. Antigenes himself was killed personally by Eunus; exactly how is not recorded. Damophilos and Megallis were put on trial in Enna's amphitheatre, but the landowner tried to talk his way out of a death sentence and the slaves' patience snapped. Two of them, perhaps maltreated by Damophilos in the past, attacked him. Hermias plunged a sword into his chest and Zeuxis lopped off his head with an axe. Megallis was thrown to the female slaves to do with as they liked. Eventually, in accordance with ancient Roman tradition, she was thrown to her death from a cliff.

The couple's daughter, however, was spared from harm. Siculus/ Constantine says she was 'approaching the age of marriage', which probably made her fifteen. She had always been kind to all her parents' slaves and she was well treated. 'Not only did no slave dare violently and shamefully to lay hands on the girl, but all of them made sure that the flower of her beauty was kept free from any outrage against her honour.' Hermias took her safely to the estate of relatives in Catana, on the island's east coast.

The exact chronology of the first Sicilian slave revolt is hazy. Eunus was chosen as leader because of his miracle-working, and he made himself king, taking the name Antiochus, the name of several actual kings of Syria. He is described by Siculus as a Syrian, and it is possible that Antioch may have been his original home. His assumption of the title served three purposes. First, it established a hierarchy among the slaves with which they were perfectly familiar; even the name was the same. Appalled though he might be, even Karl Marx could not have expected any real egalitarianism among the slave rebels; the ancient world was, if anything, more hierarchical than that of Marx's time. Second, it may have been a consciously anti-Roman act. Eunus/Antiochus must have known that Rome would send troops against him and the Romans expelled their last king – and kingship – four centuries earlier, creating the Republic instead. And third, it fulfilled the extraordinary prophecy that Eunus the slave had made, and established him as untouchable and omniscient among the men who were no longer his peers.

The first steps taken by Antiochus the king are important, because Spartacus took similar steps two generations later. A lawless rabble wandering the countryside robbing and killing would achieve nothing. Antiochus wanted something more – he wanted a state. A shadowy figure, Achaios, probably another rebel slave, was appointed a royal counsellor, given the estates of Antigenes and the task of curbing slave excesses. Antiochus' wife became his queen – like Spartacus' wife, her name is not recorded – and the citizens of Enna, now Antiochus' capital, were put to work in the forges, making weapons for the whirlwind the king knew he was about to reap.

As a symbol of his new ex-slave state, Antiochus had coins struck, bearing an ear of corn: common to Roman, Greek and Celtic civilisations as the symbol of the agricultural basis of their economy. The words read 'Basi Antio' (basileos Antiochus) – 'a coin of Antiochus'. And on the obverse is the veiled head of the goddess Demeter, whose cult headquarters were in Enna. The Romans called this goddess Ceres, 'mother earth'. The fact that the coin has a *Greek* depiction of the goddess is a reminder of the Hellenistic influence in Sicily that still existed in the generation before Spartacus.

The second outbreak in Sicily must have been sparked by the first. Its leader was Kleon, a Cilician from the Taurus Mountains in modern Turkey. Siculus glosses over Kleon's slave status, but claims he 'had been accustomed to a life of banditry from the time he was a small child'. A herder of horses, he was previously one of those who, prior to the rising, had robbed wayfarers to survive. There is nothing of the idealistic freedom-fighter about Kleon. Already a murderer, he saw a slave rising as a way of expanding his career. Gathering as many slaves as he could, he attacked Acragas (the Roman Agrigentum) in the south-east of the island and went on the rampage in the countryside.

In the Photios version of Siculus' account, it is clear that the terrified landowning classes hoped that Antiochus and Kleon would clash in a power struggle for the island and destroy each other in the process. In fact, Kleon was happy to subordinate himself to the king, handing him his 5,000 slaves as troops in exchange for a generalship in his army. The Photios version attempts a timescale; 'almost thirty days' had elapsed since Eunus' revolt. After that, any chronology falls apart. 'A short time later', the Romans were galvanised into action. The speed of their reaction, however, would have been limited by the realities of travel at the time. The Roman postal system was legendary in the ancient world, but Sicily was nearly 500 miles from Rome and even a messenger riding day and night on fresh changes of horses would have taken over two weeks to make the journey. An army marching from Rome would take twice that time to reach the island, but Antiochus' first enemy was the praetor Lucius Hypsaeus and even though he came from Rome, many of his 8,000 troops were recruited in Sicily itself and may already have been on hand.

Again, we must be wary of Roman statistics. Siculus claims that Antiochus' original force of 20,000 eventually grew to 200,000 and that consequently, by sheer force of numbers, he often defeated the armies sent against him. In other theatres of war, other commentators are happy to have a miniscule Roman army defeating an enemy countless times its number – and incurring minimal casualties – so the reason for a succession of Roman defeats must lie elsewhere. Initially these encounters took the form of skirmishes, not full-scale battles, and some of Antiochus' successes were against terrified townspeople whose city walls were not built to sustain a siege. Their resolve, such as it was, was probably stiffened by only a small garrison of professional troops. On one such occasion, out of range of the garrison's ballista bolts, Antiochus' army put on an extraordinary mime show, re-enacting the slave revolt and taunting free citizens that *they* were now the fugitives.

News of the slave revolt spread and had a copycat effect elsewhere. In Rome itself, there was a conspiracy involving an estimated 150 slaves. Over 1,000 went on the rampage in Attica (Greece), more on Delos, the slave centre in the Aegean. These local revolts, which seem to have been on a smaller scale than Sicily and poorly led, were put down harshly by the authorities on the spot.

Inexorably, however, the net closed in on Antiochus. His early successes were probably attributable to the fact that, as with Spartacus, the Romans did not take the situation seriously and they found something distasteful about an ambitious soldier/politician taking the field against mere slaves. The fact that someone somewhere in the corridors of power swallowed some pride is indicated by the fact that a consul, Publius Rupilius, was given command. He besieged the slaves in the city of Tauromenium in the north-east, where he could be supplied easily from southern Italy by sea.

Tauromenium's defences must have been formidable, or else Rupilius did not want to lose too many men in a frontal attack, because he chose more long-term methods of subjugating the city. He came from Praeneste, itself the scene of a slave revolt, and may have had some firsthand experience of the terror of it all. He was called away from Rome at a time when he was presiding over a court of inquiry into the misbehaviour of the followers of Tiberius Gracchus, and may well have resented this enforced break in his political career. No doubt he had artillery with him, the single-armed onager or ass, so-called because of its powerful kick, and the double-armed and more accurate ballista, a sort of giant crossbow. In the event he opted for the slower, but safer, starvation. Four years earlier an enemy garrison at Numantia in Spain had resorted to cannibalism in an attempt to survive a Roman siege, and according to Siculus the same thing happened at Tauromenium: 'The besieged were reduced to such extremes, in fact, that they began first to eat their own children and then their women. Finally, in despair, they did not even shrink from devouring each other.'

Kleon's brother Komanos was captured trying to effect a breakout and the city eventually fell to that other option open to Rupilius in a siege situation – stealth. According to the historian Valerius Maximus, writing in the reign of the emperor Tiberius, Komanos suffered one of the more bizarre deaths in history:

Miserable and contemptible men, who would in fact be better off dead, torture themselves during their interrogation with the fear and the dread of the death that might happen to them and worry about the form that it might take. In their minds, they sharpen the iron blade, mix the required doses of poison, take a rope in their hands, or cast their eyes to the tops of precipitous cliffs . . . Komanos needed none of this. He ended his own life by extinguishing the life in his own chest.[18]

He simply held his breath until he died. Betrayed by a Syrian called Sarapion, the Romans were let in through the fortifications and the siege was over. Predictably, Rupilius now made for Antiochus' capital at Enna, where history repeated itself, but not before Kleon died fighting heroically under the city's walls. His ripped and mutilated body was put on public display, as the cynical Voltaire would say nearly two millennia later, 'pour encourager les autres'.[19]

Antiochus managed to escape and took refuge in the mountains. Siculus estimates that he had fewer than 1,000 men and many of these, he says, realising the hopelessness of their situation in the relentless advance of Rupilius, cut each others' throats with their swords. He has no sympathy for the slave-king 'who, like a coward, had sought refuge in some caves'. He was caught, along with his baker, his bath attendant, his cook and his master of ceremonies, and imprisoned. He died at Morgantina on the island, 'his body destroyed by a mass of lice', although Plutarch contends that this happened in Rome.

A number of other tyrants died in this way; Antiochus Epiphanes (the Glorious), king of Syria (215–162 BC) who did his best to Hellenise the Jews in Palestine; Herod I (the Great) king of Judea, who, while not orchestrating anything that can be interpreted as the 'massacre of the innocents' was nevertheless a vicious and arbitrary ruler; and the emperor Galerius (AD 250–311), who persecuted Christians before something of a change of heart shortly before his death. The translation of 'lice' by Brent D. Shaw is better rendered as 'worms', and Plutarch graphically describes the death of the tyrant Lucius Cornelius Sulla accordingly:

By living in this way [drunken debauchery] he aggravated a disease which had not been serious in its early stages, and for a long time he was not aware that he had ulcers in the intestines. This resulted in the whole flesh being corrupted and turning into worms. Many people were employed day and night in removing these worms, but they increased far more quickly than they could be removed. Indeed, they came swarming out in such numbers that all his clothing, baths, handbasins and food became infected with this corruption and flux. He tried to clean and scour himself by having frequent baths throughout the day, but it was no use . . . And if we may mention undistinguished but still notorious names [who died of the same disease] it is said that Eunus, the escaped slave who was leader in the Sicilian slave war, died of being eaten by worms . . .[20]

It was the way of tyrants – a corrupt death reflected a corrupt life. Rupilius wiped out bandits all over Sicily with speed and efficiency, and the first Sicilian slave war was over.

Why is this important to our understanding of the Spartacus War? First, because it was the first of its kind. Slaves had rebelled before, but Antiochus raised an army and declared himself king, creating a state which, given other circumstances, might have survived. Five centuries after Antiochus, Paulus Orosius, the last of the Roman historians to write in Latin and a Christian, ran from the advancing Vandal invasions of Spain and wrote *Historia Adversus Paganos* (History Against the Pagans) in which he made use of Livy's account, now lost, of the first Sicilian rising. And he makes a definite statement about the danger of all slave revolts: 'Inasmuch as it is a rare kind of uprising, an insurrection of slaves is a most dangerous type of rebellion. Masses of free citizens are prompted by their aims to increase the strength of their homeland, whereas a mob of slaves is incited to destroy it.'[21]

Second, Antiochus' revolt was the first of three, a cyclical re-eruption of the slave problem. The timing between them, with Spartacus' as the third and last, suggests a response by three generations of slaves. Some of Spartacus' fellow rebels on the vine-covered slopes of Vesuvius may have been the sons of men who had risen in Sicily thirty years before and the grandsons of men who had marched with the wonder-worker Antiochus. As well as the ripple effect elsewhere cited above, Orosius tells us that

450 rebellious slaves were crucified at Minturnae, north of Rome, and 4,000 defeated by the consul Quintus Metellus in Sinuessa, some 30 miles away. If the historian is remotely right about the 20,000 slaughtered in Sicily by Rupilius, the scale of revolt was alarming indeed.

Another significant aspect of the first uprising is its religious undercurrent, echoed in the second and the war of Spartacus. Orosius, although a Christian, captured perfectly the Roman obsession with signs and portents: 'In the year [135 BC] there was born to a slave woman at Rome a boy with four feet, four hands, four eyes, double the usual number of ears and two sets of sexual organs. In Sicily, Mount Aetna erupted in great flashes of fire and poured out lava that rushed like flash floods down its slopes.'[22]

In the war of attrition that went on under Antiochus, Siculus/Constantine wrote that 'Those persons who ate the sacred fish suffered many evils.' These animals were kept in the fountain of Arethusa in Syracuse in the south-east of the island. They were part of the worship of the Syrian – and therefore slave – goddess Atagratis, who may be linked to Atar, the Persian fire god. The Romans fought back, literally, with slingshots from their ballista on which were inscribed, among names and curses, the powers of their gods. In 1808, on the slopes near Castrogiovanni, the ancient Enna, large numbers of these were uncovered by amateur archaeologists and carried the words 'Victory Athena', 'Victory Artemis', 'Victory Zeus the Thunderer' and so on. Some of these shots would have been inscribed and fired by Antiochus' slaves, but the predominantly Greek names remind us that Roman control of Sicily was only made reality by the suppression of the slave revolts there.

The second Sicilian slave war erupted twenty-eight years later, perhaps six years or so before Spartacus' birth. Although its causes are different, its pattern is startlingly similar to the first, and this is more than coincidence. Stories must have been passed through the generations, as they would have been to the men who followed Spartacus.

There had been rumblings throughout Italy in the years between the first two risings. At Nuceria near Pompeii thirty slaves were executed after a 'conspiracy' was uncovered. More tellingly, 200 rebelled at Capua, where the Spartacus rising would occur thirty years later. Again, our fullest version of events comes from Diodorus Siculus, and again there are the two, slightly different, later variants.

As the Republic's armies spread, conquering east and west and rapidly turning Rome into the 'policeman' of the ancient world, not unlike Britain in the nineteenth century or the United States today, the expansion took its toll on forces. An estimated 60,000 men had died in the war against the Cimbri tribe in Cisalpine Gaul.[23] The Cimbri and the Teutones were semi-nomadic Germanic tribesmen raiding southwards towards Rome until stopped by one of the most successful of the Republic's overmighty generals, Gaius Marius. The Senate, in some desperation, sent out demands for recruits from Rome's various client kings. Among these was Nicomedes III, king of Bithynia (modern Turkey south of the Black Sea). He complained, with some justification, that so many of his people had been kidnapped and sold into slavery by the Cilician pirates that he could not oblige. The extraordinary decree by the Senate – that any freeborn man of an allied state currently held as a slave should be freed immediately – had the effect of shooting Roman governors of provinces in their collective feet. In Sicily, governor Licinius Nerva, was bombarded with hundreds, then thousands, of requests for release. When he ignored them, a slave named Varius led thirty slaves on a night escape from their master's estate near Halicyae, slitting throats on their way. Again, the supernatural played a part. Before they were 200 strong they visited the sacred shrine of the sulphur lake at Leontini, to swear oaths to the Palikri, the twin sons of Zeus and Aetna. Sailors rowing in the currents around Sicily saw the white clouds of smoke from Etna and believed it was Hephaestus, the blacksmith of the gods, lighting his forge.

Nerva failed to liquidate the rebels, who had taken refuge on high ground in one of the island's many mountains, but, using a traitor named Titinius to infiltrate them, he was able to wipe the rising out. The governor seems to have mishandled the mopping-up operations, however, and the murder of a local landowner, Publius Clonus, sparked a second outbreak of violence that grew more rapidly than the first. Titinius was defeated in open battle, probably outnumbered, and by the time the rebel numbers had reached 6,000 they chose themselves a king. There are echoes of Eunus/Antiochus in Salvius. He too could foretell the future and played the flute in the mysterious all-female religious festivities enacted in Sicily. Siculus/Photios claims that he had 20,000 infantry and 2,000 cavalry under his command, although, as with Antiochus, we must question the skill and efficiency of these troops. Only under Spartacus, in the third and last great slave rising, would the slaves become an army to match the Romans. Salvius besieged Morgantina and beat off a night attack by Nerva, desperately recalling his already disbanding soldiers.

As with the first Sicilian slave war, the second threw up another leader, Athenion, from the area around Segesta. Unlike the prosaic thug Kleon, Athenion was another seer, an astrologer, who despite readings that he should be king of all Sicily one day, readily threw in his lot under Salvius and saved his troops from a bad mauling by Roman reinforcements sent from the auxiliary units of the Mauri from North Africa by his careful divination.

'A great chaos,' wrote Siculus/Photios, 'and a mountain of evils of truly epic dimensions disrupted all of Sicily.' Looting, rape and slaughter became commonplace as the island plunged into anarchy. There seems to have been no attempt to create an orderly state like that of Antiochus. Neither Salvius nor Athenion seem to have struck any coins and it is noticeable that, whereas Eunus took the name of Antiochus, a genuine king of Syria, Salvius opted for Tryphon, a military dictator who had taken areas of Cilicia by force forty years earlier. Tryphon nevertheless adopted the pomp of Roman consuls. He fortified the hilltop fortress of Triokala with ramparts and ditches, in the legionary style, and built himself a palace and his people a forum. He wore a purple-dyed toga (the colour soon to be adopted by the emperors of Rome) and on public occasions, *lictores* marched before him carrying the fasces, bundles of rods and axes which were the symbols of the dread punishments of the Roman law.[24]

The Senate's temper snapped and they sent the general Lucius Licinius Lucullus against Tryphon at the head of 17,000 men. His second in command was Tiberius Cleptus, a fine soldier. Lucullus had made his name in the war against the mighty Mithridates, the king of Pontus near the Black Sea, and his love of luxury, decadence and beauty were second only to that of Crassus, who fought Spartacus in the next generation. Plutarch, writing centuries later, could still refer to the man's sumptuous gardens as the finest in Rome.

Risking battle in the open at Skirthaia, Tryphon was routed, despite a valiant stand by Athenion, wounded in both knees and unable to stand. Incredibly, Lucullus did not follow up his victory and abandoned a half-hearted siege of Triokala, a failure that would lead to official reprimand and exile. The lull in Roman activity saw the death of Tryphon, and Athenion inherited the kingdom he had prophesied would be his. Lucullus' successor, Gaius Servillius, was as curiously inactive as his predecessor and he too was sent into exile. Then the Senate sent Gaius Aquillius. A political schemer and extortionist, Aquillius was also energetic and anxious to make a name for himself. Taking on Athenion in an unnamed battle, he is said to have killed the rebel slave in hand-to-hand combat, receiving a serious head wound for his troubles, and continued to grind the slaves down until the handful remaining were captured and sent as gladiators to face the beasts in the arena.

Siculus/Constantine noted: 'some people say that they brought their lives to a most glorious end when they refused to do battle with the wild animals and instead cut each other down in front of the public altars . . . Thus, the war of the slaves in Sicily, a war that lasted nearly four years, reached its tragic finale.'

There is no doubt that there were conscious echoes of the first Sicilian slave war in the second. Publius Annaeus Florus, writing in Africa in the reign of Hadrian, wrote: '[Athenion] arrayed himself in a purple robe, carried a silver sceptre and crowned himself like a king. He raised an army that was just as large as that of his demented predecessor, but he conducted his operations with even greater savagery, as if he was seeking vengeance for Eunus.'[25]

According to Florus, his own people tore him apart 'like so much plunder'.[26]

Cicero, perhaps Rome's greatest writer and orator, and closer to events than any of the commentators quoted thus far, wrote that 'The measures taken by our governors [in Sicily] and the discipline enforced by the slave masters safeguard them against the dangers of another slave war. Therefore, no internal troubles could possibly arise from the province itself.'[27]

No, the troubles arose 500 miles to the north, on the vine-clad slopes of a hill which might have been Vesuvius.

SIX

The Senate and the People of Rome[1]

The only thing recorded about Gaius Claudius Glaber in Roman texts is that he was the first luckless general who came up against Spartacus. In the Kirk Douglas film, where he is called Glabrus, he is portrayed as an ambitious fool and soon-to-be brother-in-law of Crassus, completely outmanoeuvred both by Spartacus and the vicious infighting of Roman politics. We know nothing about the real man other than he was a praetor, and that he drew the short straw.

In ancient Rome, there were up to sixteen *praetors* at any one time. The Praetor Urbanus administered justice in the city and the Praetor Peregrinus kept a judicial eye on the endless stream of foreigners drawn to Rome by its wealth and power. Explaining the origin of the term, the scholar Marcus Varro said that a praetor should 'head' the law and the army. 'Therefore,' wrote the poet Lucilius, 'it is the duty of the Praetors to go out in front and before.'[2] It was expected that the most successful *praetors* would go on to become consuls, although those who did not often became governors of provinces or generals.

In the peculiar municipal melting pot that was Rome, it was perhaps asking a lot of a man to be as comfortable leading troops in the field as he was deliberating on a point of law in a magistrate's court. However well he performed his legal duties, Glaber did not shine against Spartacus.

We do not know much about the geography of Vesuvius in Spartacus' time. The second-century historian Publius Annaeus Florus was probably born in North Africa and was writing in the reign of the emperor Hadrian in the 120s AD. His only known work is a précis of Roman history up to the reign of Augustus. He refers to Spartacus' refuge as 'an altar of Venus'. Venus, the Roman version of Aphrodite, has come down to us as the goddess of love, but originally she was associated with farming, and Florus' description is probably a reference to the multitude of grapevines that grew on the mountain. Like Appian, he assumes that mountain was Vesuvius. Appian gives us no details at all about the initial encounter between the rebels and the Romans, but the first real clash of arms is described by Plutarch: 'There was only one way up this hill [Vesuvius] and that was a narrow and difficult one and was closely guarded by [Glaber].'³

The praetor's scratch force of 3,000 would probably at this stage have outnumbered that of Spartacus. The military expert Sextus Julius Frontinus was *aedile* early in the second century and best known for his brilliant engineering work on Rome's aqueducts. His *Strategemata*, however, is about military tactics and tricks of the trade used by various Roman commanders over a 200-year period. He assumed that at the time of the skirmish with Glaber, Spartacus still only had his original gladiators. The likely number escaping from Capua was probably seventy, but other runaways would have joined the band by the time Glaber got there. Olivier's Crassus has 'Glabrus' sneaking out of Rome at night so that the people would not see their soldiers soiling their swords by marching against slaves. Fighting slaves may have been considered ignoble, but the earlier slave wars had demonstrated that the slaves were more than a match for the Roman fighters. In Sicily, the slaves had destroyed the local troops and the first units sent from Rome against them; Glaber should have had the legions with him but, as praetor, he did not command them.

The tactic of making for high places had served the Sicilian slaves well in their rebellion. Many ancient peoples took to high ground to fortify and defend, from the Celtic hillforts of Caratacus to the colossal rock of Masada in Judea. From heights like these, the glittering Roman cohorts could be seen a day's march away, the cursing, grunting *caligae*⁴ trudging though burning sand or over soggy bracken. In the face of a trained and determined Roman army, however, such places were often deathtraps. At Masada, the Legio X Fretensis built a huge assault ramp against the cliffs to the west of the fortress and wheeled their siege engines up it to smash through the walls. What followed was one of the most appalling mass suicides in history – the Sicarii[5] inside, numbering nearly 1,000 men, women and children killed themselves rather than fall into Roman hands. In the west of Britannia in AD 44, the future emperor Vespasian took the Celtic hillfort known as Maiden Castle with equal ease, if less spectacular slaughter.

On Vesuvius, Spartacus was to meet no such end. In what is probably the first recorded use of the tactic, he outmanoeuvred Glaber by, in effect, abseiling down the mountain's sheer cliffs to catch the Romans in their flank.

'The top of the hill,' wrote Plutarch, 'was covered with wild vines and from these they cut off all the branches that they needed and then twisted them into strong ladders which were long enough to reach from the top, where they were fastened, right down to the plain below.'

This takes some believing, but clearly the 'sheer precipitous cliffs' had ledges and no doubt their lower slopes were shale-covered and manageable on foot.

'The Romans knew nothing of this,' explains Plutarch, 'and so the gladiators were able to get round behind them and to throw them into confusion by the unexpectedness of the attack.'

From what followed, it was obvious that Glaber had pitched camp and should have built the obligatory ramparts and ditches. It seems that he had no siege equipment or, if he did, he was not given time to use it. We have no other details of this first major clash, but it established the fact that Spartacus was no ordinary gladiator and certainly no ordinary slave. He was a consummate general, with an intimate knowledge of how Roman troops worked and what would beat them. Modern commentators have him plundering Glaber's camp, swaggering round with the *lictor*'s *fasces*, which were the symbols of the praetor's authority, and dressing like a patrician. No contemporaries mention this and it may be confusion with Eunus/ Antiochus in the first Sicilian War.

To comprehend why Glaber underestimated his enemy, we need to understand more about what it meant to be a Roman in 73 BC, and how a little cluster of huts beside the river Tiber should come to dominate the ancient world and intelligent men's thinking for nearly two millennia.

There are two stories about the creation of Rome. One is the founding of the city by the twins Romulus and Remus, abandoned by the 'virgin' Rhea Silvia and the great god Mars and raised by a she-wolf. The famous statue of the cherubic children suckling from the wolf's teats is probably a close copy of the one standing on the Capitoline Hill in Rome in Spartacus' day. Cicero tells us that it was struck by lightning in 65 BC. The other story is that the Trojan hero Aeneas, after the destruction of his home city in the Trojan Wars, wandered far and wide and eventually founded Rome as a 'New Troy' on the banks of the Tiber. Whichever version Romans of Spartacus' time believed (and Romans were extraordinarily accommodating when it came to absorbing myth and legend) the common theme is one of violence. Romulus battered Remus to death with a spade when he jestingly jumped over the boundary ditch of the city he had just dug. Aeneas was one of the few survivors of the bloody destruction of a city which saw its women raped and its babies carried high on the points of Greek spears after a legendary ten-year siege.

More prosaically, the Latin tribe who were Rome's first inhabitants settled on the Palatine Hill about 1,000 years before Spartacus was born. They were herdsmen, their scattered archaeology containing the bones of sheep, goats, cattle and pigs. The sandy relics of their post holes tell us that their houses were circular or rectangular with in-fill walls of wattle and clay. The famous seven hills formed a series of rocky valleys down which the Tiber's tributaries splashed, and still later created marshes that were home to the teeming millions of malarial mosquitoes that Gibbon thought helped destroy Rome. The Tiber itself was navigable by ocean-going merchant ships, with their brightly painted hulls and rectangular sails, and the sea was only a few miles away.

From the outset, however, Rome was an outpost, a fortress surrounded by enemies in the tribal jungle that would take nearly 2,000 years to become Italy. To the south, in the area of Sicilia and Campania where slaves revolted and gladiators were trained, the

Greeks with their scholarship, their democracy and their libertine ways established major towns like Capua. To the north the enigmatic Etruscans, exotic craftsmen and brilliant traders, dominated the whole of the northern peninsula as far as the foothills of the Alps, where they lived in an uneasy truce with nomadic Gauls from beyond the mountains.

In the early seventh century BC, the Etruscans crossed the Tiber and a state of ongoing war forced the various Latin tribes to unite against them. Under six successive kings whose names are in part folkloric, the cluster of huts on the Palatine grew into a major city, defended with ramparts and ditches. The wattle and clay huts had given way to stone buildings constructed on a massive scale. Defence became attack as the Romans moved to end the dominance of Etruria, the Etruscan state. The king was advised by the senate, a group of noble families or *patricii*, who formed the aristocracy of the Republic long after the kings had gone and whose power survived (sometimes precariously) under the emperors.

In the days of the kings, Roman society was divided not only by class, but by tribe. There were three of these, each responsible for providing cavalry and infantry in times of war. Each tribe was subdivided into ten curia (houses) who advised the king on routine civic matters but had no decision-making powers themselves. In the class context despised by Karl Marx, who made Spartacus his hero, below the patricians and their client hangers-on came the plebeians, the ordinary people. According to Plutarch, under Numa Pompilius, the second and most peaceful of Rome's kings, the plebs acquired a degree of organisation and sophistication unequalled in the ancient world: '[He] divided the craftsmen according to their trades – flute-players, goldsmiths, carpenters, dyers, shoemakers, leather-dressers, potters and workers in copper and brass.'[6]

The barter system that was universal in the Mediterranean in the seventh century BC gave way to a primitive coinage based on ingots of copper.

The Romans' love for imposing private and public buildings was evident even at this early stage. Tarquinius Priscus (the Old) used the famous Etruscan skills and forced the plebs to labour on an ambitious public works scheme.

'The poor were set to work,' wrote the Greek historian Dionysius of Halicarnassus shortly after the defeat of Spartacus, 'in return for a miserable ration of grain; quarrying stone, cutting timber, leading the wagons filled with these materials or even carrying the materials on their backs. Others were put to digging underground conduits, constructing arches and supporting walls for them and assisting the various craftsmen, coppersmiths, carpenters and stonemasons, all forcibly removed from their private businesses to labour for the public good.'[7]

The foetid open ditch into which all the city's effluent ran became the Cloaca Maxima (the great sewer), which was so wide that a hay wagon could pass through it. Victorian copies of this astonishing feat of civic engineering are still in use today under the streets of London.

But no amount of military success and lavish public building could weigh against tyranny. Ironically, the more successful the Romans became on the battlefield the more despotic their rulers tended to be. Military power gave the later kings an arrogance and contempt for life that was to prove disastrous; their ownership of vast numbers of slaves to do their bidding only exacerbated this. Hopelessly tangled with myth and legend though it is, it is clear that the excesses of the last of Rome's kings, Lucius Tarquinius Superbus (Tarquin the Great), brought about the creation of the Republic, arguably the height of Rome's grandeur. The Romans wanted nothing more to do with kings.

The government of Rome was extremely complicated, with a series of officials drawn from the senatorial or 'knightly' class (the *equites*) whose powers often overlapped and were usually held for short periods. Serviceable though this was in preventing the rise of another Tarquinius, it meant that untried novices were expected to control the mob, provide bread and circuses, feed, clothe and water the city – and fight men like Spartacus. We have already seen the role of praetor through Glaber and the role of *aedile* in laying on the games as part of his duties of supervising markets, temples, aqueducts and baths. The quaestor was the keeper of records and controller of the treasury. Such a man was expected to be at least twenty-five and to have served as an officer in the army. The Censor held an odd position. He was a registrar, inspector of public works and tax collector. He also supervised morals.

'[The Censors],' wrote Cicero, 'shall divide citizens into tribes and list them also according to wealth, age and rank. They shall assign young men to the cavalry and infantry. They shall discourage the unmarried state, guard public morality and suspend from the senate anyone guilty of improper conduct.'[8]

The Censor checked everything from the content of plays to the state of gardens and could reduce the social rank of an offender. The Pontifex Maximus was the great bridge-builder, linking mere men with the panoply of gods, nominating Vestal Virgins and disciplining priests. This was not essentially a religious position, like that of the Pope or Archbishop in the later Christian world – Julius Caesar held this among many other posts before his enemies realised the extent of the man's ambitions and killed him.

The organisation of Roman politics was bewildering in Spartacus' time, but its very complexity may in part explain why Rome was slow to move against him. The Senate is the group with which we are most familiar, thanks largely to Victorian paintings, epic films such as *Spartacus* and the fact that the name has survived into modern American government. Traditionally, the Senate was composed of about 300 men of the patrician class, lounging on their curved marble seats in yards of draped togery or screaming at each other in fury across the floor of the house. From the fourth century BC, plebs were admitted, but the yardstick of appointment was that each man should have served in some administrative capacity. It was not actually a parliament, with legislative powers, but an advisory group, albeit an important one. It controlled the public finances and foreign policy and therefore *senatus consultum* (the advice of the senate) was duly noted and taken seriously.

The advice was given to four different committees that are the very rough equivalent of local government today. The Comitia Curiata (literally, assembly of households) represented the twenty wards set up under Rome's kings. It supervised the election of consuls, the highest of the city's governors, and was also a court of appeal. By Spartacus' time, most of its functions had been subsumed by the Comitia Centuriata. This had originally been composed of delegates from the legions' centuries (units of nominally 100 – actually 80 – men), and was therefore a military organisation. By about 200 BC it had assumed a civilian air and probably came closest to our modern parliamentary system. It had 193 seats, 88 given to the wealthiest citizens. It had the power to declare war, approve laws and establish peace treaties and literally decide issues of exile, life and death. The Comitia Tributa, open to all citizens, elected lesser city officials and was a throwback to the tribal origins of Rome. Last came the Consilium Plebis, the People's Council, representing 35 districts. Its orders were binding on the whole city.

The Roman system of government was rife with tension and internal division. It was never as simple or as black and white as Howard Fast tried to imply in his novel *Spartacus*, where the dictatorial Crassus outmanoeuvres man of the people Gracchus. That was the stuff of nineteenth- and twentieth-century class warfare and it was faithfully translated to the big screen by that old class warrior Dalton Trumbo. In Spartacus' Rome there was corruption in high places, and an ever widening gap between rich and poor. Women had no direct political power and slaves were regarded as objects under law. But the many flaws in governance and sources of discontent were papered over as long as the Republic was waging successful war.

By the third century BC, all of the Italian peninsula south of the Arno was in Roman hands, the various tribes of Latins and Etruscans the victims of a divide and conquer tactic which was as successful as it was ruthless. Most formidable of Rome's opponents were the Samnites, who occupied Campania where Spartacus would rampage unchecked 200 years later. The humiliating defeat of a Roman army in 321 BC was a shameful reminder, recorded by Livy, that, just occasionally, the invincible Romans could be stopped. In a grim retreat from their ambush site in the sheer-sided valleys of the Caudine Forks:

the consuls, half-naked, suffered the ignominious ordeal of being sent under the yoke. They were followed by their officers, in descending order of rank, then, one after the other, by the legions themselves, while the enemy, fully armed, stood round, hurling insults and cracking jokes. Many had swords brandished in their faces and some, whose attitude of indignation at their treatment offended their captors, were maimed or killed.[9]

Rome remained at war for an astonishingly long time. To the north-west of the city was the land of the Sabines, and although their relationship with Rome was probably one of assimilation over a long period, the legend of the rape of the Sabine women by the oddly all-male Roman populace probably had a basis in fact; rape and pillage are the perks of victorious warriors throughout history. The Aequians were tough, mountainous people from the Apennines who lived near the river Anio. It took the Romans seventy years to subdue them, and they had to establish a substantial garrison town at Alba Fucens to do so. To the south, in the Lepini Mountains, the Volsci proved fierce fighters, as their semi-legendary leader Coriolanus proved. Shakespeare's hero-villain drove the Romans back to their own gates before his own mother persuaded him to turn back. It was not until 304 BC, after nearly a century of on-off hostilities, that the name and culture of the Volsci disappear from the historical record.

A glance at a timeline of the Republic's history makes it clear that Rome was the most aggressive warmonger in the ancient world. In 370 BC Marcus Furius Camillus defeated the Cisalpine Gauls at the Anio. Thirty years later, Valerius Maximus Corvus destroyed Satricum, the Sabine capital. And thirty-three years after that, Lucius Corvelius Scipio Scapula defeated the Etruscans.

The list of similar battles is depressingly long. Although some of these battles could be called defensive, they quickly and often developed into wars of attrition and conquest which effectively created an empire before there was an emperor.

The most potent symbol of Rome's expansionist policy is the network of roads the Romans built as they steadily expanded the geographical area under their control. They all, of course, by proverb and necessity, led to Rome and later civilisations, who had never seen a Roman, believed they were the work of giants. Straight as arrows and dug with care to provide ample drainage and a firm surface, they were propaganda, statements of intent. The road along which Spartacus' followers would be crucified in the dying summer of 71 BC was already two and a half centuries old by that time, having been built in 312 BC by the orders of the censor Appius Claudius Caecus. The arrogant Claudius was blinded (*caecus*), men believed, because he gave the cult temple of Hercules to slaves to tend. His road to Capua was built to enable the legions to get to the troubled hills of Campania quickly, to subdue rebellion there. At first 152 miles long, the Appian Way was later extended as far as Brindisium, and the milestones along it marked the 1,000 double paces of the *caligae* whose hobnails once scraped the smooth stones.

The biggest obstacle to Roman domination was the rival empire of Carthage. 'Delenda est Carthago,' observed a grim Cato in 153 BC. 'Carthage must be destroyed' and indeed it had to be if Rome intended to be sole master of the Mediterranean world. Historian Philip Matyszak sums up the strain of the three Punic Wars – 'Rome's final victory came after sixteen years of war and cost hundreds of thousands of lives. Some of Rome's greatest families were almost wiped out and whole tracts of countryside were devastated . . . Victory encouraged arrogance.'[10] The first Punic War was almost entirely a naval one fought in the Mediterranean between Sicily and Libya where the Carthaginian Empire lay. Its people were originally Phoenician and Carthage, according to the Roman geographer Strabo, had a population of 700,000 and nearly 300 colonial cities throughout North Africa. The Carthaginians or Poeni, as the Romans called them, dealt in slaves, iron, gold, corn, dyestuffs, bronze, tin and perfumes, extending their trade routes and outposts into Corsica, Sardinia and Spain. For twenty-three years, galley grappled with galley on the breathtaking blue of the Libyan Sea and the Roman victory merely meant that the Poeni intensified their trading and colonisation in Spain.

It was the second Punic War that frightened Rome, as it produced a leader who was arguably the finest general in the ancient world – Hannibal. According to legend, he swore an oath at the age of nine to oppose Rome, and spent an astonishing sixteen years laying waste to Italy to keep it. Hannibal believed that the first Punic War had been brought to an unfair peace by corrupt politicians. At the age of twenty-six the brilliant general eschewed the largely naval posturing of the first war and invaded Italy by crossing the Alps and marching into the Po valley. In the slave Spartacus there is more than a hint of Hannibal. The Carthaginian used ambush and feint, kept a reserve well hidden for lightning attacks and was always looking for the innovative, the unexpected. Forever associated with elephants on the battlefield, it was Cannae in 216 BC that established his reputation and inflicted on Rome the worst defeat in its history.

Ignoring the cautious approach of Quintus Fabius Maximus,[11] the consuls Gaius Terrentius Varro and Aemilius Paullus drew up their estimated 80,000 men on the narrow plain near Cannae on the river Orfanto. Using the time-honoured tactic of a frontal assault spearheaded by the legions, Hannibal's Spaniards and Celts fell back. Encouraged, the *caligae* rumbled on, shields locked and javelins extended, only to find that the Celtic collapse was a feint and they found themselves surrounded, outflanked and butchered by Hannibal's Numidian cavalry. Notoriously unreliable although Roman statistics are, there is no doubt that casualties were heavy. Paullus died along with at least half his command.

Hannibal's weakness – like that of Spartacus a century and a half later – was that he was never strong enough to take Rome itself. Eventually he was beaten back to defend his homeland against the equally brilliant general Cornelius Scipio Africanus, who beat him at Zama fourteen years after Cannae. The greatest general since Alexander ended his life as a wandering freak and finally killed himself.

The third Punic War lasted only three years and was very much a mopping-up operation. It was focused on the city of Carthage itself and resulted in the end of a civilisation. The geographer Strabo recorded that after the Carthaginian surrender over 200,000 harnesses (suits of armour) and 3,000 siege engines were sent to Rome. As the smoke from their razed city blackened the African sky, the survivors were sold into slavery.

But the defeat of Carthage failed to give Rome a breathing space. It was a sad Appian who wrote three centuries later:

> The sword was never carried into the assembly [Senate] and there was no civil slaughter until Tiberius Gracchus, tribune and law-giver, was the first to fall to internal commotion . . . Repeatedly the parties came into open conflict, often carrying daggers, and from time to time in the temples, the Assemblies, or the Forum, some tribune, praetor, consul or candidate for these offices . . . would be slain. Unseemly violence prevailed almost constantly, together with a shameful contempt for law or justice.[12]

This internal violence was perhaps nothing new for Rome – after all, republican spirits had overthrown the last Tarquin in 510 BC, but what it did was to end the pretence that Rome was a republic, rather than a backdrop to the careers of a succession of violent and ambitious men. In Howard Fast's novel, the character of Gracchus stands for the man of the people. Scheming, yes, corrupt, certainly. But infinitely preferable to the appalling arrogance of Crassus. In reality there was no one like Fast's character in Spartacus' day. The Gracchi were actually two brothers, the younger, Gaius, dying perhaps twenty years before Spartacus was born. Their mother, Cornelia, daughter of the great general who had beaten Hannibal, was regarded by later Romans as the epitome of perfect womanhood. She told her sons that she wanted to be remembered as their mother, not as Scipio's daughter.

'He [Tiberius Gracchus] was a man,' wrote Vallenius Paterculis, 'of blameless life. He had a brilliant intellect, honest intentions and was . . . blessed with the highest virtues of which a man is capable.'[13]

The quiet and thoughtful Tiberius joined the hereditary priesthood of augurs when he was ten and served later as a junior officer in the final sack of Carthage. His next campaign was less successful, however, and the consul Caius Hostilius Mancinus found his army of 20,000 trapped by the warlike Celtiberians in Spain. The elder Gracchus negotiated his way out of certain annihilation and even had his account book returned to him by an impressed enemy. Rome regarded this as virtual treason, believing in the famous attitude of Spartan mothers that they would rather their sons come home dead on their shields than carrying them, if that implied defeat. Scipio Aemilianus, the destroyer of Carthage, sailed for Spain to destroy the Celtiberians, but the breaking of *his* promises to the Spanish tribe seems to have driven Tiberius Gracchus into opposition to Rome's military elite. In 133 BC, he became a tribune of the plebs. As ever, Plutarch had some wise observations to make on this post:

> It is suitable for the consul and the praetor to have pomp and circumstance, but the tribune . . . must allow himself to be trodden on; he must not have a proud manner, nor be difficult to reach. He must be indefatigable on behalf of others and easy for crowds to deal with. Therefore it is the custom that not even the door of his house can be closed, but it remains open night and day as a haven of refuge for such as need it.[14]

He was backed by some of the most influential men of his day, including ex-consuls like Appius Claudius Pulcher, who had had the temerity to lead his troops, victorious against the Cisalpine Gauls, in a triumph in Rome. Cleverly including his daughter in his triumphal chariot, Claudius was safe from attack – she was a Vestal Virgin held sacred by all Romans. Tiberius Gracchus launched himself into the much overdue land reforms.

Land was the cornerstone of wealth in all civilisations before our own. Ownership of it ensured power, wealth and status; redistribution of it appealed to the underclass because it promised a Utopian equality. In Rome, an ancient law (ironically drafted by an ancestor of Crassus) laid down that no one could own more than 500 acres. It was bad enough that this was widely ignored (although the law had not been repealed) but a scandal had occurred since the second Punic War which made matters worse. Peasants were drafted into the army in ever increasing numbers in Rome's desperate struggle for survival, and in their absence, their land fell forfeit to avaricious landlords who added the property to their estates of the latifundia, even taking parcels of public land as their own. This was all part of the wider movement we have noted already, whereby stocks of slaves were increasing to work these ever more gigantic estates, squeezing the rural freeman peasant out.

Tiberius Gracchus' proposals were that the public lands should be restored to the people to the tune of 30 acres per head. The result would be land redistribution along almost socialistic lines, the gap between rich and poor narrowed. With impressive oratory, Tiberius Gracchus thundered: 'Even the savage beasts of Italy have dens in which to lay their heads. But the men who fight and die for Italy have no part of it except the air and the sunshine . . . they are called masters of the world, who do not possess a clod of earth that they can call their own.'[15]

The proposals were carefully drafted by Gracchus' supporters, the Scaevola brothers, lawyers to their fingertips. Law and justice were on their side. The problem was that legislation via the Tribunate had to be passed unanimously and the self-interested Marcus Octavius vetoed the bill. Furious, Gracchus withdrew a compensation clause for existing landowners and proceeded to veto every other point of legislation the Tribunate was trying to pass – a fine display of filibustering 2,000 years before that term was invented. Ultimately, in a slightly dubious piece of politicking, Octavius was removed from office.

From this point on, things became ugly. The land reforms had been passed by the Tribunate, but the Senate, patricians all, refused to pay for the commission to set the wheels of reform in motion. When Attalus, the client king of Pergamum in Asia, left all his land to the people of Rome, Tiberius Gracchus swiftly voted to divert funds from there, especially as the dead king had been a friend of Gracchus' father. He was now on shaky ground. He may have outmanoeuvred the Senate in terms of cash, but he had encroached upon their other role – the conduct of foreign policy. Facing prosecution the moment he left office, Tiberius Gracchus attempted (illegally) to stand again for election.

It was high summer, with many of Gracchus' supporters on their estates and far from the city. Screaming rows over the man's fate took place in the Senate – Mucius Scaevola backing Gracchus against Scipio Nasica (the long-nosed) who saw, in Gracchus' stand, a personal attack on his father, the general. Scipio was Pontifex Maximus, the head of the priesthood. He rose from his bench, folded his toga over his head as though on his way to sacrifice. The symbolism was clear – Tiberius Gracchus *was* the sacrifice. Scipio led the senators to the tribunal Assembly on the Capitol and in the riot that followed, Gracchus and at least 100 of his followers were beaten to death with clubs and furniture. His body was dumped unceremoniously into the Tiber. Law, justice and wise counsel were gone from Rome. Anarchy ruled in their place.

The death of Tiberius Semponius Gracchus unleashed, as Appian said, troubled times in Rome that bordered on civil war. In a curious piece of double-think, the Senate allowed Gracchus' land reforms to go ahead (archaeology has unearthed several stone boundary markers with the name of Gaius Gracchus carved on them) but punished his supporters in what amounted to a witch-hunt. Howard Fast and Dalton Trumbo would both have understood.

Gaius Gracchus was nine years younger than his murdered brother. Catapulted into the political arena, the introspective youth served at the age of sixteen with his cousin Scipio Aemilianus in Numantia, before becoming a flamboyant and powerful public speaker. He also bore grudges. 'You villains who killed Tiberius,' he growled at the Senate, 'the best of brothers, watch and see how I will repay you in the same way.' He stood for the Tribunate and, despite the frantic efforts of the Senate to keep him out of the city,[16] Gaius took up the post in 124 BC.

Carrying on where his brother had left off, Gaius began a series of whirlwind reforms, confirming the land laws and establishing a monthly corn ration for the poor of Rome at a fixed – and fair – price. He sought support from the gentry class, the *equites* and country-dwellers outside the city itself, realising how feeble and corruptible Romans were. To them, he gave exclusive tax-farming rights, ensuring the continued opulence of the Republic as it systematically plundered the wealth of conquered provinces. He also ensured that the *equites* judged the behaviour and success of the governors of these provinces, thereby making senators reliant on them. This last move hit the Senate hard – it curtailed their sources of income to an extent, as well as their high-handed and arbitrary rule wherever the armies conquered.

What rattled the Senate most, however, was the extraordinary popularity of Gaius Gracchus. Elected twice for the Comitia Tributa, he stood down before serving a third term, but seems to have been elected anyway by an ecstatic populace who saw in him their liberator from the patrician monopoly of power. While Gaius was attempting to extend the right of citizenship to non-Romans and establishing a new colony, Junonia, on the site of ruined Carthage, the Senate moved against him, setting up Livius Drusus as a stalking horse and rival to Gracchus. Outmanoeuvred and out of Rome, Gaius could only watch his popularity ebb away. Under the new anti-Gracchus consuls elected that year, the Senate issued its famous *Consultum ultimatum*, in effect carte blanche for the senatorial class to do whatever was necessary to protect itself. Gracchus refused to appear before the Senate the next day, but barricaded himself with his supporters in the Temple of Diana on the Aventine Hill. There were running street fights around the Tiber's bridges before Gracchus reached a sacred grove and ordered his slave to kill him – 'what's fine, what's Roman'.[17] An estimated 3,000 of his supporters were strangled in prison in the days and weeks that followed.

Historian Antony Kamm argues 'the actions and ultimate fate of the brothers Gracchus constitutes a watershed in Roman politics. Their legislation highlighted the links between the problems of property holding, poverty, the army and the extension and retention of the empire. Their use of popular assembly to initiate legislation gave it powers rivalling those of the senate.'[18] More significantly for us, it gave Romans an awareness that men of the people could move mountains, striking blows for freedom which had hitherto seemed impossible. Spartacus was an extreme, nightmarish extension of that notion.

Into the tense and hostile arena of Roman politics emerged Gaius Marius, a 'simple countryman' who was anything but; his army reforms were extremely important in the context of Spartacus, in that they bred men like the luckless and talentless Glaber as well as geniuses like Pompey and Julius Caesar. Like many of the key players in Roman politics in the pre-Spartacus era, Marius served under Scipio Aemilianus at the siege of Numantia. Ten years later he was quaestor and four years after that tribune of the plebs, thanks to the backing of the Metelli clan. With extraordinary aplomb, he proposed making voting within the Assembly secret and when challenged by the Senate (who saw in this a breakaway move they could not control) threatened to arrest even his own patron. He was praetor in 115 BC, a post in which he was competent but no more, but quickly endeared himself to the army in the campaign against Iugurtha, the rebel king of Numidia. A master of propaganda and possessing more than his fair share of luck, Marius won the consulship in 107 BC. This was an unprecedented victory for a man whose family were rumoured to hire themselves out as labourers from time to time to make ends meet. The war with Iugurtha ended with his capture and even though it was not Marius' work, he received all the credit.

Of greater concern was the impending threat from the north. In the year before the likely birth of Spartacus, a huge army of Gauls, comprising the Cimbri and Teutones tribes, perhaps 300,000 in number, returned from pillaging Spain to skirt the Alps and enter Italy. The Romans had seen a Gallic army at their gates before when, according to legend, a gaggle of alert geese had set up such a row that the planned stealth attack was foiled. Marius remained walled up in his camp as the astonished Gauls drifted past, hooting their derision and asking (presumably via interpreters) whether the soldiers had any messages for the wives and daughters the Gauls were on their way to ravish. Marius' subsequent attack, near Aquae Sextae, today's Aix-en-Provence, caught the swaggering Teutones off guard and they suffered severe losses. An elated Rome elected Marius consul for the fifth time and on 30 July 101, Marius and Quintus Lutatius Catulus routed the Cimbri at Campi Raudii near Milan.

From this high point Marius' career took a rapid downward path. Losing support of the unpredictable tribune of the plebs, Lucius Appuleius Saturninus, and inevitably of the Senate who detested this parvenu, he went off to Asia, supposedly to fulfil a vow he had made, but leaving Rome to his increasingly pushy and successful subordinate, Lucius Cornelius Sulla.

Spartacus was probably about ten years old when the Social War broke out. Today the name is misleading. The Socii were the allies, formerly client kingdoms of Rome, whose peoples composed the rank and file of the *auxilia* who fought with the legions. In that sense the Social War, which began in 90 BC, is a prefiguring of the war of Spartacus. The Roman army would find it potentially very difficult to defeat an army that it had trained. The cause of the Social War is rather elusive, but it undoubtedly stemmed from resentment that Rome was no longer allowing outsiders to become citizens. The ever more reactionary Senate scuppered any attempt to reinstate this custom, in which outsiders were able to gain full Roman citizenship and all the advantages that implied. The murder of Marcus Lucius Drusus sparked open hostilities.

Drusus was elected tribune of the plebs exactly twenty years before Spartacus' revolt. His intention was to debase the coinage, double the size of the Senate by allowing in the *equites*, continue the land reforms of the Gracchi and reintroduce the right of citizenship. Such a radical package of reforms incensed the Senate and one of them probably paid an assassin to kill him. At a gathering at Drusus' house, someone drove a cobbler's knife into the Tribune's groin and he bled to death. Word spread like wildfire throughout the city's hinterland and the Socii, Marii, the Picentenes, the Ferentini and the Samnites rose in open revolt.

Marius was once again expected to take the field and perform miracles, but by now he was sixty-seven years old and Cornelius Sulla was breathing down his neck. For a while, the Socii established

A bronze helmet of the type worn by Thracian gladiators. The distinctive griffin crest typified this pattern and the sockets on each side of the skull originally carried upright plumes. *(Museo Archeologico Nazionale, Naples/Giraudon/Bridgeman Art Library)*

An archaeological dig near the amphitheatre at Capua, 2005. Is this the site of Lentulus Batiatus' gladiator school from which Spartacus escaped in the summer of 73 BC? *(© C.M. Trow)*

Left: The amphitheatre at Capua, showing the gates of life and death into the arena. The ruins date from the reign of the first emperor, Augustus, but Spartacus may well have fought in the arena itself. *(© C.M. Trow)*

The animal pens and access points beneath the arena at Capua. Gladiators like Spartacus waited here to begin their bouts and their bodies were carried back the same way for burial outside the town. *(© C.M. Trow)*

The Horseman in Thracian mythology was an all-important figure in the equine culture of the eastern European Celts. *(Private Collection, © Boltin Picture Library/ Bridgeman Art Library)*

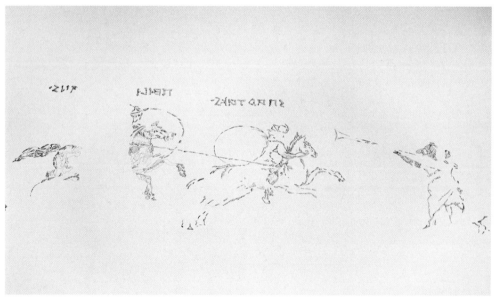

Graffiti from the House of the Priest at Pompeii showing a mounted gladiator called Spartaks. Legend has it that in his final battle, Spartacus was wounded in the thigh with a spear before death at the hands of Crassus' legions. *(© C.M. Trow)*

Photographed at Pompeii, a Thracian gladiator is seen to have conquered a *retiarius* (net fighter), symbolically placing his shield over the loser's head. *(© C.M. Trow)*

The gladiator barracks at Pompeii, showing the training area and doors to cells. In a similar complex at Capua, Spartacus was trained to kill and die for the entertainment of the crowd. *(© C.M. Trow)*

The tomb of Longinus Sdapeze of the Ala I Thracia, a Thracian auxiliary, like Spartacus, who fought for Rome. *(Colchester Museums)*

Reconstruction of Caesar's siegeworks at the Archéodrome, Beaune. The fortifications of Crassus across the Rhegium Peninsula must have looked very similar. *(© R.J.A. Wilson)*

Bust of Pompey (106–48 BC). The man who modelled himself on Alexander the Great stole the thunder of his rival Crassus by mopping up the Spartacus War. *(Ny Carlsberg Glyptotek, Copenhagen/Bridgeman Art Library)*

A scene from the House of Mysteries at Pompeii. The original owners worshipped the banned god Dionysius: Spartacus' wife was a follower of his cult. *(Alinari/Bridgeman Art Library)*

Another rebellion doomed to failure. In the aftermath of the First World War, the Spartacus League, seen here, attempted to seize Berlin in the name of the people. *(Private Collection/The Stapleton Collection/Bridgeman Art Library)*

a single state with a capital at Bovianum, but the semi-civil war became a genuinely internecine one when Marius and Sulla clashed openly in the struggle for command.

In the opening moves, Marius was initially successful, but Sulla escaped and was able to return to Rome at the head of an army to restore order. Most historians today point to Julius Caesar as the man who toppled the Republic, cutting the pretence of the previous 100 years, but Sulla was his prototype. The marble bust that is said to be of Sulla has a disconcerting stare, with large eyes and cruel mouth. The Roman sculptors were superb at catching what was probably authentic detail, but the nineteenth-century archaeologists who uncovered their works were sloppy in fixing names to un-marked pieces, so we cannot be sure of their accuracy. We know from Plutarch that Sulla had bright-blue eyes and a mass of blond hair, but his skin was fair, easily affected by the sun – like 'mulberries sprinkled with flour',[19] as the Athenians said. A playwright and perhaps even actor and dancer, as a young man he enjoyed the good life and had turned to politics (always an expensive business) as the result of two huge family bequests hard on the heels of each other.

It was Sulla who actually captured Iugurtha and quickly became disenchanted with Marius. Bribing his way to election as Praetor Urbanus in 98 BC, he spent most of that decade clashing with the rising Parthian peoples of Asia Minor before returning to Rome. His star was rising. He defeated the brilliant general Mithridates in Greece and Asia Minor and on the coins he had struck to celebrate his triumph, added 'Felix' (Lucky) to his name.

His clash with Marius had an inevitability about it and he entered Rome with an army twice in three years. The first time, most of his officers resigned rather than lead troops into the great city. It was an act of naked aggression specifically prohibited by all the Assemblies and even though we have seen many men in history come to power with swords at their back, such a thing was unheard of in Rome. His second triumphal return in 81 BC took place after the war with Mithridates was over and this time, his officers showed fewer qualms. There was a last flourish of the Social War in which the

Samnites, fearing that the patrician Sulla would revoke the citizenship granted them by Marius, fought him at the Colline Gate itself. Sulla's centre was actually driven back, but his supporter Marcus Licinius Crassus scored a decisive victory on the right flank. He then sent one of those bizarre little messages that occasionally illuminate the darkest of battlefields. The galloper, with dented helmet and foam-flecked horse, asked Sulla if Crassus' troops could stand down and eat their supper!

Sulla's first intention in marching through the Colline Gate at the head of a victorious army was to restore order in the divided and turbulent city. Now he came as an avenger. Granted the title of Dictator by the Senate – the first time in over a century that it had been given – Sulla began to clean up. A disapproving Appian wrote two centuries later:

> Sulla himself called the Roman people to assemble and harangued them with an outburst of self-aggrandisement . . . He then pronounced sentence of death on forty senators and about 1600 *equites*. He seems to have been the first to proscribe those whom he wished murdered, to reward the executioners and informers and to punish any found hiding the victims . . . Some of them, caught unawares, were killed where they were found, at home, in the street or in the temple. Others were bodily heaved up from where they were and taken and thrown at Sulla's feet. Others were dragged through the streets and kicked to death, the spectators being too frightened to utter a word of protest at the horrors they witnessed. Others were expelled from Rome or had their belongings confiscated. Spies were abroad, looking everywhere for those who had fled the city and killing any that they caught.[20]

Despite this terrifying purge, Sulla did not abuse his new-found powers to the extent that later dictators and many emperors did. He increased the Senate to 600, albeit not with the *equites* that Drusus had envisaged. He increased the number of *quaestors* and *praetors* so that the rule of law might work again. But most obviously, he increased the legal power of the Senate, so that by Spartacus' time, this was the only Assembly worth discussing. What he had actually done was to link forever the ambitious with the support of the army. The phrase 'Sulla did it – why can't I?' entered the Latin language and it paved the way for the fall of the Republic and the rise of the Empire.

When Sulla landed at Brindisium in 83 BC on his way to his second military coup in Rome, among the entourage of patricians who met him were Marcus Licinius Crassus, who undoubtedly saved his bacon at the Colline Gate and Gnaeus Pompeius – Pompey the Great of future years. These were the generals who would bring down Spartacus.

How much the gladiator slave knew of Rome's tempestuous history and politics we cannot know. But for us, it is vital to have an understanding of what had gone before to be able to put Spartacus into context. On the one hand, he was a reincarnation of Eunus/ Antiochus and all the other slave leaders who preceded him. On the other, he was a terrifying successor to both the Gracchi and to Sulla; a man of the people at the head of an army that might march on Rome: not to restore order, but to destroy her.

SEVEN

The Lowest and the Worst

Spartacus' rout of Glaber had a predictable effect. On Vesuvius, or wherever he was in the Bay of Naples, he attracted to him increasing numbers of rebels.

'And now,' wrote Plutarch, 'they were joined by numbers of herdsmen and shepherds of these parts, all sturdy men and fast on their feet. Some of these they armed as regular infantrymen and made use of others as scouts and light troops.'[1]

Two names emerge for the first time in the narratives of Appian, but not of Plutarch – Oenomaus and Crixus. They were clearly gladiators who had been part of the escape from Capua, but we know virtually nothing about them. Appian contends that both men were Spartacus' subordinates, which seems likely, although Livy, writing soon after the event, seems to ascribe greater status to Crixus than to Spartacus himself. In his *Summaries* for 95 BC he lists the man's name before that of Spartacus, and in 97 BC calls him 'the general of the fugitive slaves'.[2] Certainly, Spartacus and Crixus commanded two wings of the slave army, each going its own way later in the campaign with a different agenda and with the predictable consequences of a split command.

Historian Philip Matyszak, without quoting his sources, claims that the Thracians chose Spartacus as their leader and the Gauls chose Crixus and Oenomaus by election 'according to the tradition of their peoples'.[3] If Matyszak is right, there was a reasonable division of command in an army that was led by escaped gladiators of various races and peopled by rough herdsmen who were probably not *vernae*, that is born slaves, but prisoners of war who were likely to be any nationality other than Italian. But the slave army was a ragtag affair. Its commanders held their posts by virtue of their own personalities and reputations. They were not consuls of the patrician class born to command; still less kings with the backing of some vague notion of hereditary right. In the Napoleonic sense, some men were safe only as long as they were successful; they had to keep fighting – and winning – to stay in power. And Spartacus found himself in a particularly dangerous situation. As his followers grew in number, he had to range ever wider to feed and clothe them and each burned village or sacked villa meant that the vengeance of Rome was ever more certain.

We have no idea of the exact sequence of events. Glaber must have returned to Rome, beaten and humiliated, with whatever survivors he could muster. Certainly before the next Roman assault came, Spartacus had moved off Vesuvius. Exactly where he camped next we do not know. Again, high ground would have been likely and sensible, to give his people time to prepare for another engagement. He had plenty of choice. In the immediate hinterland of the Bay of Naples, Campania provided a range of mountains running on a north–south axis parallel to the coast. If he was sensible, Spartacus would avoid the Via Appia which, south of Capua, ran across country to Brindisium. It is likely, however, that he did move south, in the opposite direction from Rome, from where retribution would come. The defeat of Glaber was a calculated slap in the face; the greatest military power in the ancient world was not going to take this humiliation lying down.

Writers like Velleius Paterculus condemned the marauding of Spartacus' people: 'Then, as their number grew with each passing day, they inflicted serious and widespread damage on Italy.'[4] Orosius, albeit writing 500 years after the events, lamented that: 'Wherever they went, the slaves indiscriminately mixed slaughter, arson, theft and rape . . . this war against the fugitive slaves – or rather, to describe it more accurately, this war against the gladiators – was the cause of terrible horrors.'[5]

But Paterculus and Orosius had missed a salient point. Italy was already damaged, by the long years of occupation by Hannibal's Carthaginian armies and the attacks by any number of tribes during the Social War, a great deal of this focused on the Campania area.

Society moved more slowly in the ancient world and its wounds healed slowly too. The targets of Spartacus' army were those who had grown fat on the huge import of slaves in the previous century. Slaves could be maltreated, beaten or even killed, and they were not, in theory at least, eligible for service with the army. Despite the attempts of the Gracchi, land reforms had not succeeded and all over Campania were thousands of slaves: bitter, resentful and downtrodden. In the words of Karl Marx, they had literally 'nothing to lose but their chains'.[6] When villas were attacked, these men, women and children threw in their lot with Spartacus, showing no allegiance at all to their masters. When Spartacus hit the towns, not only slaves went over to him, but the free poor too. The Thracian, whether through altruistic motives or a clever piece of *realpolitik*, distributed the spoils fairly among everybody. Slave and freeman alike must have believed that they were already in the Elysian Fields.

Two hundred years later, the writer Florius mused regretfully on the events of the high summer of 73 BC:

One is able to endure even the shame of slaves in arms [the earlier Sicilian revolts]. For although slaves are persons who have been made subject to punishment in every possible way by some stroke of misfortune, they are still a type of human being, albeit an inferior type, and they are capable of being initiated into the benefits of the freedom that we enjoy. But I do not know what to call the war that was incited under the leadership of Spartacus. For when slaves served as soldiers and gladiators were their army commanders – the former the lowest sort of man and the latter the worst – they simply added mockery to the disaster itself.[7]

The appalled Florius goes on to recite a catalogue of the slave army's infamy: 'They rampaged over the whole of Campania. Not satisfied with destroying rural villas and villages, they devastated the towns of Nola, Nuceria, Thurii and Metapontum, inflicting a terrible slaughter on them in the process.'[8]

It was of course out of the question that the Roman propaganda machine would provide anything approaching an unbiased account of Spartacus and his revolt. All post-Spartacus writers in the days of the Emperors dismiss the man and his times as barbaric. Diodorus Siculus, for instance, calls him 'Spartacus the barbarian'[9] and Appian concurs that 'he was a wholly disreputable person'.[10] His was the last great slave rising that Rome witnessed; such incidents were unthinkable and probably had some vague populist link with the already discredited notion of the Republic. So Florius' audience would expect to read that such ignoble rebellions resulted in 'devastation' and 'terrible slaughter'. Such slaughter was commonly ascribed to Rome's enemies, from Hannibal to Boudicca, often accompanied by nonsensical statistics about the numbers of dead, and horror stories intended to frighten children.

It was at Nola that the first emperor, Gaius Octavianus, called Augustus, the wise, would die fourteen years after the birth of Christ. The town, in a rugged, ravine-strewn landscape, had seen fighting in the Second Punic War in the aftermath of the Carthaginians' victory at Cannae. The town lay a few miles due south of the Caudine Forks, midway between Vesuvius and the Appian Way that ran through Capua, and on through the old Samnite country and the Apennines. It featured prominently in the Social Wars, becoming an important stronghold of the rebels. It held out against Sulla's army as it advanced on Rome for the first time in 89 BC, holding off his six legions for years until the dictator withdrew five of them to march east to face Mithridates. Astonishingly, Nola held out for nearly ten years, as long as the legendary siege of Troy. Other towns had surrendered or burned themselves down; Nola had held firm. Furious at this waste of his legions' time, Sulla repopulated the place with his veterans, turning it into a *colonia* which he called Colonia Felix – Lucky's Town – in his honour.

Some of these men must still have been there in 73 BC when Spartacus attacked, but we do not know the extent to which its obviously impressive fortifications had been torn down or rebuilt by Sulla. The slave army laid siege to Nola again and sacked it. This single fact, a throwaway line in every writer from Florus to historian Tom Holland,[11] is staggering. It was one thing for a handful of runaway gladiators to wipe out a scratch army led by an incompetent who underestimated them – Rome could always put this down to omens or sheer luck. Plutarch, when writing of the minor involvement of the younger Cato in the war against Spartacus, has an interesting take on Roman failure at this point: 'the war was not one that was well commanded. Despite the effeminacy and laxity of those who fought . . .', and he goes on to extol the virtues of Cato. But for the slaves to fight their way into a town that must have been defensible and was manned by ex-legionaries, said a lot more about these runaways and their commander than it does about their opponents. We have no idea at this distance in time whether the town was taken by subterfuge or by traditional Roman-style siege equipment. No commentator mentions the slave army having siege equipment, although at various encounters during the war named after him, Spartacus almost certainly had the opportunity to use captured gear. The various types of ballista which regularly took enemy towns in the name of Rome were highly technical pieces of equipment and needed time and practice to be used effectively. Guerrilla warfare and surprise attacks were more likely Spartacus' stock in trade.

Nuceria was, after Capua, the largest town in Campania. Pompeii, Stabiae and Sorrentum were all dependent on it for trade and production. Originally an Oscan settlement, it had walls and an amphitheatre, although the exact state it was in when Spartacus came calling is impossible to determine. One of the principal settlements of the Socii, Nuceria produced its own coins, carrying the head of the river god. After a brief period of rebellion when the town went over to the Samnites in 309 BC, it remained loyal to Rome and held this position throughout the conflict against Hannibal. In 216 BC, the Carthaginians laid siege to the town and destroyed it. Its citizens were granted permission by the Senate to colonise nearby Atella (despite inevitable protests by the Atellans) and spent several years rebuilding the place. In Spartacus' time, however, Nuceria was struck again. Ironically, its very loyalty to Rome made it a legitimate target for Sulla during the Social War and he plundered it again in 89 BC.

The question hinges on how much damage Sulla – and even Hannibal – had done and how much rebuilding had taken place by the spring or summer of 73 BC. No remains exist in the modern town, but villas' foundations have been found scattered in the hills to the south, together with elaborate tombs. Like the far better-known Pompeii, it is likely to have been a rich settlement, providing Spartacus' growing following with food, equipment and valuables. It was against Nuceria that an infamous incident took place in AD 59 when the clashes between the town's gladiators led to running battles in the streets of Pompeii and prompted Nero to close Pompeii's amphitheatre for ten years. Interestingly, dull red graffiti on house 8903 in Pompeii reads 'Traveller, you eat bread in Pompeii, but you go to Nuceria to drink. At Nuceria, the drink is better.' Perhaps this was the lure for Spartacus . . .

The other towns listed by Florus as targets of the slaves, Thurii and Metapontum, are much further south in Bruttium on the Gulf of Tarentum, and logic dictates that these fell to Spartacus later in his war. In the first instance, however, the slave army had defeated a Roman army and destroyed two towns, probably in the space of months. It was high time Rome stopped Spartacus in his tracks.

This time, they sent the praetor Publius Varinius, another hapless soul whose only record in Roman history is that he became another of Spartacus' casualties. Varinius seems to have split his command in that only 2,000 men under Lucius Furius clashed with the gladiators. By this time it is likely that the rebels had at least twice that number and possibly far more, so Furius was out of his depth in every respect. Plutarch says he was routed, and for a Romanist to admit that, the defeat must have been total. Furius' troops, once broken, would have been chased all over the Campanian country-side. With the reserves that Spartacus must have had, he would have had fresh cavalry who would have cantered through the valleys below the Caudine Forks, hacking down the running infantrymen, stumbling over their shields. Legionary formations were only irresistible – and terrifying – if they were advancing forward at a steady marching pace and in sufficient numbers. Broken and scattered, they died like other men.

Why Furius' force should have tackled Spartacus alone is unknown. Perhaps he was a Custer-like fool who had such contempt for his 'inferior' enemy that he thought he could go it alone. Plutarch provides another possibility, though, in the next line of his narrative: 'Then came the turn of Cossinius, who had been sent out with a large force to advise Varinius and to share with him the responsibility of command.'[12]

Nothing is known about Lucius Cossinius either, except that he is likely to have been praetor in 73 BC. But there are two implications in what Plutarch does not say. First, the fact that Cossinius arrived with a large force implies that Varinius was perhaps not given enough men in the first place, because Rome still underestimated the military power of slaves. We know we cannot rely in detail on Roman statistics, especially in the context of battlefield casualties, but the general trend is likely to be accurate enough. If Glaber had lost with his 3,000 (and Frontinius, of course, only attributes the original seventy gladiators with Spartacus at this point), then surely Rome would have sent ever larger numbers against him, however distasteful this might be to its military pride. The second implication is that if Varinius needed Cossinius to share command, his superiors in the Senate may have considered him incompetent.

Certainly, Spartacus' engagement with him was a perfect example of how an intelligent man trained to *think* as a Roman could outwit what ought to have been a formidable force. Part of the gladiator's success must have been due to the information-gathering of his scouts. 'Spartacus watched [Varinius'] movements closely,'[13] wrote Plutarch. No doubt he did this using mounted scouts. The commander of a Roman army was nothing if not visible. He rode everywhere with a mounted escort and standard-bearers with their distinctive lion's-skin headgear, the paws wrapped over their chests. Varinius' own standard would have been a simple scarlet square flag, but it was distinctive on the field and Spartacus caught the praetor virtually napping. He seems to have been resting at a villa at Salinae – according to Sallust, actually having a bath – but whether Cossinius was there too is unclear. Different translations imply that both men were present. Gaius Sallustus Crispus, known to us as

Sallust, believed the man caught bathing in the villa was Cossinius. Sallust was a contemporary of these events. He was born in Amiternum in the Sabine country and was thirteen when the Spartacus War broke out, so he could be expected to know. On the other hand, he does not seem to have started writing until about 42 BC, thirty years later, and his work does have a rather moralising tone to it, as he clearly despised the weaker men who let the Republic fall.

Whether it was Cossinius or Varinius who was caught with his toga down, Spartacus nearly captured him and chased him all the way back to his camp. A cleverer opponent might have tried to outrun Spartacus and lead him a merry chase all over Campania, but Cossinius/Varinius appear to have had no flair or imagination and, no doubt thoroughly rattled by the screaming, whooping ex-slaves, rushed to the safety of their ramparts and ditches.

Both Plutarch and Appian dismiss the next episode in a couple of lines, but Spartacus' victory over Varinius was undoubtedly a severe blow and must have sent shock waves of panic through the narrow streets and marble halls of Rome. Sallust, however, in what is, sadly, a fragmented text, gives us a detailed insight into events.

It was now autumn and the weather was closing in. The headlong rush to the camp seems to have been a bloody slaughter, with the ringing of swords echoing in the Campanian hills as Spartacus' gladiators caught and killed Cossinius' refugee-soldiers. There was clearly wholesale desertion, and Varinius had a serious mutiny on his hands. More and more of his men melted away every day. In desperation, he sent his quaestor Gaius Toranius to Rome with news. No doubt he also asked for support and yet more reinforcements. Sallust describes his camp as 'well-defended with a wall, trench and large scale fortifications'.[14] At least he had not made the same mistake as Glaber, but Sallust believed that Varinius only had 4,000 men left behind the ramparts.

It is not clear from the Sallust text (*Histories* Books 2 and 4) who was besieging whom, because the two camps were close to each other. Most modern commentators assume that it was Spartacus who was under siege because that was the Roman way. The Latin makes rather better sense – and it fits my contention of Spartacus as a military leader – if we assume the reverse. Wind and icy rain were taking their toll on the besieged and the besiegers, and food was running as low for Spartacus as it was for Varinius. What makes Spartacus so impressive as a general is not merely his skill and daring on the battlefield (dazzling as that was) but his concern for all the nitty-gritty of logistics. One night, records Sallust, 'at about the second hour of the night watch',[15] the slaves crept away from the camp under cover of darkness. If ever we needed evidence that Spartacus had once fought in the Roman army, Sallust provides it: 'To avoid a surprise attack from the Romans while they were away raiding the countryside, the rebels, *according to regular army practice* [italics added], usually appointed night watchmen and guards and assigned the other normal duties.'[16]

This time it was different. Either Spartacus was running very low on supplies or there was an internal problem with his army, which we will consider later. He left a single trumpeter in the rebel camp and propped the corpses of his dead on stakes at the gates. In the darkness and at a distance, these men looked alive, torchlight no doubt flickering on their armour and weapons.

Daylight, however, told its own story. As surely as the Greeks from the siege of Troy (and the British from Gallipoli two millennia after Spartacus) the slave army had gone. There were no yelled insults from Spartacus' camp, no showers of stones peppering the shields and helmets of Varinius' guards. The Romans were no longer surrounded. Cautiously, Varinius sent a cavalry detachment to the nearest hill. There was no sign of Spartacus or his rabble. By this time, or possibly a few days later, Varinius seems to have been reinforced. From Sallust's comments on them, these men seem to have been no better than the weaker elements that the praetor had already lost.

'Some days later,' wrote Sallust, 'contrary to their usual behaviour, our soldiers became more confident and their tongues began to wag boastfully.'[17]

It seems reasonable to assume that Varinius' command may have grown to six or seven thousand, the strength of a legion. He broke every rule in the book by adopting their new-found bravado and leading them out in search of Spartacus.

A major problem with using Sallust's narrative is that it is very badly fragmented. We leave Varinius marching out in search of his man, his green, demoralised troops marching in silence now they have no earth ramparts and wooden stockades to shield them. They come upon Spartacus in the middle of a full-scale row with the Gauls and Germans under Crixus about strategy. That this row took place at some point is certain and explains the eventual fragmentation of the slave army (much to Rome's relief), but it is unlikely that it happened just at this point. All other sources agree that Varinius' camp was taken by Spartacus with 'a great slaughter'.[18] And that Cossinius was killed. An entirely plausible scenario is that Spartacus' quiet withdrawal in the night was a stratagem, designed to achieve just what it did – to lure a once again overconfident Varinius out of a fortification and catch him in open country. The usually perceptive and reliable Sextus Julius Frontinius, a leading strategist and military engineer of the first century AD, whose work was the basis of the better-known military theorist Vegetius,[19] has his information back to front on this score. He cites the use of corpses staked upright, but imagines Spartacus being besieged by Varinius, rather than the other way round.

Plutarch contends that Spartacus beat Varinius in a 'number of engagements',[20] but these were probably continuations of the same clash, running fights in and around the camp. The upshot was that although Varinius escaped, his horse, the *fasces* carried by his *lictores* and all his baggage fell into Spartacus' hands. He was amassing quite a collection, 'So nearly,' wrote a disgusted Appian, 'was a Roman general taken prisoner by a gladiator.'[21]

Philip Matyszak rightly laments the fact that we have no knowledge of day-to-day life in the camp of Spartacus. We know from archaeology at least, what the food situation would have been. Campania was the most fertile part of Italy – 'felix illa Campania', Livy called it – because of the volcanic minerals from Vesuvius. Electron microscopy has found traces of barley, emmer wheat, walnuts, almonds, figs, grapes, pears and pomegranates, peas, broad beans and lentils in the shops and houses of Pompeii and Herculaneum.

The fact that much of the diet of the people of Spartacus' times would have been eaten with little preparation or cooking, and much of it was raw, was a gift to an army on the move. Neither was there a problem of obtaining the more expensive or exotic foodstuffs – Spartacus' people simply took it. The same went for utensils and implements. A staple crop in Campania, then as now, is the olive. The slaves would have soaked olives in brine and eaten them raw or used them in cooking. The oil was used for lamps and had medicinal uses too. The various presses used to produce this were heavy but could have been taken from Nola or Nuceria for the slaves' future use, say in their winter camp.

When Spartacus' people were near the coast, they caught fish and were able to utilise the scraps to make a variety of sauces – garum, allec, muria, liquamen – which were widely enjoyed throughout the period. In the countryside, they made their own bread. More than thirty bakeries have been found in Pompeii, but there was no need for the elaborate, animal-driven querns and multiple ovens of professional production. Dough was pounded by hand and cooked over open fires by slaves as a matter of routine and we can assume that the runaways who joined Spartacus were slaves with a whole range of domestic talents.

All the ancient writers agree that the gladiators from Capua were a mix of Thracian, Gaul and German; three races and a multiplicity of tribes with their regional ethnic cultures, faiths and customs. What they had in common was the fact that they were slaves and on the run from their Roman masters.

The term 'Gaul' is an all-embracing one. Part of the massive influx of Indo-European tribes that had moved west during the Bronze Age, they were actually Celts, whose most westerly tribes would invade what is today Britain, France and Spain. There was a long history of hatred between the Gauls and the Latin tribes who would emerge as Romans by 4000 BC. Crixus was almost certainly from one of the tribes of Cisalpine Gaul, in the north of Italy and the foothills of the Alps. Beyond that we cannot say with certainty.

In 225 BC, these tribes had marched on Rome, among them the Taurisci, the Insubres and the Boii. There may have been others with them from Transalpine Gaul beyond the Alps, because Rome offered rich pickings. Terrified Romans, great believers in omens and prophecy, sacrificed a Celt and his wife by burying them alive in order to avoid the fulfilment of the prophecy that Gauls would one day take Rome. In the battle that followed, the Roman army was exposed to Gallic chariot warfare for the first time. Julius Caesar wrote admiringly about the British use of chariots twenty years after Spartacus. The Gaesate, spearmen from beyond the Alps, astonished everyone by hurtling across the field stark naked, gilt torcs around their necks and swirling blue designs on their skin, hacking and slashing at the Roman lines with their long swords. They needed no armour, as the Romans did, because they believed themselves immortal. They would go to their gods like soldiers. They lopped off heads when they could and stuck them on their spear-points to terrify the legions locked behind their shields. The Greek writer Polybius, who may have spoken to men who fought at Telemon, gives us the usual staggering battlefield statistics. The Gauls had 50,000 infantry and 20,000 cavalry and chariots; the casualties were 40,000 dead and 10,000 captured. Again, we cannot accept this literally, but that it was a stunning Roman victory is beyond doubt. The consul Lucius Aemilius was granted an official triumph in the streets of Rome and a jeering mob spat and snarled insults at the tall, lime-haired men from the north, with their long, curling moustaches and checked trousers.

But the Gallic threat would not go away. In the years just prior to Spartacus' birth, the Cimbri and the Teutones had gone on their travels. Again, numbers astonish and this time Plutarch is the culprit. What he is describing, however, is two bands of migratory peoples, not merely warriors, and in that sense there is a reflection here of Spartacus' people. Although the Teutones are usually lumped together with the Cimbri as Gauls, the likelihood is that they were actually Germanic. Piecing together fragments of Greek and Roman histories, the Teutones were first noted in 115 BC north of Magdeburg before wandering south into what is now Austria.

Fighting with locals as they went, they eventually clashed with the consul Gnaeus Papirius Carbo, whose command, but not his reputation, was saved by a violent thunderstorm which turned the battlefield into a quagmire. Carbo committed suicide by swallowing poison.

Four years later, with the Cimbri and Teutones permanently camped on either side of the Pyrenees, the consul Marcus Julius Silanus was roundly beaten on the Rhone, encouraging a host of Helvetian (Swiss) Gauls to join the ever growing army. In 105 BC, the armies of Quintus Servilius Caepio and Gnaeus Malleus Maximus, consuls for that year, found themselves with their backs to the Rhone at Arausio (today's Orange) and their command wiped out.

It was Rome's luck that Gaius Marius succeeded (illegally) to his second term as consul the following year. His restructuring of the Roman army made it the most highly trained, disciplined and hardened in the ancient world. Even so, the army of Quintus Lutatius Catulus, the half-brother of Julius Caesar, was defeated at Tridentum and retreated across the river Po, his army in a state of mutiny. It was only the arrival of Marius from the south that halted the Gallic advance and on the field of Campi Raurii, the years of terror for Rome came to an end. In a vivid account of the battle written by Plutarch, the Gauls' front ranks were chained together through belt loops so that the battering ram that was the Roman cohort could not smash through them. It was the height of summer and the Gauls were not accustomed to the fierce sun flashing on Roman armour or the dustbowl in which they had to fight. Jamming their huge formation into tight, immovable columns with his cavalry, Marius did not give the Cimbri a chance to use their long, deadly swords, and the slaughter was appalling. The dead were said to number 120,000 and 60,000 men became slaves. 'Never,' wrote Plutarch, 'had the scavenging birds of Italy fed on such gigantic corpses.'[22] 'For the women,' he wrote, 'all dressed in black, stood on the wagons and killed the fugitives – their husbands, their brothers, their fathers, then they strangled their little children with their own hands . . . and finally they cut their own throats.'[23]

We have no details about what Crixus himself was like. In that he eventually went his own way and broke with the wiser counsel of Spartacus, he clearly had ideas, a presence and a following of his own.

The Gauls with Crixus would have had a common bond with Spartacus' Thracians because of their Celtic ancestry. It is possible that they worshipped the same gods and shared a single notion of sacrifice. Certainly, the lifestyle of a peasant from both countries would not have been dissimilar. Language must have presented a barrier, but we know very little about the nature of 'barbarian' language at this stage, unwritten as it was.

The Germans among Spartacus' people were yet another element, although, as we have seen, they may in fact have been Celts from further north in Europe and not Germans at all. What is interesting is what each racial and tribal group brought to the nature of the war that Spartacus fought. We know from eyewitness accounts from Polybius to Caesar that the Gauls still fought naked or wore animal-crested helmets and carried oblong, bronze-fronted shields, long double-edged swords and murderous spears. They were essentially infantrymen, but their charioteers were highly skilled, dashing along the pole between the tough little ponies and hacking at an enemy before darting back to their chariots. The fact that no contemporary mentions these weapons, armour or gadgets in the army of Spartacus is clear proof that his men did not have access to their native equipment and that Spartacus knew this was not the way to beat the Romans anyway.

German military organisation and tactics changed hardly at all between the first century BC and the fourth century AD. Generals (like Oenomaus perhaps) were elected for the duration of a campaign, which accords with Appian's claim that this was his people's custom, and the army, in common with Celtic tribes, was a complex series of family, clan and tribal interrelationships. The only full-time warriors were the equivalent of nobility, well armed and equipped and required to die for their chief. Tacitus records their fanaticism and we can see it enacted by their Saxon descendants at battles from Maldon to Hastings, thegns and huscarls hurling themselves to death around the standard and the fallen bodies of their respective ealdormen and kings. In battle, the Germanii formed wedges of spearmen, not unlike the Greek phalanx, and rarely wore armour. At the heart of Germanic success against the Romans, as in the Teutoberg Forest in AD 9, when three legions were wiped out under the German chief Arminius, was the almost suicidal bravery of individual warriors and the dog-like devotion shown to leaders by their people. If the Germans in Spartacus' army elected Oenomaus, they were probably expected to die for and with him.

Much less easy to gauge is the domestic situation among Spartacus' followers. Most commentators today make the assumption that most of them were newly acquired prisoners of war, sold in the marketplace to the highest bidder having been dragged in chains from whatever theatre of war they were captured. And despite the bizarre female-led mass homicide at Campi Raurii, these slaves would have included women and children. This was the workforce that fed and clothed Spartacus' army, but they also had to be fed and protected. Again, the assumption is that they lived in a vast marching camp, probably protected with rampart and ditch in the Roman style which Spartacus would have known well. But we know that he had taken at least two towns and countless villages by the winter of 73/2 BC, and that one of them at least, Nola, was a formidable fortress in its own right. Did he winter there, with all the comforts of a Roman town, with its villas, its forum, its public baths? There were risks involved here. Determined, intelligent commanders like Caesar (and, as it would turn out, Crassus) were not deterred by bad weather and the winter months. Cities could be deathtraps if they were besieged properly. On the other hand, a camp in the open ran serious risks too.

Part of our problem is that we have no clear knowledge of Spartacus' game plan at this or any other stage. Sallust gives us a plausible insight into his mindset and his problems, but the text is badly damaged and not all of it as lucid as it might be:

[It seemed?] to others and to him . . . that they should not [wander around aimlessly lest] they be hemmed in on all sides and slaughtered to the last man . . . A few of the slaves who were prudent men and who had free and noble minds . . . praised [his advice?] and held that they ought to do what Spartacus was suggesting. Some slaves were stupid and foolishly had confidence in the large numbers who were flooding in to join their movement and in their own ferocity . . . the vast majority of the fugitives, because of their servile nature, thought of nothing but blood and booty . . .[24]

The slaves who had risen as leaders in Sicily in the previous two generations had made themselves kings, but there is no mention of this in Spartacus. If he swaggered around in Glaber's laurels and rode Varinius' horse, as some ancient writers seem to suggest, it was no more than we might expect from a winner against the odds. In his sharing out of the spoils and the frequent clashes of opinion between Spartacus and his lieutenants, we see a surprisingly egalitarian, even democratic leader, prepared to accept the will of his people. Various Roman writers, describing their enemies at different times in their long history of conquest, take delight in portraying them as bickering and brawling, killing each other over women or choice cuts of pork and often roaring drunk. Laying aside the pork, for which Romans had no particular affinity, how different was the life of their own dear Senators?

Historian Philip Matyszak has Spartacus' people moving south for the winter having defeated Varinius, gaining support from runaways including free men and women from Lucania and Bruttium. His success against Varinius now made him a household name.

'Quick, boy,' wrote the poet Horace[25] in *Carmina*, 'bring wine, that knew the Marsian[26] War/ If plundering Spartacus has spared a single jar.'

As a boy, Horace must have heard horror stories of the gladiator slave. His father was a freedman from Apulia, who may have been enslaved in the Social War. According to Plutarch, Spartacus could not persuade his people to leave Italy before the winter, so they took to raiding in Campania instead. Isolated villas and farmsteads were particularly vulnerable to attack.

'Then,' wrote Sallust, 'he persuaded [his followers] to move down into the lowland plains, which were rich in cattle, where they would be able to increase their number with select men of high quality.'[27]

It may have been now that, using a local guide, Spartacus threaded his way through the foothills of the Eburian Hills (today's Eboli Mountains) and reached Nares Lucanae, a narrow pass whose name means 'the nostrils of Lucania'. It is Sallust who gives us the only detailed account of a slave attack on a town:

At daybreak, he arrived at Forum Annii, without having been discovered by the local farmers. Contrary to the orders of their general, the fugitive slaves immediately began to rape young girls and married women, while others . . . [cut down] those who tried to resist them and who were trying to escape, inflicting wounds on them in a depraved manner, when their backs were turned, and left in their trail the torn bodies of half-dead people. Others threw firebrands onto the roofs of houses. Many slaves in the town were by nature sympathetic allies and uncovered things that their masters had hidden away or dragged out the masters themselves from their hiding places. Nothing was either too sacred or too wicked to be spared the rage of these barbarians and their servile characters. Spartacus himself was powerless to stop them, even though he repeatedly entreated them to stop and even attempted by sending on ahead a swift messenger [to warn outlying areas?]. But the slaves [were] intent on their cruel slaughter . . . and after having stayed there for that day and the following night, and having doubled the number of fugitive slaves, he broke camp at dawn and established his position in a wide plain, where he watched the local farmers leading their horses for work – it was the time of year when the autumn harvests were ripening in the fields . . .[28]

No doubt the harvest fell to Spartacus too.

There is no doubt that Spartacus' aim was freedom, but to reach it he either had to obtain ships – no mean feat for a commander with an estimated following of 70,000 by this time – or march north to the Alps to reach the overland route. That meant bypassing Rome or taking the city, and both options were fraught with difficulty. Time and weather were against him too and he stayed in the south, trying to reduce the depredations of his wilder followers and, incidentally, getting his army into shape.

'He had regular weapons forged for them,' wrote Appian, 'and he began to collect basic supplies for an army.'[29]

Within the towns under his command, Spartacus

did not permit merchants to import gold and silver, and he forbade his own men to acquire any. For the most part, he purchased iron and copper and did not censure those who imported those metals. For this reason, the slaves had large quantities of basic materials and were well supplied and able to stage frequent raids. When they next entered into hand-to-hand combat with the Romans, they defeated the Romans again and returned to their base heavily laden with booty.[30]

Florus provides more details:

With the daily arrival of new recruits, they were finally able to form themselves into a regular army. They made rough shields for themselves out of vine branches [and had possibly been doing this since Vesuvius] covered with animal hides and swords and spears by melting down and recasting their irons [slave shackles] from the slave barracks. And so that they should lack nothing required by a real army, they put together a cavalry force by training wild horses that they happened to come across.[31]

We have very little information on the training of horses by the military in this period, but the fact that it was done at all speaks volumes for the patient way in which Spartacus built up his army along Roman lines. He had seen *alae* (cavalry units) in action and understood the need for such formations in battle. They were the eyes and ears of an army on the march and however many mounts he had 'liberated' from towns and enemy units, there was always a need for more. To train wild horses, however, he must have had farriers, smiths and horse-breakers among his people.

We can only speculate on the way that Spartacus provided for these people. Like Julius Caesar, that other great military commander who was probably born in the same year as the rebel slave, Spartacus would have known all about the importance of having an army properly provisioned. Three centuries after Caesar's time Vegetius wrote: 'Time and opportunity may help to retrieve other misfortunes, but where forage and provisions have not been carefully provided, the evil is without remedy.'[32]

Both Caesar and Spartacus had to rely to a large extent on the luck of the harvest; Caesar was struggling in Gaul in 54 and 52 BC when heavy rain destroyed the standing corn. Typically of Caesar, in his account of the campaigns he put words into the mouth of his enemy, Vercingetorix: 'We ourselves have plenty of supplies, because we can rely on the resources of the people in whose territory the campaign is conducted . . .'[33]

So could Spartacus. And ten years after his war, the irrepressible Mithridates, king of Pontus south of the Black Sea, could launch an attack on Rome because 'he knew that almost all of Italy had recently revolted from the Romans because of the hatred the Italians had for them, that the Italians had fought a protracted war against the Romans [the Social War] and that they had sided with the gladiator Spartacus . . .'[34]

Producing food was what slaves did. They planted and reaped the corn, pressed the grapes for the wine, drew the water and baked the bread. They also drove the herds of cattle, sheep, goats and pigs, collected the eggs and plucked the chickens. And once Spartacus had liberated the slaves of the latifundia, all this produce fell to him; it was better than Vercingetorix's scorched earth policy, especially as it is likely that Spartacus was able to store the provisions in one or more of the fortified towns he had captured from the Romans.

The late John Peddie,[35] using Caesar's Gallic War account, has done some fascinating mathematics to gauge the size of the logistics problem for a Roman commander. In 52 BC, Caesar's baggage train was at Bibracte, in friendly Aeduan territory west of today's Autun.

Peddie estimates that it would have included ancillary troops, clerks, technicians and weapons experts, extra tentage, armour, weapons, additional horses with their own *gyrus* or circular training area, a field hospital with doctors and a varyingly sized retinue of sick and wounded, engineering stores and bridge-building equipment. Much of this would have been carried on wooden carts, hauled by mules or oxen and would have slowed the army down enormously. A baggage train was such a liability that both Philip of Macedonia and his son, Alexander, banned their use on campaign, but Caesar's carts could move at the speed of a marching infantryman and it is likely that he used them extensively. In calculating Caesar's logistics problem, Peddie points out that at the height of his war against the Helvetii in 58 BC, he finally assembled fourteen legions, giving him a command (on paper at least) of nearly 60,000 men. This does not include the huge back-up of men listed above, so that Spartacus' numbers in the winter of 73/2 BC were rather lower than Caesar's. The difference of course is that an unknown percentage of the gladiator's followers were women and children.

If we break down a legion into its marching constituents, we have each *contubernium* (eight-man unit) carrying a tent, corn-grinding mill, kettle, shovels, picks and other tools, apart from weapons and arrows. Each century (eighty men) had a *carroballista*, a mule-drawn two-wheeled cart for an artillery weapon and a second cart to carry the centurion's tent and equipment. Peddie estimates 120 auxiliary cavalry (earlier armies had more) and an approximate 250 other horses and mules for staff officers, ambulances and so on. All in all, it seems reasonable to assume that a legion had 7,500 pack animals on the march. Each man carried five days' rations of bread with an extra 15 pounds of grain and more had to be carried for the horses. Roman cavalry horses often, since the reforms of Marius, provided by the auxiliary units that made up the *alae*, needed five hours a day of good grazing, as well as 20 to 24 pounds of dried oats or barley.

Any Roman army coming up against Spartacus would have needed to calculate all this. It is likely that the slaves themselves travelled a great deal lighter. They were not, in Caesar's sense, on campaign in hostile territory; as we have seen, thousands of people welcomed them as liberators, sparking the legend of Spartacus the freedom-fighter. He used the wet and cold of the winter months to conserve his supplies, forge his weapons and to wait for spring.

The spring brought action from Rome, and the action was unprecedented. Not one but both consuls for that year of 72 BC led out separate commands to find the gladiator and destroy him. Glaber, Varinius and Cossinius had been Praetors, but the rank of Consul was the highest in the Republic and commanded huge eminence. It is a mark of the fear that Spartacus had instilled into the hearts of Romans great and small that men of this calibre were sent against him now.

Lucius Gellius Publicola was far too old for a field command by the time he marched out into Campania. He was in his sixties and had been Praetor Urbanus in 94 BC. The following year he had been proconsul of an eastern province and had fought under the general Pompeius Strabo (the squint-eyed) in the Social War. In 72 BC – and it is not clear whether this was before or after he found Spartacus – Gellius, perhaps at the suggestion of Pompey the Great, passed a law conferring the status of Roman citizenship on soldiers who had distinguished themselves in the field. It may even have a bearing on the courage needed to face Spartacus that this law was passed at this particular time. Gellius may have considered himself lucky that, in the wake of Spartacus' depredations, he was able to keep what was left of his career intact.

The other consul for 72 BC was Gnaeus Cornelius Lentulus, known as Clodianus. He had a plebeian background and was almost certainly adopted by the patrician Corneli Lentuli family. He was an avid supporter of Sulla and had marched on Rome with him in 89 BC. He too would survive Spartacus.

What played into the hands of both men was that Spartacus' force was now split and it is likely that the gladiator leader had spent weeks, even months, trying to keep his command together. From the sense of what happened in the spring of 72 BC, Spartacus seems to have been moving north, towards the Alps. His clash with the consuls was part of the calculated risk of avoiding Rome, although it is likely that there were those in his camp who argued that they had the capability to take the city itself. Whether because of a leadership dispute – Spartacus was chief only by election after all – or because of a difference of strategic opinion, the Germans broke away to find their own fortune. The likely leader of this group, estimated by Appian at 30,000 men, was Crixus. It is possible that Oenomaus was already dead by this time, either from wounds sustained fighting Varinius or an early casualty of the spring. Plutarch is in no doubt of the reason for the split – it was the 'insolent self confidence'[36] of the Gauls and Germans and it cost Crixus his life.

Gellius Publicola caught the Germans in the Garganus Mountains in Apulia and destroyed them. With the usual Roman disdain and disregard for the facts, Plutarch claims that he 'slaughtered the lot of them'.[37] Yet if Appian's figure of 30,000 dead is anywhere near accurate, they could not all have been annihilated. Some must have survived, either dragging themselves back to Spartacus or struggling north for the Alps and probably moving parallel with him.

'At this point,' wrote Plutarch, 'it was no longer the unworthiness and shame of the slave rebellion that so vexed the Senate. Rather, it was because of fear and the danger of the situation that they dispatched both consuls together to the war, much as they would send consuls to a regular war of the greatest difficulty and magnitude.'[38]

Nobody was underestimating Spartacus now. The consuls were both men of military experience and they were in command of legions: the brilliant, unstoppable regular army of Rome. Crixus was dead, smashed down, no doubt, under the tramp of the *caligae*, battered beyond recognition by the shield bosses and hacked like butcher's liver by the short swords of the legionaries. Spartacus would be next and it would all be over before the summer.

EIGHT

Running from the Field of Battle

The Garganus Mountains form the 'spur' of Italy, jutting some 30 miles out into the Adriatic. What were Crixus and his Germans doing there? The area lies north-east of Capua, where the revolt had begun months before, and not very far from that city. We know that Spartacus had turned south-west to the Bay of Naples and sacked Nola and Nuceria before hitting Forum Annii in the narrow pass of the Nares Lucanae. He had been following the Via Annia that led to Bruttium in the south. For Crixus to be this far to the north-east, it is likely that Spartacus had taken the towns of Thurii and Metapontum by this time. Both are mentioned in Florus' text based on earlier writings and both stand on the Bay of Tarentum in the 'instep' of Italy.

Like most towns in southern Italy Thurii was originally a Greek settlement, built in this case near a far older habitation called Sybaris. It was probably founded in about 452 BC and its earliest settlers included the 'father of history', Herodotus. A prolonged battle with the Lucanians further north led to the collapse of the town's democracy in the fourth century BC and a plea for help to the Romans further north still. It was among many places attacked and plundered by Hannibal's Carthaginians and officially became a Roman colony, called briefly Copiae, in 194 BC, when a great deal of rebuilding was no doubt undertaken. At the time of Spartacus, the leading landowners in the area were the Octavi. The town's greatest son, the future Augustus, was given the name Thurinus shortly after his birth.

Metapontum is better known, although the town has long since disappeared. Founded by Achean colonists on the river Bradanus about 700 BC, it was one of several towns that tried to save itself by siding with Hannibal and because of this fell into a steep decline from 207 BC onwards. Extensive archaeology has been carried out in the area since 1974 and has unearthed a grid-plan city, not unlike Pompeii and Herculaneum, that had an estimated population of 8,000 people and extensive suburbs. Historian Keith Bradley doubts that the cities in the south provided winter quarters for Spartacus, because of their poverty. This may be so, but the Metapontum finds have proved that gold, amber and copper were worked here, which indicates that there was some wealth.

There was a marked change in the agriculture of Metapontum in the Roman period. The 49 separate sites that had been excavated by the 1980s prove that pastoral farming was replacing crop-growing, providing Spartacus no doubt with his tough, armed herdsmen who knew the area like the backs of their hands and would be invaluable scouts for him. We know that Metapontum had a pumping system for water as early as the fourth century BC and ancient texts refer to the sacred spring, pool and lands of Dionysius. We cannot know, in the absence of the written record, what Spartacus' wife made of all this. This was the home of her cult; she may have felt that she had come home too.

Fifteen columns of the original thirty-two that supported the roof of the Temple of Hera still stand and excavations have revealed the bones of collie-sized hunting dogs, rabbit, fox, wild pig and red deer. Horses, mules, sheep and goats were common, but cattle more rare. Some experts believe that cattle were eaten only after sacrifice, but we do not know if this was a ritual among Spartacus' people.

We do know, however, that elements of the slave army were content to stay and plunder in the more fertile Campania, however much their commanders disapproved. Ironically, the east coast was a more sensible jumping-off point for Spartacus on his way home to Thrace, if that was his intention. If Crixus planned to take ship with his 30,000 men he was going by a circuitous route. The passes through the Alps were a long way to the north and he had ended up in a cul-de-sac. It may simply be that he went instinctively to the high ground so that he would be prepared for whatever Rome threw at him. In that sense, he was badly outmanoeuvred. Plutarch and

Appian agree that Gellius' attack was sudden; either Crixus had not posted scouts or they had let him down. But the real reason for the defeat of Crixus is that he was facing not a hastily scrambled militia or a town garrison; he was facing the full might of the legions.

On his way to greatness, Gaius Marius had reformed the Roman army. An unpopular choice as consul with some sections of the Senate, he was not voted the funds to raise new legions for the war in Numidia and hit upon the *capite censi*, the head count, which allowed poor citizens with no property qualifications to enlist. This was an important political and social change, but it and other reforms were probably under way before Marius became the catalyst. What the reforms did was to create a formidable war machine that would survive, slowly evolving and almost always victorious, for the next four centuries.

At the heart of the new army was the legion, a permanent organisation that can loosely be equated with a regiment in modern armies. These were nominally 4,000 strong and composed of heavy infantry, but accompanying *auxilia* and *alae* could easily double that number. This was the unit, brilliantly trained, equipped and organised, that had destroyed Crixus in the Garganus Mountains in the spring of 72 BC. Now they faced Spartacus, who had been one of their own. The account of Plutarch is infuriatingly terse; he dismisses this first real feat of Spartacus' generalship in a mere three lines: 'But when Lentulus, the other Consul, surrounded Spartacus with his large battlefield forces, Spartacus suddenly rushed at them and engaged them in battle.'[1]

With the help of 300 years of Roman military experience and the writings of some of the most respected commentators in the ancient world, we can put some flesh at least on to these brittle bones.

We do not know how many men Lentulus took into the field with him, or where he found Spartacus. Adrian Goldsworthy, one of the foremost authorities today on the Roman army, says that it was usual practice for consuls to lead two legions. If we add the back-up units of *auxilia* and *alae* for each one, that gives Lentulus an effective force of perhaps 20,000. This was the size of army that proved most effective against the primitive regional enemies that Rome faced in the dying years of the Republic and the early Principate or Empire. Many more than that and the army on campaign was difficult for a general to deploy effectively. The logistical problems would be immense. Against that, Spartacus would have had a similar number. Even allowing for the fact that not all of his 30,000 men were lost, Crixus' command was badly mauled and its stragglers may not have joined Spartacus in time, even assuming they were in fighting shape for a second, gruelling battle. Sallust tells us that the headstrong Crixus was always spoiling for a fight: 'Crixus and his people, who were Gauls and Germans, wanted to march directly against the enemy in order to force an armed confrontation.'[2]

Orosius credits him with a mere 10,000 men (which seems believable) and says that he 'put up a savage resistance'[3] before he was killed.

For Spartacus to have been surrounded implies that Lentulus found him, rather than the other way round, and to do that he would have used his cavalry as scouts. By Marius' time, the integral cavalry with the militia legions had disappeared and, especially in the far-flung reaches of the rapidly growing empire, native cavalry was recruited from the locality. It is anybody's guess who actually made up the units with Lentulus in the spring of 72 BC, but they were probably Sabines or Samnites in origin and would have known the country better than Spartacus, but no better than the slave-soldiers under his command.

The 120-strong cavalry unit which accompanied each legion was called an *ala* but we cannot be sure how many of them were in the field in 72 BC. Each *ala* was subdivided into thirty-man strong *turmae*, the rough equivalent of half a troop in European cavalry of the nineteenth century. They rode the tough little ponies common to all Republican cavalry, the historian Tacitus claiming that most animals were imported from Spain, although Gallic breeds, uglier and slower, were also used and even German breeds may have made an appearance in the Italian peninsula by this time. Forty years after Spartacus, the poet Virgil wrote a loving description of a war horse:

His neck is carried erect; his head is small; his belly short; his back broad. Brawny muscles swell upon his noble chest. A bright bay or a good grey is the best colour; the worst is white or dun. If from afar, the clash of arms be heard, he knows not how to stand still; his ears prick up, his limbs quiver; and, snorting, he rolls the collected fire under his nostrils. And his mane is thick, and reposes tossed back on his right shoulder. A double spine [well-muscled] runs along to his loins.[4]

Lentulus' cavalrymen did not use stirrups, any more than Spartacus' did. Today's experimental archaeologists, such as Marcus Junkelmann and Peter Connolly, are at pains to assure us that this lack of support did not hinder the Roman cavalryman on campaign or in the field.[5] This was because the rider sat in a four-pronged saddle made of wood and leather, which was probably Gallic in origin and which gave ample control, along with the single rein and simple iron bit. Lentulus' horsemen would have worn mail shirts over their tunics, of the type worn by his infantry. Their plumed helmets were made of iron or a copper alloy and they would have carried long, double-edged *spatha*, swords half as long again as the infantry's *gladius*,[6] as well as a spear and a flat, circular or oval shield made of wood, probably painted with some totemic design. Sallust makes special mention of these shields among Spartacus' troops as early as the camp on Vesuvius: 'these men [his new supporters] were very knowledgeable about the region and were used to making woven baskets from branches for their farmwork. Because of their lack of real shields, they used this same knowledge to make small circular shields for themselves like those used by cavalrymen.'[7]

These men, foraging in the wooded hills of Campania, galloped back to the army lines with the news that the army of Spartacus had been sighted.

We have no definite idea of the marching order of Lentulus' troops. Working on speculation from the eyewitness account of the Jewish historian Flavius Josephus in Galilee in AD 67, it *ought* to have followed a certain orthodoxy. But Josephus is describing the order of march of Titus Flavius Vespasianus, Vespasian, after Caesar the best general the Romans produced, and we may imagine that Lentulus fell a little short of his ideal. Josephus does not mention scouts at all. Perhaps Vespasian did not need them because he knew he would not meet the enemy on the road, or because he already knew exactly where they were. At the head of the column, sweating in the Galilean dust, came the light infantry of the *auxilia*.

We have a false idea of these men; of the units in which Spartacus himself was probably trained. They were 'light' only in the sense that their equipment was not as well made or impressive as that of the legionaries. In practice, on the road they marched at the legionaries' pace and tented alongside them. In battle formation, they tended to take post on the legions' wings, ready to turn front and parry exchanges of missiles. Auxiliaries carried the *gladius*, probably of the type excavated at Mainz in Germany, with its leaf-shaped, double-edged blade, as well as a *pugio* or dagger, and some of them, at least, were specialised slingers or archers.

There is no evidence that units were specifically trained in either weapon, but men with a good aim would certainly have been trained to improve it. Most bows that have been found are of composite manufacture, made of more than one type of wood. They were short and ornately curved, allowing only the 'Mediterranean shot' of about 300 yards, the animal-gut string pulled back to the chin.[8]

Very few contemporary commentators mention bows used in large numbers, and their relative lack of strength may have made them less useful than sling-shots. These were made of leather, firing either lead 'bullets', ovoid in shape, or the more conventional (and easily found) stones. Sling bullets used by Scipio in his war against Carthage have been unearthed, bearing legionary numbers and other inscriptions whose significance is now unknown. It is likely that, as with the case of messages on modern artillery, the inscriptions are obscene or contemptuous of the enemy.[9] Should Spartacus have attacked Lentulus on the march, these men were expected to slog it out in missile exchanges and a holding exercise until the main vanguard arrived.

Behind the leading auxiliaries marched the first of the legionaries. The image we have of these men, thanks to Hollywood and various re-enactment groups, is of the rectangular, curved shield, the overlapping plates of the *lorica segmentata*, wings and lightning flashes and lashings of red. Every element of this is wrong for Lentulus' army in the spring of 72 BC. Most re-enactors and film costume departments are working from practical modifications of the armour and weapons depicted on Trajan's column in Rome. This astonishing monument to Marcus Ulpinius Trajanus, one of the most successful emperors, is 110 feet high and was unveiled on 15 May, AD 113. On its 23 drums of Persian marble are carved 2,500 figures, mostly military and originally painted in bright colours. No two faces are alike and it forms an unparalleled source of information for the military historian of Rome. Unfortunately, it poses two problems: one is the extent of artistic licence used by its sculptors; and the other is that it was made eighty years after Spartacus. The latter is perhaps a minor problem, given the relatively slow evolution of things in the ancient world, but in terms of the physical appearance of the legions, two generations makes a difference.

Lentulus' legionaries wore a basic short-sleeved tunic of wool or linen. This may have been shorter at the sides than in the front and back and some stele or grave depictions of the period imply a curved lower hem. The soldier's tunic was a longer version of the civilian garment and was held in position by the all-important belt. The colour of the tunic is unknown. Cloth rarely survives in the archaeological record and hardly ever in its original colour. Literary sources are infuriatingly vague on the subject, probably because writers assumed that their readers *knew* all this, rather as today we have a fairly good grasp of the general appearance of soldiers in the Gulf. The scarlet so beloved of Hollywood looks very dramatic in reconstruction, but was a colour generally reserved for senior officers like Lentulus himself. What evidence there is would suggest that most tunics of the other ranks were off-white, with officers pure white, not unlike the pith helmets of the nineteenth-century British armies in Africa.[10]

Lentulus' legionaries would have worn a padded corselet, perhaps of leather, over the tunic, but none of these has survived,[11] so we can only speculate that some kind of padding was necessary beneath the mail shirt. The famous *lorica segmentata*, with its hinged, overlapping plates is unknown in the archaeological record before the early first century AD. The term itself is a modern invention, meaning sectioned breastplate; we do not know what the Romans themselves called it. The men who faced Spartacus somewhere in Campania wore the *lorica hamata*, literally 'hooked breastplate', made of iron or copper-alloy links. Each ring, 1mm thick and 7mm in diameter according to found examples, was hooked to four others. There was probably a double thickness on the shoulders and hips, where sword blows would be likely to fall, and the weight of the shirt could be anything from 22 to 33 pounds. To prevent all this from falling on the shoulders and neck, the twin belts of the legionary were essential, since they helped distribute weight and carried the sword and dagger. Belts assumed an almost totemic significance for legionaries – the emperor Augustus punished slackers in the generation after Spartacus by making them stand to attention in full pack, but without their belts – a mark of humiliation that caused muscular exhaustion too.

The most likely headgear worn by Lentulus' legionaries was the Coolus pattern helmet, itself a variant on the earlier Montefortino version. It was either forged, beaten into shape over a wooden or stone former, or spun. Iron helmets could not be spun without cracking, but the copper and zinc alloy versions worked perfectly well this way. The Coolus helmet had a domed headpiece with a strengthening bar and finial to give maximum protection to the head, large cheek-plates to protect the face and a neck-flange at virtual right angles to the skull. The very few examples of this type found by archaeologists have sockets for plumes. Feathers and horsehair seem to have been an important psychological spur on the battlefields of the Republic, and we have already noted the stylistic versions of 'foreign' headgear worn by the *thrax* and the *myrmillo* in the arena.

Like the auxiliaries, the legionaries carried the leaf-shaped *gladius* on the right hip or the shorter *pugio*, of identical shape, on the left. Enough elaborately decorated dagger sheaths have been found to suggest that embellishment of these may have been the one personal conceit of individuals in a uniform otherwise provided by the state.

The *scutum* or shield carried by Lentulus' legions was probably not yet the rectangular version, made of layers of wood with an iron boss and bronze rim. Later versions of this have been found and can weigh up to 22 pounds. The pattern of 72 BC was probably shorter and more oval in shape – of the type carried for the next two centuries by the elite Praetorian guard. On the march, Lentulus' legionaries carried their shields cased in leather, probably decorated with totemic designs or at least the legion's number.

The final weapon the legionaries carried was the *pilum*, the heavy-blocked, small-headed throwing javelin designed to puncture the shield and body of a running enemy. Convention has it that Republican troops carried two spears, the second the *hasta*, a shorter, broader-bladed weapon that could be thrown, but also served as a stabbing weapon. In the field, for reasons of practicality, it is likely that only the *pilum* was used as routine. Re-enactors have, over the last few years, helped us understand the shortcomings and advantages of various pieces of Roman armour, weapons and equipment, but we cannot take their experiences too far. What 21st-century man finds irritating or inconvenient may well have been readily accepted by his first-century BC counterpart.[12]

In Lentulus' line of march, if he followed an approximation of Vespasian's a century and a half later, would come the camp markers, the men from each century with stakes to mark out the lines of the marching camp. At the end of a day's round, it was standard to build a defensive work of earth ditches and ramparts, topped by palisades carried in roped sections on the pack mules. The fact that Spartacus had surprised Glaber and taken his camp with ease implies that he had not bothered to do this properly. A full-blown consul, especially facing a man who had already destroyed three Roman armies, was not about to make the same mistake. There is nothing in Plutarch or Appian, however, to suggest that the Romans camped within sight of the slave army, posturing for hours or days as they often did before battle was joined. Again, the fact that Spartacus was surprised may indicate that he was on the move. Next in Vespasian's line of march come engineers, the equivalent of a Pioneer Corps, whose task it was to clear away brushwood and repair or even construct roads. Vespasian was operating in very different country from Lentulus and such a unit, though probably present, would have less to do relatively close to civilised Rome.

Then came Lentulus, with his senior officers and bodyguard. The single scarlet flag, the *vexillium*, dangling from a plain pole, marked the position of a general. The excellent military artist Angus McBride has painted a depiction of a consular general in this period, based on the statue of Lucius Cornelius Balbus, a contemporary of Spartacus, who was made a Roman citizen in 72 BC: the very year in which Lentulus took on the gladiator rebel. He wears a scarlet tunic, the stylish *paludamentium*, a fuller, tailored version of the legionary outfit and a scarlet cloak, worn in the manner of a toga, thrown over the left arm and probably secured by means of a brooch to the shoulder. Boots worn by generals were either scarlet or black. Of greatest interest is the muscle-breastplate, of bronze, hinged at the shoulders and sides and bound with scarlet strapping high on the waist. This may be pure artistic convention (although they are shown frequently for senior officers) in that no actual examples have been found. As with the luckless Glaber, in front of the Consul's horse would have trudged his *lictores*, carrying the rods and axes of the *fasces*, the symbols of his power. Ironically, Spartacus already had a set of these too!

Behind Lentulus rode the bulk of the *alae*, the cavalry we have already discussed, shields on their backs and eyes alert for every movement. Then came the siege train. We have no idea of the extent of this or whether Lentulus had any meaningful siege equipment. Vespasian needed siege weapons because he knew that the Jews would defend their cities such as Jerusalem, which he would sack in AD 70, and Masada, where the famous last stand was made. We do not know what intelligence Lentulus had of Spartacus' movements, still less his intentions. With hindsight, it looks to us as if the gladiator was already making a run for it to the north, to the Alps and freedom. Lentulus could not be certain of that. What if

Spartacus retreated to Nola or any other fortified town he had taken? Siege weapons were of limited use in the open field, but what if he had to pin the slaves down for a prolonged period and starve them out? The Consul probably had the basics with him – the *carroballista* of the *contubernia* and one or two larger field pieces.

Next in Vespasian's column, and very likely in Lentulus', came the legates of the legions with their *praefecti*. It was not until the reign of the emperor Augustus that officer ranks in the legions were formalised but they clearly followed a pattern already adopted, quite probably by 72 BC. The *legati* were usually hand-picked men and in the close-knit nepotistic world of the Republic, possibly relatives and certainly friends of Lentulus. They were the rough equivalent of lieutenant-colonels today, commanding their 'regiment' in the field. Each legion had six tribunes, usually young men on their way to a political career. Long years of fighting, however, both against Carthage and in the Social War, had given the legions a stability and experience that the pre-Marian army lacked. Under the *legatus legionis* and riding alongside him in search of Spartacus, was the *tribunus laticlavius*, usually a novice in his twenties. Then came the *praefectus castrorum*, an old hand who was usually promoted from the centurion ranks. The *tribuni augusticlavii* were the junior officers, the lieutenants of their day, with no particular role other than to plug gaps and learn from the whole experience.

Behind them, the legions marched. We do not know exactly how many tramped through the Campanian country, slave-hunting, that spring and summer. Twelve legions are listed as having been raised in the late Republic, but exact dates of their formation are unknown. I Germanicus was disbanded in AD 70 because they had supported the revolt of Gaius Julius Civilis, a Batavian (German) auxiliary commander who used the unit to proclaim an 'Empire of the Gauls'. It was a reminder that the army was a political weapon in the hands of ambitious men and that retribution was swift and final. Those who survived the punitive campaign against them saw their standards smashed and their legion wiped from the record. II Augusta, which probably acquired the nickname Gallica from their clashes with the Cimbri and Teutones, were given their title by

Augustus, but may have been simply II Legio prior to that. III Augusta Pia Fidelis (faith and hope) certainly acquired that title under Rome's first emperor, but again were probably created earlier. III Cyrenica were either raised in Libya or, more probably, fought against the Libyans in the destruction of Carthage. Likewise V Macedonia earned its laurels against the Greeks. VI Victrix (the victorious) was obviously an impressive unit, but where and when the name was acquired is unknown. X Fretensis was named for the straits between Italy and Sicily and may have been the legion that put down the second slave rising on the island in the generation before Spartacus. XIII and XIV were both called Gemina, indicating that they were part of 'twin' units raised at the same time. XIV would go on to earn the nickname Martia Victrix (winner of the war) for their suppression of the revolt by Boudicca of the Iceni in Britannia in AD 61. Any of these legions could have been with Lentulus in the spring of 72 BC. The men marched six abreast in their cohort formation, the silver eagle standard carried by the *aquilifer* at the front, and the cohort standards, the *signi*, behind that.

Auxiliaries, the foot soldiers of the Sabine and Samnite tribes, marched next, some of the men who had fought Rome in the Social War, but were now given citizenship, pay, blisters, calluses and as much hard-tack as they could eat.

The rearguard, ever wary of ambush and surprise attack, formed the end of Lentulus' column. They were auxiliaries and legionaries intermingled with cavalry, the *cohors equitata* which foreshadowed the *corps d'armée*, the mixing of roles used with such brilliance eighteen centuries later by Napoleon.

For Lentulus to have surrounded Spartacus, the gladiator's scouts must have let him down. Again, there is no mention in any source of a camp, so we must suppose that the slave army was caught in the open. Even so, the time it would take a Roman army to *surround* an enemy implies that the area was probably wooded. Lentulus would have held a swift *consilium*, a council of war, and given his orders. These would be relayed by the *legati* to the *tribuni*, who would gallop to their centurions for word to be spread among the cohorts. Speed – and silence – were essential.

No doubt the consul expected Spartacus to surrender. It is extremely unlikely that he would have enough men to pen the slaves in completely and Spartacus would have been looking for weaknesses in the circle. The conventional Roman battle line was the legionaries in the centre with auxiliaries and cavalry on the wings, but the ground may have precluded such a neat formation. Lentulus was probably brought up with the fixed-notion tradition of the *triplex acies*, a formation not dissimilar from that of a football team. The ten cohorts that made up the legion formed itself into three lines of four, three, three pattern, the units overlapping and marching at the measured tread of the centurions at their head, probably two and a half miles an hour, increasing to three on contact with the enemy.

Spartacus would have recognised the centurions with their *phalerae* (decorations) flashing on their mailed chests, their transverse-plumed helmets, the bronze greaves on their legs and their knurled sticks. He could hear their harsh, barked orders to the ranks behind them, shields at the level, stripped now of their leather covers and bright with cohort paint. At the rear of each cohort, he knew, the *optio* was watching the lines. It was at the rear, not the front, that men began to waver in a battle. The men at the front were penned in by the fighting, hacking to stay alive or trapped by the standing dead on each side of them. The *optio* too carried a stick and used it on the back of any man not keeping pace with the rest or whose face was not looking forward.

From various accounts, we have a reasonable idea of the Roman army in action, but Spartacus' slave army is a blank book. The portrayal of them in the Kirk Douglas film, wearing a mishmash of looted, stolen and 'home-made' armour, is probably not far from the truth. Several ancient writers refer to Spartacus employing smiths and iron workers, so his arsenal may have been considerable. Exactly how Spartacus fought is unknown. It is likely that when Crixus, with his Gauls and Germans, fought Gellius days before, the old methods of tribal warfare would have been used. Both Gauls and Germans essentially used the same technique. They would scream insults at the Romans, hurling stones, arrows and abuse in equal measure, 'psyching themselves up' for the killing that was to come. Then they would launch themselves, men on foot or in the saddle, crashing through the solidity of the shield lines. The noise and the impact of the charge were the only psychological weapons these tribes had. If they failed and the cohorts stood firm, then it was only a matter of time before the Romans drove them back.

The historian Dio Cassius, writing in the late second century AD, puts words into the mouth of the general Gaius Suetonius Paulinus which were probably very similar to the orders the man would have given. Paulinus was in command of the legions facing the warrior queen of the Iceni at Manduessedum in AD 61. 'Pep talks' like this were not merely the stuff of Shakespeare; they formed – and still form – an important psychological element of command. Dalton Trumbo's words in the mouth of Kirk Douglas on the eve of the final battle jars a little – 'We have come a long ways together . . .' – but there is a stark realism about the words of Colonel Tim Collins to his men in the Second Gulf War: 'We are going to Iraq to liberate and not to conquer. We will not fly our flags in their country. We are entering Iraq to free a people – and the only flag that will be flown in that ancient land will be their own. Show respect for them.'

Paulinus may have been outnumbered at Manduessedum, but he and Dio Cassius could not find any such laudable aims in his speech. The Romans were the conquerors; they had not gone to Britannia to liberate, but to conquer. The message was more prosaic: 'Keep in close order. Use your javelins, then march on. Bring them down with your shield bosses, kill them with your swords.'[13]

Lentulus must have given similar instructions to his men too, but he was probably astonished by the very fact that the slaves intended to take him on. He would have been doubly astonished to realise that the rebels were mirroring his battle lines, forming into centuries and cohorts before his eyes. Above all, they were *silent*, like his own troops. Only later would Romans adopt the Germanic habit of sending up a guttural roar on the battlefield, and then only seconds before the lines hit. Spartacus was a highly skilled general, and as such he would have adopted the Roman method of fighting to the letter. It is this that all other commentators have missed and it is this alone that explains Spartacus' astonishing success.

When Roman met Roman in the field, as Pompey the Great would against Caesar in the years ahead, then it was superior generalship that decided the outcome, not tribal tactics. And Lentulus, the Consul, was no match for Spartacus the slave. We really cannot know what it was like to fight a battle in this period. Hollywood has done its best, but the only time we see Spartacus in battle in the Kirk Douglas film, the brilliant rolling fire-logs quickly give way to a mass of hand-to-hand duels without structure or coherence. If it was really like that, then the Romans would never have won a battle. A gladiator against a soldier would always have the edge because of his superior training and the tricks of his trade. The whole strength of the legion was in maintaining its formation in the thick of the fighting. The first cohorts would have hurled their *pila* into the slave ranks, but Spartacus would have held his ground and returned fire. There would be no headlong Gallic rush against the shields so that the legionaries could bat his men aside, stab with their swords and march over them. He had enough equipment taken from Glaber and Varinius to match Lentulus' legions blow for blow and he had had all winter to train his men for this moment.

There can be no other explanation for what happened next. Had Spartacus used an unusual stratagem, like the retreat from the siege of Varinius' camp or abseiling with vines down Vesuvius, one of the ancient writers would have commented on it. Lentulus survived the battle and he would have been keen to trumpet the fact that Spartacus had used underhand tactics to secure his victory, if that had been the case. Lentulus did not, and no one else has either. The only other possibility is that Spartacus did in fact use the age-old tribal full-frontal screaming assault; but to do that, he would have needed to have outnumbered Lentulus to an unlikely degree.

'He defeated Lentulus' legates,' wrote Plutarch laconically, 'and captured all their supplies.'[14]

Again, this is important. The baggage train was the lifeline of an army on the march; countless mules, engineering equipment, corn, barley, wine, meat, weapons and medical supplies all found their way into Spartacus' hands. It is not recorded what Lentulus did next. His legions were shattered and in the darkest watches of the night, he must have rued the mistakes he had made. Plutarch tells us nothing about these possible mistakes, and Appian does not mention the battle at all. Like all the battles of the Spartacus War, this one has no name. There is no further mention of Lentulus in the accounts of this war. It is likely that he gathered his battered, bleeding cohorts together, grateful that he probably still had some of his eagles, and limped back to Rome to face the spitting mob and the opprobrium of the Senate.

It was the summer of 72 BC and Spartacus was going home. Exactly where he defeated Lentulus is not recorded, but it was probably somewhere in the foothills of the Apennines and the slave army was moving north. A truly great commander, even a beaten one, would have kept mounted scouts trailing them, reporting on their progress; but Lentulus was not a great commander and only one army now stood between Spartacus and safety north of the Alps.

Philip Matyszak muddies the waters here by suggesting that Lentulus and Gellius had been carrying out, perhaps unknowingly, a pincer movement, with Spartacus trapped between them. He says that the gladiator defeated one, then the other, in Napoleonic style, since the Corsican often faced two enemies simultaneously. There is no record of this being the case, although Appian is probably his source:

Spartacus . . . exerted great efforts to make his way through the Apennine mountains to the Alps and then to the land of the Gauls . . . One of the Consuls got to the place before him and prevented his escape, while the other Consul harried the rearguard of Spartacus' army. Spartacus turned on them one after the other . . . and defeated each Roman army in turn, with the result that the Romans were forced to flee from the field of battle in great confusion and uproar.[15]

'Great confusion' is what we are left with. Appian, writing over two centuries later, clearly believed that both Lentulus and Gellius had been smashed by Spartacus. This is unlikely, especially as he makes no mention of the third army that was now on its way to deal with the renegade slave. Bizarre enough for Lentulus, the shamed commander, to be allowed to continue in his consular career, but would Gellius have been so lucky? As the victor over Crixus, he could at least claim some respect, but if Spartacus did not fight him, where was he?

One possibility is that he joined the 10,000-strong force commanded by Caius Cassius Longinus, described by Plutarch as the governor of Cisalpine Gaul. This is one of the most famous Romans of them all, the 'lean and hungry' conspirator of Shakespeare's play, who would plunge his dagger into the dying body of Julius Caesar on the Ides of March twenty-eight years later. Most commentaries record Cassius' career as beginning in earnest as quaestor in Marcus Licinius Crassus' campaign against the Parthians in the early 50s BC, but there can be little doubt that this is the same man. The Alps are the most prominent mountain range of western Europe. Their name derives from the high pasture lands where nomadic herdsmen of the neolithic period grazed their animals. From the Italian side – and Spartacus may have been as far north as the river Po by the time Cassius caught him – the summer vineyards give way to deep gorges where the melting snow sends cascades of crystal water through pine-covered ravines. There were chestnut groves, flower meadows and above all, a clear, sweet air. If Spartacus was this far north, his huge army would have been between 5,000 and 7,000 feet above sea level, gazing up at the dramatic peaks, crystal white in the summer sun that marked the Venetian Alps and beyond them the Dolomites. Beyond that lay the longed-for homes of the Gauls, the Germans and the Thracians.

Spartacus' most likely route, assisted no doubt by local slaves who joined his band, was the Brenner Pass that divided the mountains of what would become the East and West Tyrol in the centuries ahead. But since Hannibal no one took it for granted that the Alps kept Italians safe. The Carthaginian general had crossed the mighty mountains with his elephants and subjected the Republic to years of pillage and depredation. To Spartacus and his people the Brenner represented freedom.

We have no idea where or when he met Cassius or what nature the battle took. But there is some evidence that Spartacus carried out another stratagem which may have been intended to avoid a pitched confrontation. We have no idea how many men he may have lost against Lentulus and what state of battle-readiness his troops were in. Inexplicably, he seems to have halted, swung round and retraced his steps back into Picenium. This would have drawn Cassius after him, and perhaps given the slaves a chance to outmanoeuvre him and march to the north-western passes of the Alps. It was this feint that led to the legend of the march on Rome. After the defeat of Lentulus – or was it Gellius too? – there seemed little the gladiator rebel could not achieve. But Rome was a tough prospect – serious Gallic armies and even the great Hannibal had failed to take it. While Spartacus' army numbered up to 100,000 men, its progress was hampered by the many women and children accompanying them. It had, at best, the bare minimum of siege equipment and few people skilled in its use. Spartacus' experience at Nola and the camp of Vesuvius convinced him that he did not have the material to take Rome. The doubling back by Spartacus is perhaps the most inexplicable single action in the two and a half years that he fought Rome. Having swung south, it may be that the lure of 'safe' towns and the luxuries of Campania beckoned too strongly. It may be that there were rebellious influences among his people who once more refused to heed his wiser counsel, seduced by the plunder and the promise of an easier life.

In the event, Cassius clung to him like a leech. If Plutarch is right about the Proconsul's 10,000 men, then he *had* to be supported by Gellius' troops even to contemplate taking on Spartacus. By now it was common knowledge, certainly in central and northern Italy, that the legions had been routed, and Cassius must have been wary in the extreme. Appian remarks that many deserters, presumably from Lentulus' luckless command, flocked to Spartacus, 'but he accepted none of them'.[16] From one perspective, this was short-sighted. Spartacus had already proved that Roman armies could be beaten using Roman tactics – and who better to do so than these *caligae*, the rank and file of the cohorts, with mail on their backs and experience under their belts? On the other hand, these were Romans, the natural enemy, and he had made them run once already. What was to say they would not do so again, when the going got rough?

Spartacus destroyed Cassius' cohorts, probably made up of auxiliaries, without the deserters' help – 'another of those victories', writes Philip Matyszak, 'which leaves the military historian slack-jawed with incomprehension'.[17]

It was now, with the north open to him and the Alps a safe haven, that Spartacus came to a new – and fateful – decision. Like the classic hero of a Greek tragedy or a Shakespearean play, he was in fact responsible for his own downfall. Just as Adolf Hitler, the failed artist and architect, discovered a new world through demagogy and politics, Spartacus the bandit, the slave, the deserter, became Spartacus the legend. And perhaps, like many men before and since, he began to believe in his own mythology. A conservative estimate makes him, in the high summer of 72 BC, the destroyer of four Roman armies – it may have been six. Military historians may try to defend the Roman record by dismissing these clashes as against inferior troops who did not take their slave opponents seriously, but the success rate is truly breathtaking. What we have in Spartacus is another Hannibal, another Caesar, and he proved now that he was just as ruthless as either.

'As an offering to the dead,' wrote Appian, 'Spartacus sacrificed 300 Roman prisoners on behalf of Crixus . . . he torched all unnecessary supplies, killed all prisoners of war and slaughtered all pack animals.'[18]

Here we have echoes of Philip of Macedon and of Alexander, who burned their wagons to give them speed on the march. And we have, too, a reminder of the importance of religious ritual, not just to Spartacus himself, with his priestess wife, but to ancient commanders generally. Such men regarded omens as equally important in their planning as numbers of troops, water supplies and bushels of barley. And sacrifice was regularly carried out, not only to propitiate the gods but also for the purpose of divination. We know little about Thracian mysticism, but Roman is well chronicled. The elder Pliny was concerned to note that 'There are memorable instances on record of the times when unlucky portents impeded and spoiled [the ceremony] and when there was a mistake in the prayer; then suddenly, the head or the liver or the heart, has disappeared from the entrails, or these have been doubled, while the victim was standing.'[19]

Human sacrifice was rare in Rome and seems to have been carried out at times of desperation when it was believed only the special sanctity of a life could appease the pantheon of gods. After Cannae, the defeat by Hannibal in 216 BC, two Vestal Virgins, normally irreproachable, were convicted of sexual relations with men. One was walled up alive and one of the men was beaten to death by the Pontifex Maximus. Perhaps human sacrifice was more acceptable in the 'barbarous' state of Thrace, or perhaps Spartacus wanted to make a point. The whole of northern Italy now lay before him, untapped as a source of plunder, and he meant to take advantage of it. Crixus was avenged. He took his people south again, away from the long reach of the Roman arm, into the mountains around Thurii in the 'instep' of Italy and probably spent the winter in the city.

One by one, the remnants of the armies of Lentulus, Gellius and Cassius Longinus straggled back to Rome. It was bad enough that the legions had been beaten; the fact that this happened not in some vermin-infested outpost but on Rome's doorstep and under the command of two consuls and a proconsul was almost impossible to bear.

'This news,' according to Plutarch, 'roused the Senate to anger.'[20] Enough was enough. They sent for Marcus Licinius Crassus.

NINE

Marcus Licinius Crassus

Laurence Olivier's portrayal of Crassus in the film *Spartacus* is everything we expect of a Roman general. With his impossibly white armour, riding his impossibly white horse, he is devious, haughty, decadent, perverted and above all, disgustingly rich. In fact, this last fact is probably the only one that Fast and Trumbo and Olivier got right. In his own day, he was known as 'Dives', 'the rich', and he may well have been the wealthiest man in Rome.

For a time, between 60 and 53 BC, Marcus Licinius Crassus was one of the three most powerful men in Rome in a political sense, yet we know relatively little about him. He is almost as much of a blank sheet as Spartacus. Crassus' contemporaries, Julius Caesar and Gnaeus Pompeius, are well chronicled, but we have few sources for him apart from a chapter in Plutarch's *The Fall of the Roman Republic*. Caesar wrote *The Gallic War*, which was in part an autobiography, but Crassus left no such record. Like Spartacus, we have no visual representation of him, although (unlike Spartacus) any of the unnamed marble busts found by archaeologists in Rome since the Renaissance may be his likeness.

Plutarch does not tell us when he was born, but it is likely to have been 115 or 112 BC, making him about fifteen years Spartacus' senior. One of the problems of stamping reality on an historical character like Spartacus, who has been the subject of such an iconic film, is that audiences/readers have a fixed view of physical appearance. Kirk Douglas was forty-four when he made *Spartacus*; Laurence Olivier was fifty-three. Take about fifteen years off them both and we may be getting close; Douglas should have made *Spartacus* when he was actually starring in the boxing movie *Champion*; Olivier was the right age for Crassus when he was sorting out the French at Agincourt as Henry V.

'Marcus Crassus' father,' says Plutarch, 'had held the office of censor and had been honoured with a triumph.'[1]

Publius Licinius Crassus was a Tribune of the Plebs when Marcus was a boy, and he proposed a law regulating private expenditure. He became consul in 97 BC at the time when the Senate passed a resolution forbidding human sacrifice. The triumph to which Plutarch refers marked the elder Crassus' victory over the Lusitani, a warlike tribe in Further Spain (today's Portugal). It was held in 93 BC, one of those glorious spectacles at which Rome excelled. Lasting for days, triumphs were granted by the authorities to generals whose campaigns had furthered the cause of conquest or saved the Republic. The elder Crassus would have ridden like a god in his four-horsed *quadrigae* chariot, his *legati* behind him wearing the decorations (*ornamenta triumphalia*), then his legions and finally, in chains, the captured leaders of the Lusitani who would be spat at and rough-housed by the mob before being sold into slavery – the fathers of the men who joined Spartacus.

Despite the glories of a successful military career, Publius Crassus seems to have been parsimonious. There is conflicting evidence on this. Historian Tom Holland has the elder Crassus involved in a lucrative import–export business and implies that the whole family earned the epithet dives. Marcus and his two brothers were brought up in what Plutarch describes as a small house. Both the brothers married during their parents' lifetime (like Spartacus, we do not know the name of Crassus' mother) and all of them apparently lived cheek by jowl, which explains, says Plutarch, 'why Crassus was so temperate and moderate in his own way of life'.[2] Whereas Olivier's Crassus was unmarried and had an eye for his female and male slaves, the real Crassus married Tertulla, the widow of one of his brothers (when is unknown) and had sons by her.

'Indeed,' says Plutarch, 'with regard to his relations with women, his conduct was as exemplary as that of anyone in Rome.'[3]

Since the chronicler then goes on to discuss a scandal involving a Vestal Virgin, we may wonder whether he has his tongue in his cheek. Vesta was the Roman goddess of the hearth, with its association with the sacred flame of fire. The Virgins, recruited from Rome's noblest families, took vows of chastity for thirty years, were given special privileges within the city, tending Vesta's temple and its eternal flame and officiating at the goddess's festival, the Vestalia, on 7 June. We have already seen how seriously Rome took the breaking of a Virgin's vows, and Crassus may have got off lightly.

It may be no more than coincidence that this sordid court case took place in 73 BC, but that was the year Crassus took six legions in pursuit of Spartacus. Was this an attempt by his enemies, depending on its exact timing, to strike a blow against Rome's richest man while he was militarily preoccupied? Or was it, post-Spartacus, an opportunity to take something away from the lustre of his success? Even in the case of the Vestal Virgin, however, Crassus' motive was not one of lust, but greed.

'Certainly,' wrote Plutarch, 'the Romans say that in the case of Crassus many virtues were obscured by one vice, since it was such a predominant one that other evil propensities which he may have had were scarcely noticeable.'[4]

The particular Virgin was Licinia, who was prosecuted for her behaviour by one Plotius. It seems to have been Crassus' defence that he was interested, not in the lady, but in her 'very attractive' house in the suburbs. Greed was not a crime in ancient Rome, whereas sex with a Vestal Virgin was. Whether anyone gave the woman a medical examination to prove Crassus' innocence is unknown, but not only was he acquitted, he 'did not let Licinia alone until he had acquired the property'.[5]

Long before this, however, the Crassus family had become embroiled in Rome's deadly politics. Publius Crassus, like any self-respecting Roman, fought in the Social War in 91/90 BC. He became censor in 89 BC. In that year, along with Lucius Caesar, elder brother of the more famous Julius, he proposed the citizenship measure which was one of the sops that brought the Social War to an end.

Young Marcus would have been around twenty by now and was already poised for an illustrious career, but politics intervened. In the civil war that developed by 87 BC, the elder Crassus joined forces with Sulla, Marius' pushy subordinate. That was the year when open conflict broke out between Marius and Sulla and with the support of Lucius Cornelius Cinna, the former marched on Rome. Although Plutarch contends that Marcus Crassus was 'very young' and that Marius and Cinna's supporters killed his father, he seems to have been wrong on both counts. Licinius Crassus committed suicide in the fine old Republican tradition – exactly how is not known. His elder son was probably killed in the anti-Marius purge that the new dictator carried out. Marcus fled to Spain.

Plutarch maintains that Crassus knew the area well, having spent time with his father there as a boy, and that he had friends there. Spain in fact was in just as much turmoil as Rome itself, with loyalties divided between Marian and Sullan factions, so that suspicion was everywhere and the son of a leading player in the city's politics had to tread warily. He found the estates of Vibius Paciacus, an old friend of his father's, somewhere on the coast and hid in a cave with food supplied to him by a slave. Clearly Paciacus was in a difficult position; by keeping Crassus hidden away he hoped to avoid any possible retribution that might come from his enemies.

Bizarrely, Plutarch spends an entire paragraph describing the cave in which Crassus hid, although he is not likely to have seen it. Whether this was an attempt at geophysical analysis, or mere padding, we do not know. According to Plutarch, Paciacus seems to have been a generous and thoughtful benefactor. He also continues to stress Crassus' youth, so perhaps the estimates of his birth date are wrong and he may only have been in his late teens, making him perhaps five years Spartacus' senior. Paciacus sent two female slaves to attend to the boy's needs and the story may have been relayed to Plutarch by the historian Fenestella, who wrote under Augustus and knew one of those slaves, by then an old woman, personally.

This shadowy existence went on for eight months, but news of the death of Cinna persuaded Crassus to return to public life. By this time it was 84 BC. The dictator was killed by his own mutinous troops as he was preparing for a campaign against the Liburni tribe in Isturia. Coming out firmly for Sulla, Crassus assembled a scratch force and began to attack various Marian towns. This was quite bizarre. No ordinary citizen had ever raised a private army before and it may have numbered two and a half thousand men. One city, Malacca, was allegedly sacked by him but Crassus denied this for the rest of his life. From Spain, he crossed the Straits of Gibraltar, then still known as the Pillars of Hercules, to Libya, to join forces with Quintus Caecilius Metellus Pius.

Like most successful men of his time, Metellus had fought in the Social War. The son of a great general, Metellus Numidicus, he had earned the nickname Pius (the devoted) by begging the people of Rome to allow his father, exiled by Marius, to return to the city. In 87 BC, with Marius marching on Rome, the assemblies begged Metellus to take command against him. The problem was that the role should have been reserved for the consul of that year, Gnaeus Octavius, and, clearly a stickler for protocol, Metellus refused. The fickle troops, already well aware of their importance as players in the endless power-struggles, went over to Marius en masse and Metellus sailed for Africa.

Plutarch tells us that Metellus and Crassus quickly quarrelled, but does not explain why. Both men were exiles and on the same side, but their dissimilar temperaments may have made them uneasy allies. In the event, Crassus returned to Italy to join Sulla in his march on Rome. The young man's role in this camp was to raise an army from among the Marsi, one of the tribes of Rome's hinterland recently defeated – and given rights of citizenship – in the Social War. Not unreasonably, Crassus asked Sulla for an escort. The country was teeming with enemies and life was cheap. Sulla's reply was far from friendly: 'I give you as an escort your father, your brother, your friends and your relations who have been put to death without law or justice and whose murderers I am going to punish.'[6]

Crassus seems to have been stung by this rebuke, as Sulla no doubt intended him to be, and went on to become one of the dictator's most loyal and successful subordinates.

We have already seen the future triumvir's success commanding Sulla's right wing at Rome's Colline Gate, when his rout of the enemy literally turned the tide of battle. Tarnishing all this, however, was the greed which Plutarch notes. One of the towns that Crassus took, Tuder in Umbria, became his personal property, the spoils disappearing into Crassus' own coffers. Sulla, a far more typically generous Roman, was appalled. In the killing spree that followed Sulla's assumption of power, Crassus benefited hugely.

'During the period of the proscriptions,' wrote Plutarch, 'and the selling up of confiscated property he again got himself a bad name by demanding gifts and by buying up large estates for low prices . . . It is said that in Bruttium he actually added a man's name to the proscription lists purely in order to get hold of his property.'[7]

Whether this was true or not, Sulla never trusted Crassus in public affairs again. This was to play directly into Crassus' hands. He could – and did – distance himself from what was, after all, a vicious military dictatorship. He could be seen to owe allegiance to no one, and that made him all the more dangerous. If Sulla fell, Crassus would not fall with him. If someone else rose, Crassus was free to rise with him.

At this stage, Crassus was worth an estimated 300 talents, a modest enough sum for the time. As consul in the year after the defeat of Spartacus, he dedicated a tenth of his fortune to the god Hercules, which would probably have involved paying for his temple to be embellished and tended and, incidentally, would have been the equivalent of Crassus buying his way into heaven. In the same year, he provided street parties for the plebs and gave out enough money to 'every Roman citizen to live on for three months'.[8] It is tempting to think of this as some sort of popularity contest or tax-dodge; in the event, Crassus' account books (sadly, now lost) show that he was worth 7,100 talents on the eve of the war with Parthia in 55 BC.

Plutarch writes disapprovingly of the source of Crassus' wealth: 'since one must tell the tale, however damaging, he amassed most of his property by means of fire and war; public calamities were his principal source of revenue.'[9]

Sulla's proscriptions probably went on until about 80 BC. After that, natural disasters were music to Crassus' ears. He 'observed what frequent and everyday occurrences in Rome were fire and the collapse of buildings owing to their size and proximity to each other'.[10]

By Crassus' day, the Comitium in Rome's central Forum had been extended by Cato's Basilica Portia, the first of its kind in the city. Sulla's Curia Hostilia, home of the Senate, was brand new. A water clock told the time at the Basilica Aemilia, so it was no longer necessary to wait for the solemn announcement by the Accensus, recording from the Senate's steps that moment at midday when the sun was halfway between the Rostra and the Graecostasis. On the Palatine, magnificent new houses were springing up, among them probably Crassus' own, belying Plutarch's reference to his moderation. Elsewhere, in the shopping quarters, streets were impossibly narrow and houses crammed into every available space. The fire during which the later emperor Nero was wrongly supposed to have played his lyre, and which was attributed to the new sectarian danger, the Christians, was only the most famous of hundreds of fires in Rome's long history. Plutarch noted that

[Crassus] therefore bought slaves who were architects and builders, and then, when he had more than 500 of them, he would buy up houses that were either on fire themselves or near the scene of the fire; the owners of these properties, in the terror and uncertainty of the moment, would let them go for next to nothing. In this way most of Rome came into his possession.[11]

Plutarch is adamant, however, that Crassus owned only one house himself, giving the lie to the magnificent countryside villa in white marble we see in Kirk Douglas' *Spartacus*. The real Crassus knew exactly how expensive it was to maintain multiple properties, noting that 'people who were fond of building needed no enemies; they would ruin themselves by themselves'.[12]

In Howard Fast's fictionalised version of the story, there is a close antagonism between Crassus and Spartacus. The Roman pauses with his friends at Capua en route to Rome and pays handsomely to watch pairs of gladiators fight to the death for their amusement. Among them is Spartacus. Further, Crassus buys the slave girl

Varinia, unaware that she is Spartacus' woman. None of this, of course, is true, but once Crassus and the gladiator were matched on the campaign trail, there must have been a relationship of sorts between them. And, thanks to Plutarch, we know a great deal about Crassus' attitude to slaves. It was in slaves, rather than land and silver mines, that Crassus' real wealth lay.

> There were great numbers of them [wrote Plutarch], and they were of the highest quality – readers, secretaries, silversmiths, stewards, waiters. He used to direct their education himself and take part in it by giving them personal instructions. Altogether his view was that the chief duty of a master is to care for his slaves, who are, in fact, the living tools for the management of a household. And in this he was right.[13]

This smacks of good economic sense rather than humanitarianism. Slaves, especially the intelligent sort that Crassus bought, were expensive and if they died or ran away through bad treatment, they represented a financial loss. Clearly, Plutarch was referring to Crassus' own domestics, not a dangerous renegade like Spartacus who appeared to possess skills that no civilised Roman would wish to acknowledge. The man was a general and a leader of men. Given other circumstances, he would be lolling on the benches of the Senate or riding out on campaign with his *lictores* in front of him in search of some foreign tribe to destroy.

But Plutarch tells us more about Crassus. His relatively ordinary tastes were probably a mark of his inherent meanness.

> His house was open to all; and he used to lend money to his friends without interest; but when the time came for repayment, he was quite relentless about demanding it back . . . The people he invited to his dinner parties were usually ordinary people and not members of the great families; and these meals were not expensive, but they were good and there was a friendliness about them which made them more agreeable than more lavish entertainment.[14]

No doubt many of Plutarch's comments on Crassus derive from the post-Spartacus years, as he became ever more embroiled in politics and rivalries with the great men of his day. Plutarch noted that

> He became one of the best speakers in Rome, and by care and application, was able to surpass those who were highly gifted by nature. He never appeared in the law courts without having prepared his speech beforehand . . . and often when Pompey and Cicero and Caesar were reluctant to speak, he undertook the whole management of the case himself, thereby gaining an advantage over them in popularity, since people thought of him as a man willing to take trouble and to help others.[15]

Historian Tom Holland sums the man up brilliantly:

> Crassus was assiduous at cultivating men on the make. Whether he wished to help promote them to high office or merely have them serve him as patsies or ciphers, he would treat them all with the same menacing geniality, keeping open house, avoiding airs, remembering the name of anyone he ever met. In the law courts he would tirelessly plead for defendants who might later provide him with a return. A debt taken out with Crassus always came with heavy interest.[16]

There is little doubt that Crassus wanted to be loved. Unlike the haughty Olivier character, who clearly does not have a friend in the world, the real man deliberately courted popularity: 'However humble and obscure a man might be, Crassus, on meeting him, would invariably return his greeting and address him by name.'[17] Crassus' friendly demeanour makes his extreme greed all the harder to understand. He had other virtues, too: 'He is said to have been well read in history and also to have been something of a philosopher, attaching himself to the doctrines of Aristotle.'

In the stormy years ahead, in which the triumvirate of Pompey, Caesar and Crassus dominated the Roman world, Plutarch believed that it was the 'sober and conservative' elements in the city who backed Pompey, the 'violent and easily unsettled' types that supported Caesar, while Crassus stood between them and took advantage of both. Perhaps this is why, ultimately, the others eclipsed him. It seems to be the way of triumvirates; in the one that followed Caesar's assassination in 44 BC, everyone has heard of Shakespeare's hero Mark Antony and of Octavian who became the emperor Augustus – but who remembers Lepidus?[18]

'Crassus was strong,' wrote Plutarch, 'because he was popular and because he was feared – particularly because he was feared.'[19]

In the parlance of the time, like the dangerous bulls in the market stalls and on the estates of the latifundia that men gave a wide berth to, Crassus had 'hay on his horns'.[20] It is likely that a large proportion of senators were actually in financial debt to Crassus. In that sense, he commanded respect and obedience; everyone regarded him as a friend because they were afraid to do anything else.

Crassus was praetor in 73 BC and appointed to the command of the army as proconsul in the following year. Appian implies that no one wanted the job. The astonishing successes of Spartacus in 72 BC and the fact that he was holed up for another winter, glutted with the spoils of war, probably at Thurii, made the Senate dither, fumble and look the other way. No doubt there was a lot of hot air expended but 'when it came to hold the selection of new commands for the praetor, a morbid fear seized all the men and not one of them would proffer his name for the position'.[21]

This 'morbid fear' was of Spartacus, who had by now assumed the monstrosity and supernatural powers always reserved for ultra-successful warriors. Mothers hushed their frightened children with horror stories about him – the thing lurking in the darkness of their bedroom corners was the gladiator rebel who ate babies for breakfast. But men also failed to come forward because slave-killing was a dirty business and it won no laurels. As for Crassus himself, his motivation may have been a personal one. He might have been, as Philip Matyszak suggests, patriotic, but he was also related to Cassius Longinus whom Spartacus had trounced in Picenium; for Crassus, the coming clash may have been personal. And there was something else. News from Spain was that Rome's new darling, the mercurial Gnaeus Pompeius, was putting down the opposition there. How soon would it be before he came home at the head of his victorious legions, demanding a triumph? Crassus needed military glory to offset his rival. There is a suggestion, certainly inherent in the Kirk Douglas film, the Howard Fast novel and even in modern histories, that all the previous generals who marched against Spartacus were small fry and that Crassus was *the* general par excellence. In fact, he had fought a handful of unremarkable engagements in Marian towns and had won a partial – albeit crucial – victory at the Colline Gate. That, however, was sixteen years earlier and Pompey's laurels were remarkably fresh. Spartacus was a golden opportunity for Crassus to reinvent himself.

He raised six fresh legions, in addition to the two granted to him by the Senate, giving him a command of upwards of 70,000 men, heavy infantry, cavalry, auxiliaries and siege equipment. This was probably the largest army ever fielded by the Romans in Italy itself and it was a mark of Crassus' and the Senate's determination to rid themselves of the scourge of Spartacus once and for all.

We do not know where the slave army was or when Crassus set out in pursuit of it. Logic would dictate the spring of 71 BC, but references to the weather in some of the ancient accounts would seem to make it earlier. Unlike most ancient peoples reliant on dry ground for travel, the Romans could move whenever they liked because their road network was excellent in all weathers. The Via Appia ran south to Capua and then turned south-east, crossing the peninsula to Brindisium. The Via Annia continued south-west, following the line of the coast to Bruttium. The location of the battle is unknown, however. It is also not known whether Spartacus wintered in Thurii, but Appian's information that he prevented merchants from trading in gold and silver and dealt only in iron would indicate that he spent several weeks or even months there. Unlike bread baking and even cloth spinning, which could be done on the move, iron production for his weapons and armour required anvils, forges and fires of fierce heat; towns provided these things as a matter of course. Plutarch insists, however, that Spartacus was 'bearing down on Picenium',[22] though from which direction is uncertain. If Spartacus abandoned Thurii, and it was his winter quarters, to raid again in the relatively unpillaged north, this would make sense. Alternatively, he may have decided to try for the Alpine escape again. Without any information from his camp, we can only speculate. Oenomaus and Crixus were both dead; does this mean that Spartacus was a despot now, with ultimate power of life and death over his people? Or was the ragtag army still clinging to their tribal custom of arguing things out in council around their camp-fires? In the weeks that followed, two new leaders of the slave army emerge – Castus and Grannicus. The first-century historian Frontinius describes these men as 'leaders of the Gauls' and it seems that they were Crixus' and Oenomaus' successors.

It is clear from Plutarch that two of the defeated Consular legions of the previous campaign season were still in the field. Demoralised and no doubt riddled with desertion, these men may have followed the slaves south or stayed in the mountains in the middle of the peninsula, shivering under their cattle-hide tents through the winter months. Crassus' first job was to find his enemy and to do that he took the calculated risk of splitting his force, rather as Lentulus and Gellius had done without much success the previous summer. During the campaign of 71 BC the legate Mummius, whose name is found only in Plutarch, took two legions to find the slaves. His brief was simple; he was to find Spartacus, and trail him, presumably sending his fastest scouts to locate the bulk of Crassus' army, and to keep the general informed of the slave movements. On no account was he to engage the gladiator in battle or even skirmish.

With an appalling predictability, Mummius ignored the order. If Spartacus' army remained intact – and it only seems to have frag-mented later in the spring – he would have outnumbered Mummius' two legions perhaps five to one. It was no contest. Plutarch writes that 'Many of his men were killed and many saved their lives by throwing away their arms and running for it.'[23]

We have no way of knowing whether these units were the remnants of the army of 72 BC or whether they were two of Crassus' new legions. If they had met Spartacus before, they would have been wary of him, half beaten already. If not, they would have been full of the false overconfidence that Mummius himself probably exuded – and it was a weakness of Roman commanders at all levels that each thought himself to be invulnerable and immeasurably better than the last incompetent who had failed. Either way, the result was the same. Again, the men at the back of the cohorts would have cracked first, terrified by the silence of the slave enemy, their measured onward tread, facing their own shields, their own swords, their own javelins, Glaber's stolen eagles flashing in the weak, late winter sun. The *optiones* would have thrashed the turning men with their sticks, screaming orders to hold the line. The centurions at the head would have tried the same, before they had to turn to face death on the blades of Spartacus' gladiator cohorts. Men who might have queued three years earlier outside an amphitheatre and paid good money to watch these men die now knew what it felt like to be on the receiving end. The worm had turned.

A shamefaced Mummius crawled back to Crassus with however many of his cohorts he could still command. The great commanders in history are those on whom the gods smiled – Napoleon famously asked whether a man he was about to promote to the rank of marshal was lucky – and men like this could disregard orders, take initiatives, dazzle. Mummius was not one of these men. Plutarch records that 'Crassus gave Mummius a very rough reception after this',[24] and his punishment of the cowards under him was far harsher. First, the general rode among the crestfallen, wounded, exhausted men, exacting a promise that they would never again abandon their weapons in the field. Philip Matyszak claims that in typical Crassus fashion, he charged them a deposit on their swords and shields to hold them to the oath. Then he killed every tenth man.

Decimation was an ancient punishment for troops who had cracked on the battlefield and the grim custom had fallen into disuse. The offending cohorts drew lots and every tenth man was symbolically chosen to die for the cowardice of the rest. Legend has credited Crassus with wiping out thousands in this way, giving decimation its modern meaning of total destruction; Appian quotes

4,000, saying that Crassus was 'not in the least deterred by their numbers'.[25] Most modern commentators are happy to accept 500 as a likely figure. Embarking on a difficult campaign against a strong and clever army this could have been foolhardy in the extreme, but Crassus had a very strong point to make. There is some confusion in the neo-contemporary record. Some suggest that this fate was meted out for the units of the previous year who had failed so dismally under Lentulus and Cassius. It seems more likely – and certainly more impressive as a striking statement of intent – that it was Mummius' wavering troops who were decimated. They may, of course, have been the same men. The condemned went down under the cudgels and swords of their comrades, with all the legions paraded in hollow square to witness it. 'Those who lose their lives in this way,' wrote Plutarch, 'are also disgraced . . . and the actual circumstances of their execution are very savage and repulsive.'[26]

No one spoke of them again once the gravediggers had hammered the last shovelful of earth back into place.

As for the survivors, Crassus had not yet finished with them. These men were given rations of barley, not wheat, for the rest of the campaign. This was horse-fodder, and there was probably no intended irony in the fact that it formed the staple diet of gladiators too. More disturbingly, the offending cohorts had to pitch their tents outside the ramparts of Crassus' camp. If Spartacus caught them napping, they would be the first to die. And in fact, in the final engagement, the gladiator did attack troops digging a trench outside the camp's perimeter.

Having established himself as a no-nonsense commander to rival the men who would be his co-triumvirs in the years ahead, Crassus marched in search of the slave army. In the good weather of the spring, he could make 25 miles a day, but in what was still probably winter this may have dropped to 15, depending on the size of his baggage train. He seems to have learned from the Mummius experience not to split his command again.

Not so Spartacus. Appian records that a breakaway band of his army became isolated and Crassus picked them off. The chronicler clearly had no idea who these men were, where Crassus found them or why they were separated. It may be that Spartacus was trying to control Crassus' movements, harass his lines or at least slow him up. In the event, the idea backfired. Crassus killed two-thirds of the 10,000, according to Appian, and resumed his march. As with Crixus in the previous year, men not commanded by Spartacus tended to fail against the training and focus of a Roman army, although if Appian is right about numbers, the 10,000 were woefully outnumbered by Crassus and his victory must have been predictable. It must have given his troops heart, however. This was the first victory over any unit of Spartacus' army for nearly a year and between those events, at least four Roman armies had been beaten and the last had suffered the further humiliation of decimation.

In view of the events that followed over the next four months, the idea has arisen that Spartacus was on the run and his nemesis, in the shape of Crassus, was bound to succeed. Yet in the early spring of 71 BC, the odds were actually still with the slave army. Spartacus may still have had a force of 70,000 with him, although as always this is impossible to prove, and marching south as he now was, had only one army behind him and nothing between him and the sea. He reached the Straits of Messina and took stock of his position.

In the Kirk Douglas film, much is made of Spartacus' dealings with the Cilician pirates. A rather shifty, but in the end honest, Herbert Lom offers Spartacus ships to take all his people off the Italian peninsula in return for chests of gold and silver – the loot of Roman towns and villas sacked by the slaves. Both Appian and Plutarch claim that the gladiator's real intention was to sail to Sicily and stage a third slave rising there, 'since the previous slave war had recently died down and only needed a little fuel to make it blaze out again'.[27]

There was a lot of sense in this, although Plutarch's claim that Spartacus intended to do this with only 2,000 men is difficult to reconcile. There were Roman troops on Sicily and though they may not have been of the calibre of Crassus' legions, they would need to be subdued quickly and decisively if the slaves were to be persuaded to rise for the third time in as many generations. Then there is the egalitarian element in Spartacus. He was no Utopian socialist, born ahead of his time, but he did share out plunder equally among his men and seems to have acted in a humanitarian way to stop the worst excesses of pillage. Would such a man leave the vast bulk of his people to the grisly fate he knew lay in store for them, to run to comparative safety with a small elite group? No doubt Plutarch's thinking is sound in another sense; the slaves of 71 BC were the sons of those who had rebelled in 113 BC and the grandsons of the rebels of 132 BC. But Spartacus had to get to Sicily first.

The governor of the island in 71 BC was Gaius Verres, one in a long series of overzealous controllers of imperial provinces who made difficult situations worse. Changing sides in the Social War, which was a defining moment for many men in Spartacus' time, he became the quaestor in Cilicia seven years before the slave war and proceeded to plunder it and the areas beyond the frontier for his own ends. With the instincts of a natural turncoat, he gave evidence against his master in Cilicia, the governor Gnaeus Cornelius Dolabella, and saw him convicted for extortion. In 74 BC he was in Rome, accepting bribes from all and sundry and continued to govern through extortion when made governor of Sicily. Exasperated, the islanders turned to Rome's greatest orator, Marcus Tullius Cicero, a man more or less of Spartacus' age.

In a withering attack on the man's appalling corruption, the orator slammed him in *Against Verres*:

What are you saying? That Sicily was freed from a war of fugitive slaves by your brave actions? Surely, you don't imagine that you're going to share the glory . . . with Marcus Crassus or Gnaeus Pompeius? Yes, I suppose that your arrogance is of a scale that you would actually dare to say something of that sort. You would have us believe that you were able to prevent bands of fugitive slaves from crossing over from Italy into Sicily? Where? When? From what direction? Did they attempt their landing with rafts or real ships? I've never heard of anything of the sort.[28]

Two centuries later, Florus had. He said of the slaves in the 'toe' of Italy, 'Since they did not have ships to take them, they tried to cross the swift-moving waters of the strait between the mainland and the island by using rafts made of wooden beams and barrels lashed together with thin vine tendrils, but in vain.'[29]

The implication here is that the swift and deadly current of Messina drove them back, slaves perhaps dying as the flimsy rafts capsized and the breakers rolled over them. Cicero, much nearer to events and more likely to be accurate, has a different take: 'But I have heard that the energetic actions and planning of Marcus Crassus, that bravest of men, prevented the fugitive slaves from lashing rafts together, with the result that they were not able to cross over to Messina.'[30]

Cicero's eloquence causes further problems. Was he so intent on denouncing Verres that he praised Crassus too highly? No other commentator from the time says anything about Spartacus' attempt to cross to Sicily, but it is unlikely that Cicero, a brilliant lawyer on the make, would have invented the story. In view of what Crassus did next on the Italian mainland, however, it is difficult to see how he could have stopped the slaves from making rafts. The key to the situation lies in Cicero's almost throwaway line – 'that bravest of men'. When the orator condemned Verres in Rome, the city had been spared the risk of attack by the unspeakable Spartacus, because Spartacus was dead. The two men whom Cicero praises, Crassus and Pompey, were the twin pillars of the state. It would be another decade before Julius Caesar joined them. What was more natural than that Cicero should claim all sorts of achievements for these men, knowing perfectly well, as he did, that their monstrous egos would not let them contradict him?

And, true to the propaganda of haughty Rome ever since, nowhere does Cicero mention the name of Spartacus. But if the orator's eloquence was based on fact and not just hyperbole to smear Verres, Spartacus' possible arrival in Sicily *did* cause anxiety and even ripples of revolt. Cicero criticises Verres for not contacting the Senate, but he believes that various slave conspiracies were formed, citing an example of slaves belonging to a Sicilian named

Leonidas. As governor, Verres presided over their trial and found them guilty of 'intent to seize arms and to raise a war'. Unbelievably, he then released them! Cicero taunts his jurymen in the case of Verres – and us, his readers, two millennia later – by asking how the governor could have profited by this bizarre move. His implied answer was that Verres did it to prove he could overthrow the decision of a Roman court – that he was, in fact, a law unto himself.

The point here is not Verres' cranky and tyrannical governorship, but the impact of the Spartacus War: 'When he saw that the minds of the slaves in Sicily were teetering on the edge of rebellion because of the slave war in Italy . . . And it was a great and violent war.'[31]

Appian is wrong when he says that Crassus overtook Spartacus, and we can discuss Cicero's assertion that Crassus destroyed the gladiators' rafts as so much sycophancy. The truth was that the Cilician pirates, ever fickle, had taken at least some of Spartacus' money and run. The slave army was stranded in Italy. There is probably a great deal more politics in this situation then we will ever realise. Some modern commentators find this a contrivance and believe it unlikely that any such deal was struck, but Plutarch seems sure of his facts. We cannot know the differing pressures on Spartacus at various times to get his people home to safety. Perhaps there was a plan for the women and children and faint-hearted to sail with the Cilicians to freedom (despite their notorious predilection for slave-trading) and for Spartacus' warriors to raise his standard in Sicily. We know that Marcus Crassus was fabulously rich. Had he been able to intercept Spartacus' messengers and made the Cilicians a counter-offer to sail away which they could not have refused? A man with fingers in so many pies would have little problem with this.

Spartacus knew that Crassus was behind him, somewhere to the north, and he turned to face him.

The peninsula of Rhegium was a potential graveyard for Spartacus. Countless commanders have found themselves out-manoeuvred, with water on three sides of them and the enemy ahead. It was now that the engineering skills of the Roman army, which Spartacus could never hope to match, came into their own.

Twenty years after the Spartacus War, Julius Caesar was on his way to conquering Transalpine Gaul. The army of Vercingetorix was huge and Caesar ordered a containing wall called a *circumvallium* to be built. It was 10 Roman miles (each Roman mile was 1000 paces) long and contained 8 camps, one for each of his legions, and 23 smaller forts. The huge attacking fortifications at Alesia have been reconstructed today and are impressive. At every 130 yards along the length of the palisade on top of the ramparts an observation tower 12 Roman feet high was built with sharpened stakes pointing outward to deter would-be attackers. There were two parallel ditches in front of the ramparts, one filled with water and beyond that a patchwork of sharpened stakes hidden in sand pits which the legionaries called 'lilies' because of their shape. Caesar had a peculiar complication in these lines because while he was besieging Alesia, the Gallic army was besieging him, so a second line of defences (*contravallium*) was necessary.

At Rhegium, Crassus had no such problem. He had succeeded in penning Spartacus south of him, because the gladiator had no escape route and the general knew he had nothing to fear from behind. Plutarch takes up the tale: '[Crassus'] observation of the place made him see what should be done and he began to build fortifications right across the isthmus. In this way he was able at the same time to keep his own soldiers busy and to deprive the enemy of supplies.'[32]

No doubt keeping his troops busy was a vital part of Crassus' psychology. There is an air of shakiness about his command. His men were nervy, aware that with slaves generally and with Spartacus in particular, they held the proverbial wolf by the ears. Decimation might have provoked the survivors to action, but it left men feeling vulnerable; who would be next? The longer the wait before the battle, the greater the risk of a fall in morale and an increase in the rate of desertion. Spartacus in the meantime had nowhere to go. Plutarch says that he was contemptuous of the Roman earthworks going up in the crisp early spring mornings in front of him, but this indifference may have been feigned to buoy up the spirits of his own people.

Plutarch comments on the industrious Roman preparations for battle:

The task which [Crassus] had set himself was neither easy nor inconsiderable, but he finished it and, contrary to all expectation, had it done in a very short time. A ditch, nearly forty miles long and fifteen feet wide, was carried across the neck of land from sea to sea, and above the ditch he constructed a wall which was astonishingly high and strong.[33]

The chronicler gives us no other figures. Were there two ditches rather than one? Were there towers at intervals, like the ones Caesar built? All we know is that the whole edifice was four times longer than Caesar's at Alesia and literally bisected Rhegium, extending from Scolacium in the east to its opposite point in the west, today's Gulf of Squillace to the Gulf of Santa Eufemia. Neither Plutarch nor Appian tells us exactly where Crassus' ramparts were, but the Scolacium latitude marks the narrowest width of the peninsula and is about 40 miles east to west.

For as long as he dared Spartacus stayed put, but inevitably supplies began to run low. For his part, Crassus must have been anxious that no new deal should be struck with the Cilicians or his elusive quarry would be gone for ever. The final stages of the Spartacus War are confusing. Plutarch's is the fullest and most rational account, but Appian has Crassus defeating Spartacus in open battle *before* the lines went up and even puts forward the theory that Spartacus defeated Crassus and it was *this* which led to the desperate measure of decimation. Both battles are possible; neither is likely.

The gladiator waited for a stormy night with snow driving down from the north and staged his breakout. Even this tactic, so typical of Spartacus, is shrouded in controversy. Plutarch's account, again, makes most sense, but Appian's is more detailed. For several weeks, Spartacus probed Crassus' defences. On one day, Appian tells us, 'Crassus killed about 6000 of Spartacus' supporters in the early morning'.[34]

Withdrawing to lick his wounds and wait for dark, Spartacus tried again in the evening and again the move failed, with another similar line of casualties 'towards the twilight hours'.[35] Even allowing for the fact that the slaves must have been in the open and the Romans crouched behind their wall, Appian's casualty rate is laughable: 'Only three men from the Roman army died and seven were wounded, so great was the change in the soldiers' eagerness for victory because of their recent punishment [decimation].'[36]

Over those weeks Spartacus staged sudden, sharp attacks all along Crassus' line, no doubt varying the time and place to cause maximum havoc. If there were waverers in his ranks, Spartacus strengthened his resolve by crucifying a prisoner in the open ground before Crassus' lines. Death was slow on the cross and could be prolonged. It was the inevitable punishment for rebellious slaves and the gladiator was warning his people that this would be their fate if they lost.

Appian comments that Spartacus was waiting for cavalry reinforcements during the siege and because of this shortage of horses did not commit his whole force against Crassus. This is a curious assertion because the only conceivable places that riders could come from were Rhegium to the south or from the north, *behind* Crassus. Since Appian implies that this cavalry unit did arrive, they can only have been raised in Rhegium as there is no mention of Crassus' lines being breached from the north.

At last, on the night of driving snow, Spartacus attacked in force, filling in the ditch with earth, tree branches and the corpses of his men. Appian relates that this was achieved through a cavalry charge, but taking a wall, ramparts and ditch was hardly a cavalry tactic and it must have been accomplished by men on foot. We do not know what losses Spartacus incurred; Plutarch says he got a third of his army across, past Crassus and out into central Italy.

It was probably before this, as the fortifications went up, that Crassus seems to have lost his nerve and written to the Senate, sending the letter by trusted riders with changes of horses, to ask for reinforcements. The men he asked for were Lucullus from Thrace and Pompey from Spain.

Lucius Licinius Lucullus was probably three years older than Crassus. He had the first cherry trees in Italy planted in his garden and the first known examples of plate glass for his windows.

Related to the powerful Metellus clan, he had staunchly supported Sulla in the Social War and, unlike Crassus, was trusted totally by the dictator. In 88 BC, he was the only senior officer who threw in his lot with him on his intended march on Rome. Two years later, as Sulla went east to fight Mithridates, Lucullus was with him in what was in effect a commissary-general's role. He had the wholly unenviable job of squeezing cash and warships out of Rome's allies in the east. As unofficial admiral, Lucullus carried Sulla across the Hellespont to negotiate with the rebel king at Dardanus. Back in Rome by 79 BC, Lucullus was *aedile* with his brother and staged some of the most lavish games the city had seen. No doubt gladiators like Spartacus died in the sand before him as the mob roared their approval of the splendour of the games and the bonhomie of the *aedile* who understood it all so well. The seventies were good to Lucullus. He became literary executor to Sulla when he died in 77 BC, and the guardian of his children. He ruled Africa as propraetor for three years and was consul in 74 BC, backing Pompeius who was fighting in Spain.

Later that year, which was the year before Spartacus broke out of Capua, Mithridates went on the warpath again. Rome's client king of Bithynia, Nicomede, died that year and Rome quickly ceded his kingdom, something they had done many times before and would do again throughout both the Republic and the Empire. Mithridates would have found himself with fully fledged Roman neighbours, with armies and all that that entailed, so he stole the moral ground, not to mention the initiative, by invading Bithynia himself.

This was the third time the Romans had faced Mithridates and Lucullus' co-consul, Marcus Aurelius Cotta, was defeated by the king at sea and forced to scramble ashore to take refuge in Chalcedon. On land, Mithridates fared less well against Lucullus himself and his fleet was badly smashed by a freak storm in the Black Sea. For the first year of the Spartacus War, Lucullus marched and counter-marched all over Pontus without success, but in 72 BC, an alliance with Deiotarus, leader of the Galatians, brought the rout of Mithridates at Cabira. Leaving his army behind, Lucullus returned to Asia – Plutarch specifically says Thrace – where there was financial chaos caused by Sulla's earlier crippling fines on the province. Technically, Lucullus was at something of a loose end in that Mithridates had been defeated. Even so, it is a mark of Crassus' sense of panic and the Senate's sense of urgency that they should recall a general and his army when they were still subduing an entire province with substantial pockets of resistance. Odder still – and yet more evidence of his mounting hysteria – is the fact that Crassus sent for the man he probably hated most in the world – Gnaeus Pompeius Magnus: Pompey the Great.

TEN

Gnaeus Pompeius Magnus

'On one occasion,' wrote Plutarch, 'when someone said "Pompey the Great is coming!" Crassus merely laughed and said "As great as what?"'[1]

Unlike Spartacus and even Crassus, we know exactly what Pompey looked like. He stares out at us from his marble bust through piggy eyes in a broad, flat face. The mouth is weak and petulant, the hair combed forward in a deliberate attempt to emulate the greatest general in all antiquity – Alexander of Macedon, the Great.

If Sulla was the blueprint of an arbitrary despot and would-be emperor, Pompey and Julius Caesar were the prototypes. Both men were egotistical and ambitious to an extent that makes Spartacus and Crassus appear positively modest; and both men paid for it with their lives.[2]

Pompey started life with a disadvantage. Whereas the elder Crassus was respected and genuinely improved the lot of Romans high and low, Pompey's father, Gnaeus Pompeius Strabo ('the squint-eyed') was arguably the most hated general of the Republic. Leaping from side to side in the power-struggle between Marius and Sulla that followed the Social War, his attempts to act as power-broker, if that was what they were, came to nothing. Plutarch says that the elder Pompey was killed by a thunderbolt, with all the delicious superstitious capital that that engendered, as if this was a fitting end for a monster. In fact, it is likely he died of plague contracted shortly after taking the city of Asculum in 89 BC; and the lightning story may be based on the fact that his tent was struck during a storm. Plutarch believes that the people's hatred of the elder Pompey was based on his insatiable love of money (although he

187

does not record them bearing a similar antipathy to Crassus), and it was so strong that the mob actually dug up the dead man's body and dragged it through the streets of Rome.

None of this seems to have rubbed off on the elder Pompeius' soon-to-be-famous son. Pompey the younger was generous and friendly, with the same yearning as Crassus to be loved by all and sundry. Whereas Plutarch does not describe the physical appearance of Crassus, he waxes lyrical on the young Pompey: 'His hair swept back in a kind of wave from the forehead and the configuration of his face round the eyes gave him a melting look, so he was supposed (though the resemblance was not a close one) to resemble the statues of King Alexander.'[3]

Plutarch also mentions that Pompey had a reputation as a ladies' man, of whom people said that 'Flora, the courtesan, when she was getting on in years, was always delighted to tell people about her early intimacy with Pompey; she always had the marks of his bites on her, she said, when she went away after having made love with him.'[4]

Romans of the patrician and *equites* class were almost expected to have various dalliances like this, but the young Pompey seems to have taken things too far. 'He was accused,' says Plutarch, in an unusually gossipy aside, 'of having relations with married women and of neglecting public business and betraying public interests in order to gratify them.'[5]

Like Crassus, young Pompey was drawn inevitably into the centre stage of Roman politics because of his father's position. He was only seventeen when an attempt was made on his life. The ever ambitious Pompeius Strabo was fighting against Cinna in the clash between him and the consul Octavian. He was sharing a tent with Lucius Terentius, whom Plutarch describes as a friend. Since Terentius was actually a hit man in the pay of Cinna, we are entitled to ask how deep friendships ran in the last, murderous days of the Republic. Somehow, the younger Pompey got wind of the attempt, placed a guard around his father's tent and left a heap of bedclothes on his own camp bed. Terentius crept in and attacked the bed, soon realising that there was no one in it and his bird had flown. The whole camp was in uproar. Pompeius Strabo's guard were all for killing their general, since assassination was clearly the order of the night. It was the young Pompey who pleaded with them, weeping, not to kill his father and not to desert. Plutarch relates – and the story is so odd as to be probably true – that Pompey lay across the gates of the camp all night, daring his father's soldiers to march over him. Most, ashamed at their behaviour, stayed put. But Plutarch says that 800 soldiers ignored his plea and left; presumably treading on the heroic boy as they passed through the gates.

With the elder Pompey dead, those who had hated the father wanted, at least metaphorically, the head of his son. He was charged with *peculatum*, misappropriation of funds, acquired when his father had sacked Asculum. Plutarch lists items including hunting nets and books. This has been a ploy throughout history. When John Churchill, the extraordinarily successful British general in the reign of Queen Anne, was thought to be gaining too much power, his opponents accused him of falsifying troop numbers to draw the pay of non-existent soldiers. Undoubtedly, Churchill was guilty of this – it was a well-established perk throughout the army, although technically illegal. This was also the case with Pompey; every general helped himself to 'souvenirs' from the sack of a town. Bringing charges against him for doing so would be for political reasons only. In the event, the praetor overseeing the case was Paulinus Antistius. It seems an extraordinary state of affairs, but not, apparently, to Romans at the time, that Pompey became engaged to the man's daughter while the case was under way. When Antistius announced the not guilty verdict, the watching crowd roared 'Talasio!', the ancient greeting used at weddings.[6]

The year 87 BC was the one in which Pompey went over to Cinna, as the Sullan consul against Octavian, but there was a poisonous atmosphere in the camp and Pompey left so quickly and quietly that a rumour started that Cinna had had him murdered. The young man went home to his father's estates in Picenium in the east. This was always an option for men whose involvement in Rome's internecine politics made the city too hot for them.

Events there moved quickly. Cinna himself, having established some sort of equilibrium which Plutarch saw as a vicious dictatorship, was killed in a mutiny of his troops in 84 BC. A centurion approached the consul with his sword drawn and Cinna offered his valuable signet ring to spare his life. 'I have not come here to seal documents,' Plutarch records the centurion as saying, 'but to punish a wicked, lawless tyrant'.[7]

He cut him down.

Gnaeus Papirius Carbo, Cinna's co-consul, now held sway in Rome, but the vengeful Sulla was amassing supporters to march on the city. The 23-year-old Pompey, never having held an independent command, raised troops in the Picenium region, amounting to between one and three legions.[8] At Auximum he raised his standard, kicked the pro-Carbo officials out of the town and began to select his *legati* and centurions.

It was on his way to join Sulla that Pompey established his military reputation. He was faced with three separate armies: those of the pro-Carbo generals Gaius Carrinas, Tullius Cloelius and Lucius Junius Brutus, known as Damasippus. Had these three combined their forces, they would probably have defeated the brash, untried Pompey and that might have been the last history heard of him. In the event he moved first, engaging Brutus' troops and routing him. Plutarch asserts that Pompey placed himself at the head of his cavalry and charged Brutus' Celtic auxiliaries. It was not the place of a general to risk his life in this way and older, more experienced men stayed behind their lines where they could direct operations in some safety. A commander struggling for his life in the front line had no idea what was happening elsewhere on the field. Pompey unhorsed the Celtic leader, however, and drove the little ponies back, crashing into Brutus' infantry, who panicked and ran.

No doubt Pompey's first real blooding was a success and increased his reputation among his followers, but Brutus' troops were not the steady cohorts of the legions. There were large numbers of non-Romans among them and certain units were demoralised and mutinous. All this was underscored by the fact that Carrinas and Cloelius quarrelled, probably over military differences, and melted away, offering no battle. Pompey's next opponent on the march to Sulla was Lucius Cornelius Scipio Asiaticus, consul in that year of 83 BC and of the family of the famous Scipio Africanus, whose military exploits were still admired wherever all-conquering Romans met. This Scipio may or may not have been a chip off the old block. The armies were already drawn up just out of javelin range when most of his men defected to Pompey and Scipio ran for his life.

The meeting of Sulla and Pompey was one of those carefully staged moments that all who were there would remember for the rest of their lives. Armour was polished, plumes trimmed, shields repainted. Pompey's troops looked splendid, for all they were in the middle of a campaign. The cohorts lined up as Sulla trotted past them, chanting 'Imperator! Imperator!' (conquering general). That was expected. What was not was Sulla's response. He dismounted and dropped to one knee, covering his head with his cloak, calling Pompey 'Imperator!' in turn. No wonder Crassus resented this upstart in the months and years ahead. On the strength of one battle this young man, with no official position and too young to sit in the Senate, was being treated like another Alexander. Nearly 2,000 years later, however, Karl Marx was distinctly unimpressed. 'Pompey was a real shit,' he wrote to his friend Friedrich Engels in February 1861, '[who] acquired an undeserved reputation only by claiming, as Sulla's "young man", Lucullus' victories [in Asia Minor] and then Sertorius' [in Spain].'[9]

Once Sulla had established himself in Rome – with Crassus' victory at the Colline Gate, not Pompey's, the boy-general was sent in pursuit of Carbo. His search took him by a rather circuitous route, as he sailed first to Gaul to reinforce the campaign of the ageing Metellus Pius. His role, said Plutarch, was to 'put fresh fire and spirit into Metellus'.[10] The chronicler gets carried away with his hero, claiming that his successes in Gaul were so numerous that he could not list them because of the need to record all the man's later victories. Crassus must have been spitting blood. Pompey was with Sulla in the siege of Spoleto against the Marian general Carrinas, who had failed to face him months earlier, and he finally caught up with Carbo at Clusium.

Pompey's streak of ruthlessness shows clearly in his treatment of the fallen consul. For some reason he came down hard on the Mamertines, who held the town of Messana. When they objected to his high-handed tactics, he replied with a famous line, parroted countless times throughout the centuries in word and deed: 'Stop quoting the laws to us. We carry swords.'[11] He had Carbo, a man who had been consul three times, dragged in chains through the streets of Rome and insisted on a show trial at which he, Pompey, sat illegally as judge. Carbo's death was bereft of dignity. Suffering from a 'looseness of the bowels', probably dysentery, he asked permission to relieve himself before the executioner cut his throat. Pompey refused him even that.

Plutarch is anxious to be fair to his man. The dictatorship of Sulla was never ambivalent and the dictator himself, blond and blotchy, was not known for his forgiving ways. Pompey was a loyal lieutenant (unlike his father) and had no qualms about being his master's avenging angel. However, he did give strict orders to his troops not to ravage the war-torn countryside through which they passed. He commanded that their swords be sealed to their scabbards and punished any man whose seal was broken.

Sulla now sent his 'butcher boy', his *adulescens carnifex*, to Africa, where the proscribed Marian general Gaius Domitius Ahenobarbus, an ancestor of the future emperor Nero, was in hiding with a sizeable army. Pompey's force was huge. Plutarch records that he sailed with 120 warships and 800 transports, laden with supplies, money, siege equipment and weapons. The invasion force was roughly the same size as that Caesar would take to Britain 20 years later. Pompey had six legions, a force of the same size that Crassus marched out against Spartacus. An estimated 7,000 defectors left Ahenobarbus' camp, comprising over a legion, and the clash, when it came, happened in a downpour in which Pompey used the freak weather to his advantage. Driving his cohorts through the waist-high waters of a flash flood, Pompey himself narrowly escaped death when he was slow in responding to a soldier's demand for a password. Not for the first time Plutarch records a wildly improbable level of slaughter, although for once he qualifies the number with the embarrassed 'it is said'. According to him, only 3,000 of the rebel troops survived out of an army of 20,000. In the sacking of the enemy camp, Ahenobarbus was killed and the army hailed Pompey, as Sulla had, as Imperator.

With his blood up and all sorts of political possibilities ahead for a successful general, Pompey invaded Numidia. In forty days he destroyed the army of King Bogud and replaced him with the puppet-king Hiempsal, something of a scholar who wrote works on anthropology and ethnology in the Punic (Carthaginian) language.

Sulla must by now have realised that his protégé posed a considerable threat to him. He ordered Pompey to send all but one legion home; he was to remain in Africa with a skeleton outfit until he could be replaced as commander. No one knew better than Sulla how easy it was for a general to march his victorious troops on Rome. Pompey dutifully ordered them home. They refused to go, and even when he threatened to kill himself rather than disobey an order, hailed him as 'Pompeius Magnus': Pompey the Great.

In the event, Pompey came home with his troops and asked for a triumph. This was almost the last thing Sulla wanted – a hugely popular general leading five legions through the streets of Rome; a man who still held no senatorial rank and was only twenty-four. Pompey made an extraordinarily unwise remark to the dictator. 'He asked Sulla,' wrote Plutarch, 'to bear in mind the fact that more people worshipped the rising than the setting sun.'[12] Sulla gave way and was no doubt delighted that when Pompey tried to enter the Colline Gate with a *quadrigae* drawn by elephants, the terrified animals got stuck. Amid the manic trumpeting, the great general had to revert to the usual four horses.

Pompey's domestic arrangements were naturally dictated by politics. One way for Sulla to keep this ambitious young man loyal was to incorporate him into his family. Accordingly, he ordered him to divorce the praetor's daughter Antistia (whose father had by this time been murdered by the Cinna–Carbo–Marius faction) and marry his own stepdaughter Aemilia. Although she was married already and pregnant by her husband, that divorce too was arranged. It all came to nothing – Aemilia died in childbirth.

Never as much of a political judge as his mentor, Pompey backed the unstable Marcus Aemilius Lepidus, who was standing for the consulship in 78 BC. Sulla was furious, and Plutarch quoted him as warning Pompey: 'It is about time . . . that you woke up and gave your attention to what is happening. What you have done is to make your opponent stronger than yourself.'[13]

By this time, Sulla had more or less retired from active politics and on his death his enemies – of whom there were many – tried to prevent both a state funeral and his burial in the Campus Martius, the field of Mars, where all Roman heroes were buried. It was Pompey, cut out of Sulla's will, but never an ungracious loser, who insisted that full honours were given to the man at his passing.

Now Pompey had reason to rue his support of Lepidus two years earlier. In the context of Spartacus, Lepidus is an interesting man. Even before Sulla was dead, he began to repeal much of the legislation he had passed and was faced, along with his co-consul Quintus Lutatius Catulus, with a rebellion in Etruria, north of Rome. Sulla had granted the veterans of his army plots of land as a reward for their loyalty, but this meant that the locals were, in many cases, dispossessed. Ten years after the Social War and four years before the rising of Spartacus, more turmoil near Rome added further enemies to the Republic's long list. Both consuls were sent to put the trouble down, but Lepidus threw in his lot with the rebels. His intended march on Rome was dismissed as the ravings of a lunatic, yet both Marius and Sulla had done it in recent years and were hailed as saviours by their followers, rewarded with huge power and influence. Lepidus' problem was that he did not have their ability, and he grudgingly swore an oath to the Senate to behave himself. Partially to get him away from central politics, Lepidus was made governor of Gaul, but he spent his time beyond the Alps raising troops with the help of Marcus Junius Brutus, father of the assassin of Caesar. Unable to wait for Gallic reinforcements, Lepidus marched on Rome and was roundly defeated by Catulus. In the meantime, however, Brutus took most of his army across the Pyrenees into Spain before landing in southern Italy.

Here, in Rhegium, where Spartacus would find himself trapped six years later, Pompey was waiting. Brutus was killed in battle and Lepidus was defeated at Cosa, sailing for his life to Sardinia. Later that same year, Pompey was made proconsul and sent to Spain to aid Metellus Pius against more rebel troops under Quintus Sertorius, an old crony of Cinna. This ex-praetor had set up what amounted to an independent state in Hispania Interior and eagerly accepted Sulla's enemies who fled Rome for their own safety. Claiming proconsular status, he set up a Senate that rivalled Rome's, proclaiming that this, and not the corrupt regime of Sulla, was the *true* Republic.

It was to have been an action replay; Pompey the young lion, backing up the elderly and ill Metellus to bring Sertorius back into line. In fact, Sertorius had the measure of them both. Plutarch quotes him as saying, 'I shall only need a cane and a whip to deal with this boy, if I were not afraid of that old woman'.[14]

The 'boy', outmanoeuvred by Sertorius at Lauro, had no choice but to watch the rebel burn the city. As so often, Pompey's instructions were to wait for Metellus to reach him, and as usual Pompey disobeyed. In the battle that followed at Turia, Pompey was again in the thick of it, charging with the cavalry. Wounded in the hand, he lost his horse and only saved his life because his would-be captors stopped to argue over the animal's valuable harness. It was perhaps lucky for him that the 'old woman', Metellus, arrived the next morning and Sertorius' force melted away like the will-o'-the-wisp he was on campaign.

According to Plutarch, Pompey was received by the 'old woman' as a great general, exactly as Sulla had received him five years before. Yet again, along with Crassus, we must wonder why. There is no doubt that Sertorius, with a tactical skill that bordered on genius, was more than a match for the 'butcher boy', but he was murdered by what amounted to a palace coup in the year of the Spartacus War and his place taken by his killer, Marcus Veiento Perperna. This man had all the ambition and none of the flair of his predecessor and Pompey had little difficulty in defeating him. Letters in Perperna's possession which could have implicated large numbers of rich and powerful Romans – perhaps even Crassus himself – who had been in contact with Sertorius' rival government, were burned by Pompey without being read and the rebel was executed.

It was at this point, with Pompey's campaign in Spain virtually over and Lucullus' likewise in Pontus, that Crassus' desperate letters arrived by galloper. The exact sequence of events in the Spartacus War is not known and the picture is a complicated one. We must assume that Crassus sent these requests for help either before the breakaway slave force was defeated or as he was building his fortifications across the Rhegium peninsula. Depending on *exactly* where Pompey was in Spain and the favourability of the winds, it must have taken Crassus' messengers the best part of a month to find him. If Lucullus was in Thrace, he would have heard the news much later, as Crassus' men would have had to sail across the Aegean and possibly up the Straits of Marmara past the Gallipoli peninsula to locate the man.

Spartacus' breakout from Rhegium changed the situation. Crassus was now faced with a dilemma. Had Spartacus stayed put, then Crassus would have had to swallow his pride as far as Pompey was concerned and wait until the reinforcing legions arrived, so that the slaves would be bound to lose. In that event, men would have said, as they always said, that Pompey was the real victor and that Crassus could not cope without him. Now that the gladiator was on the loose, however, there was a sense of panic in Crassus' army. Like Pompey at Turia, like Custer at the Big Horn two millennia later, he wanted to destroy Spartacus on his own. Perhaps he even dreamed of men hailing him as Imperator one day too. And of course, at the back of his mind, as with all Romans, was the niggling fear that the gladiator might move on Rome after all.

Judging from both Plutarch's and Appian's accounts, Spartacus probably escaped with a third of his force, perhaps 40,000 men, under cover of darkness. If this was done quietly, they would probably have been largely infantry – horses are noisy. Daylight prevented any further success, however, and the next wave must have been halted at the ramparts by Crassus' troops: hence the 6,000 dead in the morning. The slaves would have pulled back out of javelin shot and Crassus' men would have known better than to chase them, especially if Crassus was aware that several thousand men were somewhere in his rear, and they tried again as the light began to fail – a further repulse with heavy losses.

Crassus had succeeded in splitting Spartacus' command. Leaving perhaps two legions at the fortifications to contain those still trapped to the south – and that must, in the main, have been the old, the women and children – he turned north, chasing Spartacus before the man did the unthinkable and attacked Rome. But disunity had again hit the slave army. It was the inevitable weakness that plagued an army of this sort – the weakness that undermined Karl Marx's dream of world revolution. A man like Spartacus *could* have toppled Rome in 71 BC, but he would need thousands with him, thousands who thought as he did and would be distracted by nothing. Such solidarity has rarely existed among men driven by desperation, hunger and fear – and it never lasts for long.

Crassus' scouts reported, as they darted back to the marching column in that spring of 71 BC, that the slaves had scattered and that some units were quite small. It is now that we learn the names of the other two members of Spartacus' leadership – Gaius Grannicus and Castus. Modern scholarship assumes that both these men were Gauls, the successors of Crixus and Oenomaus, but they could have been Thracian or from any of the Socii still alienated by Rome's arbitrary government over the previous fifty years. Crassus detached a legion to take this force, separated as it was from Spartacus, near the town of Croton, at the 'Lucanian lake'. 'There are stories about this lake,' wrote Plutarch, 'whose waters, they say, turn sweet for a time and then return to being bitter and undrinkable.'[15]

The problem with locating the battle here is that Croton is in the 'instep' of Italy, a matter of two days' march away from Crassus' lines, if that. Lucania is many miles to the north, so it is not possible to determine the exact site of this battle. Plutarch places the conflict in Lucania itself, a theory that makes more sense, but also supposes that Spartacus' force was charging all over Italy with no cohesion at all.

Frontinus provides more detail than anyone else, with the following account: 'Near the town of Camalatrum, in the war of the fugitive slaves, Licinius Crassus planned to lead his troops out against Castus and Grannicus, the leaders of the Gauls. He dispatched twelve cohorts under his legates Gaius Pomptinius and Quintus Marcus Rufus to circle around behind the mountain.'[16]

Philip Matyszak claims 30,000 dead in this engagement, but this seems positively Appian in its exaggeration. Livy gives us 35,000. The Romans had crept up to high ground, presumably under the cover of trees, with strips of linen around their helmets so that the sun did not glance off them. Two women, however, 'sacrificing', according to Plutarch, 'for the enemy',[17] saw them and raised the alarm. Sallust has a slightly different version: 'in the meantime, just before daybreak, two Gallic women, avoiding contact with the group, climbed up into the mountains to spend their menstrual periods there . . .'[18]

Plutarch may have misunderstood the Latin of his source, whether that was Sallust or someone else whose work is now lost to time. Or perhaps he was being coy. There is nothing incongruous about the two versions however – women having their periods were thought by many ancient peoples to be highly dangerous and were often sent away from the rest of their community at that time. In Spartacus' day, certainly among the Romans, if not the Gauls, menstruating women were thought to be able to make fruit fall from trees, bees fall in their swarms out of the sky and plants wither. Their menstrual blood was sometimes used as part of elaborate sacrifices to the moon and, more importantly in the context of the battle that was to come, their glance could blunt swords.

This, says Plutarch, was the most stubbornly contested battle of all, and it seems likely that both Crassus and Spartacus joined the later stages of it, ending in what seems to be a draw. Again, it is Frontinus who fills in the infuriating gaps of other neo-contemporaries. 'When the battle had already begun, these men [the Romans] suddenly rushed down from the enemy's rear with a terrifying shout and so shattered [Castus' and Grannicus' troops] that they fled from the field of battle pell-mell in all directions and never stood to make a fight.' [19]

For the Romans to have taken the high ground and out-manoeuvred the slaves makes sense. Their thunderous, screaming assault does not; it was not the Roman way of the battlefield and Frontinus should have known that. Adding to the confusion of the scene near the Lucanian lake, Frontius has Crassus himself building stockades around two of his legionary camps in the foothills of Cantenna, near Spartacus' camp. Then, taking a leaf from the gladiator's book, he crept away in the night and changed front. By the morning of the attack, his cavalry under Lucius Quintus were sent out to harass Spartacus and keep him away from the forces led by Castus and Grannicus. Frontinus reports this as a complete success, implying that Quintus' cavalry's retreat was a deliberate feint to draw Spartacus head on against Crassus' infantry. History, of course, is written by the ultimate winners, and the most headlong rout can be turned into a cunning, intended plan if the other side is dead and cannot disagree.

The outcome was that the eagles and regalia lost by Glaber were retaken by Crassus' cohorts and Spartacus withdrew to the mountains of Petelia. 'In [this battle],' wrote Plutarch, 'Crassus killed 12,300 men, but he only found two of them who were wounded in the back. All the rest died standing in the ranks and fighting back against the Romans.'[20]

What modern commentators have overlooked is that this too could have begun at least as a Spartacus-inspired trap. A small unit, apparently resting near a lake, their women seemingly occupied in religious observance. And then the sudden arrival of Spartacus, galloping to the rescue like the Seventh Cavalry. It all seemed a bit too coincidental. And again, the veiled reference to Spartacus' Roman tactics – 'All the rest died *standing in the ranks*' [italics added].

Spartacus was being trailed by an unknown number of Crassus' troops led by Quintus Marcus Rufus, who we know was a legate. He was either accompanied by the quaestor Gnaeus Tremelius Scrofa or he led a separate command. Once again, Spartacus did the unexpected. Rounding on the Romans, he smashed them again. Plutarch comments that 'the Romans were entirely routed and they only just managed to drag the quaestor, who had been wounded, to safety'.[21]

Once again, Spartacus was inflicting formidable punishment on armies that ought to have bested him with ease.

The last weeks of the Spartacus War are bewildering in their speed. We do not know exactly where Rufus and Scrofa were defeated, but it looks as though Spartacus was now marching south-east towards the port of Brindisium, by which he might have arrived in Italy about four years earlier. Thirty-three years later, in altogether more peaceful times, the poet Horace took the same journey, except that he was travelling by carriage and along the Appian Way from Rome. His slaves abused the waterman, who in turn abused the slaves and bored everybody with tall tales of their mistresses. The water itself was 'most vile'[22] and the gnats and the fenland frogs made sleep impossible. Then Horace's eyes became infected and he had to use 'black ointment'. The bread was good at Equotuticum, as opposed to Canusium, where it was gritty. It poured with rain. No doubt Spartacus' increasingly desperate men cared little for details such as these. Bread was bread, however gritty it was, and runaways with a price on their heads watching for Romans do not sleep well anyway. The weather was immaterial.

As we know, Appian places heavy emphasis on the fact that Spartacus was 'waiting for cavalry',[23] but the context is not clear. Were those slave reinforcements due to harass Crassus' rear while the slave army was still penned in at Rhegium? In which case, how did Spartacus contact them? Or were they joining him fresh after the latest Roman defeat, not slaves, but an *ala* of auxiliaries from some disgruntled tribe? Historian Antonio Santosuosso believes that Spartacus' plan at this stage was to join forces with the Samnites, still hostile to Rome since the Social War. Appian was of the opinion that the cavalry had joined Spartacus before he arrived at Brindisium, only to find another potential way out blocked by Lucullus' army, newly disembarked from Thrace.

We have no figures concerning these troops, but it is likely that Lucullus had at least three legions – a potential 30,000 men. Crassus, approaching from the north, probably still had four legions with him, depending upon the losses incurred by Rufus and Scrofa. In these last weeks, Pompey landed with his troops from Spain too, but again we have no details of precisely where he was or when or how many troops he had with him. Three or four legions is not unreasonable, and his probable line of approach was from the west.

Throughout the story of Spartacus, we have been plagued by the infuriating numbers game played by the Romans. I believe that Spartacus was now hopelessly outnumbered by the three armies converging on him. In fact, in terms of actual fighting men, he might have been outnumbered by Crassus alone; Pompey and Lucullus were merely the icing on the cake. But it was icing that Crassus did not want.

Spartacus turned back from Brindisium, marching now north towards Crassus. Plutarch describes the slaves' overconfidence, saying, 'They refused any longer to avoid battle and would not even obey their officers. Instead, they surrounded them with arms in their hands as soon as they began to march and forced them to lead them back through Lucania against the Romans.'[24]

Spartacus the general may now have realised that his day had come. It seems reasonable to assume that his army was now almost entirely made up of actual warriors. The bulk of the women and children, including his own wife and any children they may have had in the previous three years, were probably left behind in the south, although whether Crassus maintained the fortifications across the peninsula is unknown. The ennui so effectively demonstrated in the Kirk Douglas film may have gripped him even if his men had remained optimistic. We follow the camera around the gladiator's circling campfires. We see the children asleep under the stars, the firelight on their quiet, trusting faces. We see the old men and women smiling in their sleep, Spartacus' officers poring over maps, putting the finishing touches to their plans for the next day's battle, the tears in Spartacus' eyes.

The attack came, says Plutarch, as Crassus' men were digging a ditch. This is not likely to be a second attempt to corral Spartacus, because with Lucullus and Pompey both on the march in Italy, Crassus needed to end this quickly. More likely, the ditch was just the outworks of Crassus' marching camp. Spartacus sent messengers to Crassus, asking for negotiation. What his terms were we do not know. Only Appian mentions this, and he implies that the offer came even before Spartacus marched on Brindisium. Whenever it happened, if it happened at all, Crassus would not treat with slaves, and he drew up his cohorts.

In the Kirk Douglas film, the battle begins with Crassus' legions marching forward in their tight formations – tiny moving extras on a rolling valley side in the days before computer animation cheapened the whole art of re-creation. As one, their shields face front and they march on at the deadly measured tread towards Spartacus' line. The slave army is drawn up, several lines deep on the crest of a hill, giving them the advantage of height. As the first cohorts appear, there is no hurling of javelins, which we know Crassus' men would have done in reality. Instead the front lines stand dithering as Spartacus' troops light the huge, pitch-covered logs they are carrying and, with a running man at each end, roll the flaming logs into the massed ranks. We see no centurions at the front, no *optiones* at the rear. But against those rolling, terrifying walls of fire, the legions break, as terrified men would have broken, from the back. As we watch, fascinated, Spartacus' infantry rushes forward, not in the steady, silent Roman fashion, but like the Gauls and Germans and Thracians they were, running, yelling, charging the crumbling Roman line, leaping over the fire logs in their enthusiasm to spill Roman blood. Perhaps, in the end, it was like that.

Then, fresh forces appear on the scene. Roman horsemen galloping forward. Crassus' second in command obligingly lets us know who they are. 'The army of Lucullus,' he says and Laurence Olivier remains impassive on his impossibly white horse, watching it all. 'The army of great Pompey.' Olivier's Crassus does not wince. The lethal animosity between the two men is not part of Dalton Trumbo's screenplay. Lucullus and Pompey are just names; neither of them actually appears on screen.

The only enemy facing Spartacus on the final battlefield was that of Crassus. Pompey was probably at least a day's march away;

Lucullus may never even have left Brindisium. The gladiator ordered his horse to be brought forward and butchered it dramatically in front of his men, cutting its throat with his sword. If they won, he shouted, the Romans had plenty of good horses which would be theirs. If not, he did not need a horse at all.

Appian believed that Spartacus' army was still large and 'the fight was long and bitterly contested, since so many tens of thousands of men had no other hope'.[25]

In a rash move for a period when battles were often decided by the death of a leader, Spartacus made a headlong assault on Crassus' position. Olivier sits astride his horse on a hill, well away from the action. It is likely that Crassus would have been behind his legions, directing operations under his scarlet flag. Despite his aspirations to military glory he was actually no Pompey, leading with his cavalry from the front. Spartacus would have had to have hacked his way through so many lines of the hated *caligae* to reach him. And the old skills he learned at Batiatus' school at Capua came flooding back; lead with the left foot, swing the body, a clean kill to the throat, the heart, the head. How many men went down before him we do not know. Plutarch records two centurions who attacked him simultaneously – Spartacus killed them both.

'Spartacus himself,' wrote Appian, 'was wounded by a spear thrust in the thigh, but went down on one knee, held his shield in front of him and fought off his attackers until he and a great number of his followers were encircled and fell.'[26]

Plutarch has a similar end for the gladiator who took on a nation: 'Finally, when his own men had taken flight, he himself, surrounded by his enemies, still stood his ground and died, fighting to the last.'[27]

Even Florus, a writer who has nothing but contempt for the Spartacuses of this world, admits that the slaves 'died like men, fighting to the death as might be expected of those commanded by a gladiator. Spartacus himself fell as is proper for a general, fighting most bravely in the front rank.'[28]

Is it this warrior we see, etched into the plaster of Pompeii, shown, wrongly, still mounted, with a spear thrust in his thigh and his name, in Oscan – Spartaks?

'Crassus had had good fortune,' wrote Plutarch, 'had shown excellent generalship and had risked his own life in the fighting; nevertheless, the success of Crassus served to increase the fame of Pompey.'[29]

We will never know how 'good fortune' and 'excellent generalship' balanced themselves or to what extent Crassus actually risked his life, but this may be a reference to how close Spartacus came to killing him. And there was something odd about Spartacus. His very facelessness meant that he was as elusive in death as he had been in life. In the Kirk Douglas film, he survives the battle with Crassus and his followers refuse to save themselves by identifying him – hence the famous 'I am Spartacus' of Trumbo's screenplay. In reality, his body was never positively identified. The gladiator slave had destroyed six Roman armies and created an astonishing legend which Rome wanted to obliterate. Not being able to display a bloody corpse made that difficult and gave rise to an enduring legacy. Two things place this in perspective; the first is that Spartacus was, in the words of the film brochure, 'a general without stars'. We have no evidence that he wore elaborate armour or distinctive dress, setting him apart from his people, unlike the *quaestors*, proconsuls and consuls he had defeated. On the field, his hacked body would have looked just like several thousand others. And secondly, the power that was Rome took a calculated risk. The lack of a body meant he may have survived to keep his cause alive. Such rumours have been common throughout history – Boudicca, warrior queen of the Iceni, has no known burial chamber, so she is still alive; the ever shadowy Arthur is not dead, but merely sleeps under a hill in Wales, waiting to be summoned when we need him again; Vlad the Impaler's battlefield death was so shrouded in confusion that he became the Undead – the inspiration for the whole Gothic horror genre. But the Senate was prepared to take the risk that Spartacus might live on in legend, because the alternative was worse. Conquered kings and warriors were brought to Rome in chains, as living proof that no army was a match for those of Rome. The British leader Caratacus marvelled at the magnificence of Roman architecture and was allowed to live out his days there.

Vercingetorix, the Gallic king, was publicly displayed before being ritually – and publicly – strangled. But these men were rulers of their people, men of substance and if not exactly the equal of Romans, at least worthy opponents. Not so Spartacus. Spartacus was a slave, the dregs of his race; exposing his corpse in the Forum would give him a status in death out of all proportion to events. And everyone wanted to forget the whole affair as soon as possible.

Everyone except Gnaeus Pompeius Magnus. We do not know how many of Spartacus' troops survived him. Appian says that there were still a sizeable number on the run in the mountains, and that they formed themselves into four groups and 'kept up their resistance until there were only 6000 survivors'.[30] This implies a series of skirmishes as part of Crassus' mopping-up operations, but where any of this happened is unknown. Without Spartacus, his people probably disintegrated into a disorganised rabble and Crassus' legions made short work of them. Plutarch estimates that a further 5,000 slaves were trapped by Pompey's army and that the general, either with Pompeian ruthlessness or Plutarchian hyperbole 'killed them all'.[31] It was Pompey's timing that gave him the edge over Crassus. He sent a dispatch to the Senate to the effect that although his rival had defeated the slaves in open battle, it was he 'who had extinguished the war to its very roots'.[32] He demanded a second triumph, ostensibly for his war in Spain, but probably to garner his share of the glory for obliterating the army of Spartacus. Crassus, displaying rather more dignity, declined to be involved. Even so, the man could not win; Plutarch says 'indeed it was thought that he acted rather meanly and discreditably when he accepted for a war fought against slaves, the minor honour of a procession on foot, called the ovation'.[33]

Writing two centuries later, Aulus Gellius elaborated on the situation:

> The reason for awarding an ovation, rather than a triumph, is either because a war was not proclaimed according to the proper rituals; because it was not fought with a real enemy; because the enemy had a humble or unworthy name, as in the case of slaves or

pirates; or because the enemy's surrender was too quick and the victory was, as they say, 'bloodless' and 'without dust'.

. . . so Marcus Crassus, when he had brought the war with the slaves to an end and had returned to Rome to celebrate an ovation, disdainfully rejected the myrtle crown [of an ovation] and used his influence to have a decree of the Senate passed that he was to be crowned with laurel [the mark of a triumph].[34]

In the meantime, the last of Spartacus' followers – both Appian and Plutarch claim that there were 6,000 of them – were brought in chains along the Appian Way towards Rome. They never got there. Crassus' legions set up crosses at regular intervals by the roadside and crucified them. Two millennia of Christian art and religious mysticism have lent an aura of magic to death by crucifixion. We know, however, as medieval and Renaissance painters did not, that a human body cannot be supported by nails driven through the palms of the hands and that almost everything about the description of Christ's 'passion' at Calvary is incorrect.

George Riley Scott contends that crucifixion was practised by many ancient peoples including the Phoenicians, Scythians, Persians and Carthaginians. The wooden cross which we associate with Jesus and which has given Christians their most potent symbol, was probably a capital 'T' constructed of two posts fixed at right angles to each other. By the time of Jesus' execution in AD 33, the court officials flogged the victim and made him carry the cross piece (i.e. one piece of timber), not the whole structure. 'When the place of execution was reached,' writes Scott, 'the victim was stripped naked and forced to stretch himself upon the ground on his back, with his head resting on the cross beam and his arms stretched out along its length.'[35] Ropes were then lashed around the wrists and although Scott, writing in 1940, maintained that nails were driven through the palms of the hands, we now know that this was not the case. With ropes in place nailing the hands is pointless, except to add to the pain of the whole process. Without ropes, the weight of the body would tear the flesh from the metatarsals and the victim would drop. Scott says that to prevent this, a large wooden peg was driven into the upright beam on which the feet rested and that nails were driven through both feet in a 'crossed over' position shown in depictions of Christ's death. Without the peg, in fact, death was relatively quick, because the weight of the body would constrict the lungs and the result would be suffocation.

> Death [writes Scott] was slow and unutterably agonizing. It represented a form of torture for days on end, which was sometimes prolonged by giving the criminal food and drink . . . The legs were sometimes broken by heavy blows; the face and breast were torn by hooked implements; the body prodded with pointed rods or stakes. Sometimes sticks were forcibly pushed into the anal orifice or the urethral passage and then withdrawn. Another variation consisted of smearing the face with honey to attract insects.[36]

The exact nature of the crucifixion depended on the degree of contempt and vindictiveness of the crucifiers. We do not know exactly what Crassus' orders were or how much he left to the ghastly imaginations of men whose comrades had been cut down by these renegades.

One thing is certain; their bodies were left to rot in the fierce sun of a Roman summer, flies gorging on the ripped, bloated, blackening corpses. In the ordinary little town of Santa Maria Capua Ventere, there stands a new milestone on the pavement by the side of the main street. It reminds us that this metalled road, with its traffic signs and its constant stream of cars, lorries and scooters, was part of the Appian Way. Looking right from the milestone, we see the toppled ruins of an amphitheatre, the base of which stood when Spartacus fought there. Somewhere under the modern tarmac, the blocks of flats and the shops, are the remains of the gladiatorial school of Lentulus Batiatus, where Spartacus was trained for the arena. Two and a half years after it started, the revolt of Spartacus was finally over.

ELEVEN

The Legend of Spartacus

In the whirlwind of intrigue, war and murder that was the Republic of Rome, the men who knew Spartacus did not last long. Many of the Romans who fell with him in that last unnamed battle would have paid into a burial club during their time with the eagles, with deductions taken from their pay. In practice, when a legionary died, the body was carried by his friends of the *contubernium*, on a couch to a place beyond the ditch perimeter of the camp. Here, couch and body were placed on a pyre and burned. The ashes were collected into an urn made of glass or earthenware, and the mourners held a solemn wake around the site.

It is unusual to find grave-markers which record the reason for a soldier's death, but a very telling one marks a monument to the centurion Marcus Caelius Rufus, who died along with three legions in the Teutoberg Forest nine years after the birth of Christ. His brother had the stone inscribed that 'should they ever be found, his bones may be interred here'.[1] There are no markers to the men killed by Spartacus since, to the bitter end, the establishment refused to believe that the slaughter of slaves was much above killing rats. In any case, the sheer numbers involved precluded elaborate, individual ritual. The dead were cremated en masse, in enormous fires whose smoke must have blotted out the bright Campanian sunshine.

The remains of the last 6,000, those crucified by Crassus along the Appian Way, would have hung, discoloured and bloated from their crosses throughout the sweltering months of that summer of 71 BC. Travellers from the south on their way to the great city or those leaving Rome bound for the 'toe' of Italy would have wrapped their cloaks and togas around their mouths and noses against the gruesome smell and sight, and they would have cause to remember Spartacus.

Of those slaves who survived as prisoners and were returned to their masters, we know nothing. They were broken men, but they were dangerous too. They had tasted freedom and the blood of Romans. Could they ever have been trusted again? Perhaps their masters chained them with double locks in their *ergastulum* cells; perhaps they sold them on; perhaps they had them executed. It would be a surprise if *none* of them ended up in the arena.

Of Spartacus himself, there was no trace. His was one of the thousands of bodies burned in the vast, communal funeral pyre after that last battle. We have no knowledge of the fate of the anonymous wife, the priestess of Dionysius who was probably at his side throughout the whole of the war named for her husband.

The people and the Senate of Rome breathed a collective – and huge – sigh of relief. Although Spartacus' followers raided the countryside around Thurii as bandits for ten more years, they were scattered, isolated, leaderless. The magic of leadership had gone and with it, the unimaginable threat of slave revolt. Or had it . . . ? Pompey had his triumph – for the 'real' war against Sertorius in Spain; Crassus had his ovation – for hunting down slaves. Yet again, the 'butcher boy' was the darling of the Senate and the mob; yet again he had stolen a march on Crassus. Neither man would disband their victorious armies; both men ran for consulship. And both were appointed. Appian takes up the story: 'The population of Rome, who discerned the seeds of fresh civil war and were afraid of a pair of armies encamped outside the city, begged the consuls, as they sat in state in the Forum, to be reconciled with each other.'[2]

It was Crassus who cracked first, rattled perhaps by soothsayers' warnings and the wailing of the crowd. With a considerable degree of magnanimity he said, according to Plutarch,

My friends, I do not think that I am lowering or demeaning myself in any way if I take the first step in the direction of friendship or goodwill towards Pompey, a man to whom you gave the title of 'the great' when he had scarcely a hair on his chin, and whom you honoured with a triumph before he was even a member of the Senate.[3]

The gesture may have been magnanimous, but the language was as barbed as ever.

Crassus continued to use his money to impress and to buy friends. He held a great feast in Rome in honour of Hercules where 10,000 people sat down to eat in a vast street party. 'Each man,' wrote Plutarch, 'was presented with an allowance of grain enough to last for three months.'[4]

In his darker moments, however, Marcus Licinius Crassus must have remembered that for all his money, his reputation and consulship rested on having defeated Spartacus. And the irony was that he could not actually crow about this – Spartacus was probably every bit as much of a general as Sertorius in Spain or even Mithridates in Pontus Euxinus. But Spartacus was a slave, an 'unworthy enemy', and this victory just did not count.

But the ghost of Spartacus would haunt Rome for a while yet. Ten years after the gladiator escaped from Capua, Lucius Sergius Catilina (Catiline) may well have invoked his name for a cause of his own, but a cause not dissimilar in some ways from that of Spartacus himself. Catiline was a firebrand of the patrician order with money in his purse and a chip on his shoulder. Fighting under Pompey's father Strabo in the Social War, he seems to have heartily enjoyed enforcing the proscriptions that followed, hacking off the head of an opponent and parading it – still breathing, some said – on a pole through Rome. His time as quaestor before the Spartacus War and praetor after it was followed by a governorship in Africa, but he found himself on trial for extortion (rather like Verres) when he tried to stand for the consulship. Involved in a plot to murder those standing on election day, he was saved from further prosecution by the scheming of Crassus and spent the next four years wheeling and dealing in Roman politics and gaining the support of Caesar, now very much the coming man in the city. When the orator Cicero was elected consul in 62 BC, Catiline organised a revolt. Among his followers were disgruntled patricians from his own class, veterans of the Social War and, most significantly, slaves. Catiline's attempt to murder the consul was rumbled by Cicero's spies on 7 November and he fled the city to join the forces of Gnaeus Manlius in Etruria.

By January of the following year, Catiline was defeated and killed in battle near Pistoria in the foothills of the Alps.

The link with Spartacus is explained by Gaius Suetonius Tranquillus in his *Life of Augustus*. 'On the way out to govern his province [Macedonia] [Gaius Octavius, father of the future emperor Augustus] destroyed the fugitive slaves who were remnants of the forces that had once fought for Spartacus and for Catiline, and who now were occupying the countryside around Thurii.'[5]

For Catiline's slave followers to have fled south rather than north with the legions of Manlius, there had to be some kind of organisation and communication. Was the name of Spartacus, ten years on, still strong enough to raise the storm?

What of the men who fought Spartacus, who, in their arrogance, were nearly destroyed by him? Livy has a melancholy list from the Roman point of view: 'The consul Gnaeus Lentulus fought unsuccessfully against Spartacus. The consul Lucius Gellius and the praetor Quintus Arrius were defeated in battle by this same Spartacus . . . the proconsul Gaius Cassius and the praetor Gnaeus Manlius also fought against Spartacus, but with no success.'[6]

Livy fails to mention Glaber, who first fell victim to the fugitive gladiator's brilliance. We have seen already that he vanished without trace after the trouncing he received on the slopes of Vesuvius. Gnaeus Cornelius Lentulus, known as Clodianus, survived the humiliation of a slave defeat and went on to become censor in 70, together with Gellius. In 67 BC he served as a legate under Pompey in his purge of the Cilician pirates. Rome, usually so unforgiving of its failed sons, seems to have made an exception for him. Quintus Arrius, technically propraetor in 72 BC, destroyed Crixus' breakaway army of Gauls and Germans but was outmatched by Spartacus himself. Neither Plutarch nor Appian mentions him, clearly singling out Gellius as the loser in that he commanded as consul on the day. Gellius himself rose or fell with Lentulus and as co-censor in 70 BC drove out sixty-four members of the Senate in an anti-corruption purge which would have delighted the Gracchi brothers a generation earlier. Gaius Cassius may have felt he had something to make up for after his defeat by Spartacus. His was, in

72 BC, the only army between the slaves and their possible escape route north through the Alpine passes. A staunch supporter of Crassus, he fought in Syria and Judea in 52 BC and repulsed an invasion by the warlike Parthians a year later. In the internecine struggle between the triumvirs Pompey and Caesar, Cassius joined the former and was given command of the fleet. Ever the wily politician, however, he made his peace with Caesar and became praetor in 44 BC, when he emerged into the spotlight as the most bitter opponent who plunged his dagger into the would-be emperor. Shakespeare took up Plutarch's view of him sixteen centuries after the event. 'Caesar said "I'm not much afraid of these fat, long-haired people. It's the other type I'm more frightened of, the pale, thin ones"' – by which he meant Brutus and Cassius.[7]

In the political confusion that followed Caesar's assassination on the Ides of March, the conspirators lay low for a while; however retaliation against them was by no means as swift as Shakespeare implies. It was a full two years before the Caesarian faction caught up with Cassius and Brutus at Philippi in Macedonia. Believing the day to be lost, Cassius committed suicide, not realising that 'in another part of the field' Brutus had defeated Octavian. This battle ended forever the myth of the Republic; Octavian became Augustus and the greatest empire in the ancient world became a reality.

The last named in Livy's list of victims of Spartacus, Gaius Manlius, is a complete unknown, unless this is a misreading for Gnaeus Manlius, a tribune in 66 BC who sent the butcher-boy Pompey out against Mithridates of Pontus Euxinus and Tigranes of Armenia to extend the sway of Roman power still further.

The general who had least to do with the final defeat of Spartacus, but whose arrival at Brindisium drove the gladiator north again into the teeth of Crassus, was Lucius Licinius Lucullus, he of the first plate glass and cherry trees in Italy, the owner of unrivalled gardens in Rome. A highly capable soldier, he spent the sixties extending Roman occupation in Asia, but found himself at logger-heads both with greedy Roman money-lenders and mutineers within his troops. Much of the land he conquered was reclaimed by native kings as Lucullus had insufficient troops to stop them.

He returned to Rome in 65 BC, but was kept waiting two years for his triumph. Nearly as rich as Crassus, or at least Pompey, he retired to the magnificence of his garden, acting as a patron to mediocre poets and dying insane, completely upstaged by the mighty clash of Pompey and Crassus.

The man who claimed to have rooted out the Spartacus War, the great Pompey, went on to fulfil his destiny. An uneasy partner with Crassus as co-consul in 70 BC, he neither held a qualifying post in administration nor was he a member of the Senate, but he was the darling of the people and the *equestrian* class, and his second triumph was the height of his fame. Cashing in on his youth and military skill (Crassus, for one, was highly dubious of the latter) he left the wheeling and dealing to his co-consul and waited for a chance to prove his prowess again. His role in the Spartacus War had been limited, despite his extravagant claims, and unlike Crassus he had never faced the gladiator in the field.

His opportunity to shine came in 67 BC when the Senate gave him carte blanche to operate, over a three-year campaign, against the Cilician pirates. These men were the scourge of the Mediterranean, especially its eastern coast, trading the slaves they took by force from all over Rome's eastern provinces and near neighbours. Their systematic and frequent attacks on grain ships from North Africa and Sicily led to a law against their activities, the *lex de pirates*, which in turn led to an all-out punitive raid on them in Cilicia itself four years before Spartacus broke out from Capua and possibly about the same time as he crossed the Aegean to be sold as a slave. Destroying their strongholds actually made things worse, because now their ships were their homes and the sea their backyard. They were only too willing to throw in their lot with Mithridates and promise Spartacus safe passage off Italy because it gave them a chance to rattle Rome and to make money into the bargain. Pompey's attack on the pirates was ruthless and efficient and he completed it in three months, not the three years granted to him by the Senate.

It was against Mithridates and Tigranes of Armenia that Pompey finally proved his mettle. Both these kings were thorns in the side of

Rome's eastern expansion and he dealt with them piecemeal, controlling the whole of Asia Minor by 62 BC. In that year, he was awarded another triumph in Rome but failed to establish the veterans' colony he wanted to build in the east. Two years later, when the remnants of Spartacus' people around Thurii were heard from for the last time, the unlikely first triumvirate was created of Pompey, Crassus and Julius Caesar.

This was a marriage most definitely not made in heaven and Crassus' death in 53 BC exposed the naked competition and aggression of the pair of survivors in a bid to outdo each other. Pompey's star was already falling when he clashed in open battle with the greatest of Rome's generals at Pharsalus in Greece in 48 BC. On 28 September, having collected his wife, he sailed into exile in Egypt. Plutarch allocates two pages to the man's end. Pompey's trireme could not land on the shore and he was taken by a small and apparently friendly escort by rowing boat to the sand. The king of Egypt was Ptolemy XIII, the brother and husband of Cleopatra. His was an impossible position. Egypt was a client kingdom of Rome; if Ptolemy welcomed Pompey, Caesar would furious. If he arrested Pompey, Caesar would dominate. Either way, Egypt's fragile semi-autonomy would disappear. Allegedly remarking that 'dead men don't bite', Ptolemy seems to have panicked and sent assassins to finish the matter. The first to strike was Septimus, who had served as a centurion under Pompey, lunging from behind with his sword. Another ex-comrade, Salvius, hit him with his dagger and the slave Philippus held his hand as Achillas, the Greek entrusted with the killing, hacked off the general's head.

'He neither said nor did anything unworthy of himself,' Plutarch recorded, 'only groaned a little and so ended his life in his sixtieth year and only one day after his birthday.'[8]

The slave Philippus washed the now-naked body in sea water and burned it in a wrecked fishing boat as a funeral pyre, which was still burning the next day. An anonymous old comrade of Pompey helped him. 'I find this happiness at last,' Plutarch records the man as saying, 'to touch with my hands and to prepare for burial the body of the greatest Imperator that Rome has seen.'[9]

Pompey's head was taken to Caesar, who was horrified. When he was shown his rival's signet ring with the engraving of the sword and the lion, he burst into tears. Cornelia, Pompey's wife, eventually obtained his ashes and reburied them in the grounds of his villa at Alba. There was no such solemnity for Spartacus and no one knows where his ashes lie.

Marcus Licinius Crassus grew ever more bitter as Pompey's star rose. Sidelined time and again by the younger man with his gift for self-publicity, much of what Crassus did for the rest of his life was motivated by his hatred for the people's darling. He should have blocked Pompey's arrogant standing as consul in the year after the Spartacus War because the move was unconstitutional. This single failure meant that Crassus never dominated the political scene as Pompey did and Caesar would twenty years later. Instead, Crassus played a curious game of hiding in the shadows, perhaps intending to be the string-puller behind whatever puppet was available at any given time. If he could not oust Pompey face to face, he would plot against him from behind. So while the butcher boy was busy dispatching Cilician pirates, Crassus was literally buying the backing of the ever indebted Caesar by paying the coming general's bills. When Catiline attempted to murder the consular candidates two years later, it was Crassus who bribed his prosecutors. Never fool-hardy enough to follow the rebel into open rebellion and death, his continued support of Caesar as consul in 59 BC led to the triumvirate in which, once again, Pompey and Crassus were partners. This time, however, Crassus was very definitely the 'third man' and the tripartite arrangement was, to say the least, shaky.

Since the Colline Gate, when the young Crassus had saved the day for Sulla in his march on Rome, the richest man in the Republic had rested on his military laurels. He had been given a mere ovation after the defeat of Spartacus, walking solemnly on foot through the thronged streets rather than riding in a *quadrigae*. While Pompey and Caesar went on to win laurels without number and Rome erected statues to them both, Crassus had to content himself with the mere defeat of slaves. The deep irony here is that Spartacus the gladiator was probably an infinitely greater general than the opponents of Pompey or Caesar – Mithridates in Pontus and Vercingetorix in Gaul; it was just that obsessively hierarchical Rome refused to see it that way.

Perhaps with this in mind, Crassus insisted on a five-year command in the east, having served as co-consul with Pompey for a second time. In 55 BC, as Julius Caesar was sailing along the south coast of Britannia looking for a likely landing place, Crassus was riding with his legionary columns through Syria, plundering the temple in Jerusalem and invading Parthia. It was unfortunate for Crassus that he took on one of the most formidable enemies in the ancient world. The Parthians used heavy cavalry in preference to almost any other category of soldier. Some accounts of battles suggest that on occasion no infantry was used at all. These Parthian cataphracts were terrifying in appearance. The horses were draped with mail and plate armour covering their entire bodies and their riders armed with a long lance that could skewer a horse's chest or slice a man's head off. Their unarmoured horsemen were light archers famed for their speed and expertise in the saddle, especially the Parthian shot delivered at enemies behind or on the rare occasions that the archers retreated.[10]

Crassus found himself caught at Carrhae, today's Haran in Turkey. With him were seven legions, perhaps 4,000 Arab cavalry and a further 4,000 auxiliaries, more or less the number he took out against Spartacus. But this time, the gods were not smiling on Marcus Licinius Crassus. The cataphracts smashed through the solid ranks of the legions, breaking their formations as Spartacus had all too often twenty years before. Crassus' own son, Publius, followed the fate of Crixus and allowed himself to be cut off from the main force. He and 5,000 others died on the cataphract lances.

The Parthian commander, Surena, gave the Romans a night to bury their dead and for Crassus to mourn his son. The man seems to have lost his nerve in those hours of darkness. A Pompey, a Caesar or a Spartacus would have rallied his shattered, frightened ranks, walking among their tents, checking their wounded, honouring their fallen comrades. Instead, Plutarch tells us, 'Crassus had covered up his face and was lying by himself in the dark'.[11]

Attempting an orderly retreat at daybreak, Crassus was eventually forced into negotiations with Surena. In the exchange, Crassus was on foot and the Parthians, the eternal cavalrymen, were mounted. They brought him a horse and as he tried to mount a scuffle broke out. A Parthian called Pomaxathres hacked the general down and lopped off his head and right hand as he struggled on the ground. The head and hand were sent back to Armenia and a mock Roman triumph was held at Seleucia, in which a prisoner called Paccianus, who resembled the dead general, was forced to ride, dressed as a queen and to answer to the name 'Crassus' and 'Imperator'. In front of him, Parthians dressed as *lictores* rode camels and from their bundles of rods and axes dangled the bloody heads of defeated legionaries. The women in the obscene parody shrilled songs 'on the theme of the effeminacy and cowardice of Crassus'.[12]

Crassus' head was to make one final appearance. In a Greek-influenced banquet, days after the Roman defeat at Carrhae, Euripides' play *Bacchae* was being performed for the entertainment of the Parthian generals. While a male actor whirled and screamed in the part of a maenad, a female devotee of Dionysius, the head was tossed into the sand and thrown and kicked from player to player. 'This, they say,' wrote Plutarch, 'was the farce played as an afterpiece to the tragedy of Crassus' expedition.'[13]

There is a delicious irony here. The head of Crassus, the conqueror of Spartacus, mutilated and used as entertainment for a baying mob. And, flinging it into the air, a maenad, like Spartacus' own wife. But that may be a fancy too far. We can be sure however that any of the survivors of the slave army hearing of Crassus' fate would have managed a grim chuckle. It is possible that 10,000 legionaries fell prisoner to Surena, men in chains at the mercy of their masters; 20,000 died. Spartacus was avenged.

When the extraordinary intellectual burst of enthusiasm, skill and activity that we call the Renaissance tried to rekindle the glory of ancient civilisations, it inevitably began in Italy. Rome had been the centre of all things great and the crumbling ruins of its power, cloaked in ivy and crawling with feral cats, had stood as silent reminders since the Visigoth king Alaric had done what many men hoped Spartacus would do and destroyed the place in AD 410.

One by one, the ancient texts that tell the fragmented story of Spartacus were found in libraries great and small, translated, annotated, understood, left to historians of the future to make their own conclusions on them: Cicero, Sallust, Livy, Plutarch, Appian, Paterculus, Florus, Frontinus, Athenaeus and Orosius. Between them, they chart the story of the slave who became a gladiator and the gladiator who became a rebel. The earliest accounts are corrupt, rambling, like a half-remembered dream. The longest, those of Plutarch and Appian, did not focus specifically on the story of the slave-rebel and are self-contradictory. To later writers, Spartacus was just a name and so he comes down to us as all things to all men.

It was not until that second burst of intellectualism, the Enlightenment of the eighteenth century, however, that serious note was taken of Spartacus once more. The French *philosophes*, and especially Jean-Jacques Rousseau, began writing about the concept of freedom as we understand it in a modern sense. So perhaps Rousseau was thinking of Spartacus in the famous first line of *The Social Contract*: 'Man was born free and everywhere he is in chains.'[14]

Since later conservative thought branded Rousseau a rabble-rouser and libertine and even blamed him for the outbreak of the French Revolution, the idea of a slave revolt could still arouse panic in the hearts of men seventeen centuries after Spartacus tried it. The French politician and historian Charles de Brosses was fascinated by all things Roman. A study of classical antiquity was essential for any intellectual at the time; a knowledge of Greek and Latin the mark of the gentleman in European society. In May 1768 de Brosses presented a paper – the Second Servile War, or the Revolt of Spartacus in Campania – to the Académie des Inscriptions in Paris. A fellow member of the Society, Jean Lévesque de Burigny, was producing one of the first serious works on Roman slavery and slave revolts at the time.

But it was François Marie Arouet de Voltaire, the embodiment of the Enlightenment, who put Spartacus centre stage for the first time since he had been the sole talking point in the streets of Rome. Voltaire, in his copious correspondence during the course of 1769, described the war of Spartacus as 'a just war, indeed the only just war in history'.[15] The notion of the just war is one with which historians are now familiar; less than ten years after Voltaire's claim, the Americans used the concept to explain their stand against the alleged tyranny of George III and the British.

At the beginning of the decade in which Spartacus was becoming, in enlightened France at least, the subject of serious scholarship, he made his first appearance on stage as a character of fiction. The Théâtre Français in Paris put on Bernard Saurin's *Spartacus, tragédie en cinq actes*, opening on 20 February 1760. In a later edition of the published version of the play, Saurin wrote that his intention was to 'evoke a great man . . . who would combine the brilliant qualities of the heroic men of justice and humanity . . . a man who was great for the good of men and not for the evil that they suffered. His real aim was the abolition of slavery, whose chains he broke.'[16]

This is the image of Spartacus that has persisted to the present day, echoed by Howard Fast, Dalton Trumbo and Kirk Douglas.

Late eighteenth-century society focused on Spartacus because already he was a symbol, perhaps *the* symbol, of the evils of slavery. No one was thinking of the slaughters perpetrated by Spartacus' people, of his butchery of Roman prisoners, of his goading wealthy Romans whose villas he had sacked to fight each other in mock gladiatorial displays. They were thinking of the appalling tyranny of Rome which allowed slavery in the first place, rather as the rebel Englishman Tom Paine defended the French Revolution and criticised its opponent Edmund Burke by claiming that he 'pitied the plumage, but forgot the dying bird'.

And the notion of slavery and freedom was not confined to scholarly and literary debate, or to the subject matter of stage dramas. African slavery was still a reality in Europe and America and in 1791 the first known slave revolt since that of Spartacus took place on the French island of Haiti. Pierre Dominique Toussaint l'Ouverture became the 'Black Spartacus'. We cannot make many parallels between slave leaders of different races who lived eighteen centuries apart, but there are similarities. Like Spartacus, l'Ouverture was a noted horseman, and he was married. L'Ouverture, like Spartacus, had a natural ability as a general; in one week in January 1798, he won seven skirmishes against a combined Anglo-Spanish force. There, however, the similarities end. L'Ouverture was the son of slaves, unlike Spartacus the freeman, although the Haitian was freed at about the same age that Spartacus was when he broke out from Capua. We know from records that he leased fifteen hectares and, ironically, thirteen slaves who grew coffee.

Just as the principles of liberty, equality and brotherhood overturned the corruption of the *ancien régime* in France, so the French colonies felt the ripple effect. Avaricious slave owners on Haiti – rather like those on Sicily in the generations before Spartacus – refused to accept any form of egalitarianism and their slaves went on the rampage as a result. L'Ouverture joined them in August 1791 and soon became a leader among them. When the revolutionary government in Paris abolished slavery throughout the French colonies in 1794, l'Ouverture orchestrated a dazzling campaign, like that of Spartacus, and won seemingly impossible victories. His mixed army of black, mulatto and white soldiers routed first the British and then the Spanish.

By 1800, l'Ouverture (the sobriquet comes from the breaches he could punch through lines of enemy troops) drew up a constitution for Haiti. But l'Ouverture was not allowed to remain undisputed master of his island. The French wanted it back, rather as Rome went to great lengths to win back Sicily and to take Campania back from Spartacus. The Black Spartacus was given 'safe conduct' to France and died in the grim cells of Fort-de-Joux, Doubs, in 1803.

It is unlikely that Toussaint l'Ouverture saw in himself echoes of Spartacus; it is very likely that he had never heard of him – but certainly Frenchmen at home made the connection and the slave-owning community around the world must have watched in awe and fear as the man's military victories mounted. The British abolished the slave trade in 1807 and slavery itself in the next generation.

Alone of the western powers, the United States held on to the 'peculiar institution' and had to fight a civil war to eliminate it.

But Spartacus was not merely a symbol of the heroism of slaves; he became an icon of freedom against tyranny of any kind. When Karl Marx made him his hero, he compared him favourably with the Italian freedom-fighter Giuseppe Garibaldi in his letters to his friend Friedrich Engels. Garibaldi fought in central Italy, his red-shirted guerrillas criss-crossing the same mountains of Campania where Spartacus fought. He entered Naples in triumph, standing in an open-topped carriage like a latter-day Pompey in his *quadrigae*. Was Spartacus welcomed in the same way at Nola or Nuceria nearby? The hugely popular novel *Spartaco*, written in 1874 by Raffaello Giovagnoli, had a preface by Garibaldi himself and was translated into umpteen languages.

Spartacus' story reached the stage in America in 1831, when Robert Bird's *The Gladiator: A Tragedy in Five Acts* was performed in New York. Its popularity was astonishing; in twenty years it had been staged over 1,000 times and was still playing to packed houses until well after the civil war that brought slavery to an end. What is fascinating is the way that Bird completely missed the salient point that Spartacus was a brutal military commander as well as a hero, and that men died in his name and by his hand. The year of the slave rebellion by Nat Turner, alluded to in Chapter Five, was also 1831. Bird was so horrified by rebellion that he wrote:

At this present moment there are 600 or 800 armed negroes marching through Southampton County, Virginia, murdering, ravishing and burning those whom the Grace of God has made their masters – 70 killed, principally women and children. If they had but a Spartacus among them – to organize the half million of Virginia, the hundreds of thousands of the states and lead them on in the Crusade of Massacre, what a blessed example might they not give to the excellence of slavery![17]

Spartacus had ceased to be a slave in the eyes of the novel-reading and theatre-going public. He was a Democrat, urging war against corruption. He was a nationalist freedom fighter championing the cause of the underdog against foreign armies of occupation.

When Karl Marx adopted Spartacus as a hero of the people, his place in leftist ideology was assured. If all history was a class struggle, then the story of Spartacus fitted very neatly. He was a member of the proletariat, those hopeless, downtrodden creatures who had 'nothing to lose but their chains'. Crassus, Pompey and all the rest were the bourgeoisie, owning the means of production and exploiting the proletariat for all they were worth. Lenin, who put Marx's theories into practice – with suitable adaptations – in Russia in 1917, went further when he wrote

> The history of slavery contains records of wars of emancipation from slavery which lasted for decades . . . Spartacus was one of the most outstanding heroes of one of the very greatest slave insurrections, which took place about two thousand years ago. For several years, the seemingly omnipotent Roman empire, which rested entirely on slavery, experienced the shocks and blows of a widespread uprising of slaves who armed themselves and joined together to form a vast army under the leadership of Spartacus.[18]

The decades that followed under Josef Stalin saw Spartacus elevated still further in Russia to become the most famous figure in ancient history. As the leader of the last great slave uprising, he was the political and symbolic forerunner of Lenin and of Stalin himself. In 1936 a seminal Marxist interpretation was written by Russian historian Aleksandr Mishulin – *The Spartacus Uprising*. The historian named his son Spartak in the gladiator-slave's honour. And of course we have already seen how the name was used by revolutionaries of the left in Germany led by Karl Liebknecht and Rosa Luxemburg.

In the twentieth century, an interesting dichotomy developed in the legend of Spartacus. On the one hand, he was the hero of at least three silent films, all of them Italian and made during the First World War, probably as morale boosters. Audiences were invited to identify with Spartacus 'the Thracian' as the embodiment of Little Italy struggling against the monstrous tyranny of the Crassus of that day – the superpowers of Austria-Hungary and Germany. On the other hand, because of his adoption by the Left, America in particular was hostile to him. We have already noted the FBI's interest in writers like Fast and Koestler and the McCarthyite mania that was only just dying out when Kirk Douglas made his film in 1960. The opposition to that film, from Hedda Hopper and the Legion of Decency, leave the impression that somehow the man was not *quite* a fit subject for the young to regard as a hero.

A number of epic poems have been dedicated to Spartacus, at least a dozen stage plays, countless paintings and engravings with highly inaccurate Victorian and Edwardian renderings of gladiatorial armour, a ballet by Aram Khachaturian (usually performed by the Bolshoi company, perhaps in memory of their folk hero of the Left), various jazz improvisations and a rather average made-for-television movie in which Goran Visnjic is suitably stoic as Spartacus. Brent D. Shaw, professor of classical studies at the University of Pennsylvania, finds 'decadence and decline' in much of the music that has been linked to Spartacus – 'It seems that the romantic myth of Spartacus has had its day.'[19]

The man's name has been hijacked by the gay community, especially in Amsterdam, and today's websites show glistening young men with the bodies of gladiators smiling serenely out of a guide that offers tourist havens for relaxation – some of them, no doubt, in central and southern Italy, where Spartacus fought and died. And the words of rebel British MP George Galloway crackled over the airwaves in the run-up to the general election of 2005. Speaking on behalf of the Respect Party and apparently on behalf of all races, he confidently quoted the words of the beaten slaves on that Spanish film-set hillside, the words that were never spoken, the words of Dalton Trumbo, for all the world as if they were true – 'I am Spartacus'.

As so often with iconic figures of the past, we are left with a bewildering array of tantalising glimpses but very few firm sightings of Spartacus. We have some facts. He was from Thrace, but exactly where and from which tribe is unknown. The date of his birth must be guesswork; his parents' names are not recorded. Perhaps he was Sparadakos and perhaps he spent his childhood as a shepherd in the mountains of Thrace – among mountains he was born and in mountains he died. He may have served with the Roman army, where his quick, fertile brain combined the experience of cutting-edge warfare with the timing and instincts of a born general. He rebelled and deserted – why is unknown, but I have suggested that he was ordered to march against his own people. Caught and sold into slavery, he became a gladiator in Capua, trained to die for the pleasure of the mob. Again, he broke out, taking on ever larger and more desperate armies until finally they brought him down.

This is virtually all we know. His wife's name remains a mystery as does the air of the supernatural that floats over them both. To some at least, he was Hero, the all-powerful god called the Horseman, and in what is perhaps the only attempt of a portrait of him, roughly executed on a plastered wall in Pompeii, he is shown in the saddle, galloping, with shield and spear in hand. We do not know exactly which type of gladiator he was; nor do we have details of Lentulus Batiatus' school at Capua. Was it the *lanista*'s over-zealousness that drove Spartacus to escape? Or was he a natural-born rebel who took orders from no one?

What was his relationship with Oenomaus, Crixus, Grannicus and Castus, the men who served under him? To some he was an egalitarian freedom-fighter, sharing the spoils taken equally among his people. That they flocked to him in their tens of thousands is testimony that they loved him.

And what is beyond doubt is that Rome trembled. Modern commentators have dismissed Spartacus as a dreamer, an idealist who had no chance of toppling Rome. But that is to accept Karl Marx's version of him, to see him as a proletarian revolutionary bent on the creation of a Utopian Marxist state. Spartacus was a realist. He fled to the high ground for survival, where he could see his enemy's strength far off. He fled to the coast, not once but twice, in an effort to evade superior forces. At least once he reached the

Alpine passes that would have taken him to freedom. He never seriously intended to march on Rome, still less destroy its civilisation – only the centuries would do that.

Historian Philip Matyszak sums him up: 'Spartacus was daring, a truly remarkable general and an inspiring leader of men. He was a brave and ferocious fighter and dealt fairly with his friends. On this the historical sources agree. But they do not say, and we should not suppose, that Spartacus was a good man, or a particularly noble one.'[20]

Terms such as 'goodness' and 'nobility' are notoriously subjective and relative. Today we remember Spartacus, not the man who beat him, because the Crassuses of this world – greedy for wealth and power – are ten a penny. Spartacus belongs to a more select group, one of a band of brothers who, for whatever reason, take on impossible odds and almost win. It is the courage and the inspiration that we most admire, because cynical and worldly-wise as we are, we need our heroes. And over 2,000 years ago such a hero rose up out of oppression, challenging tyrants in his own personal quest for freedom.

He was Spartacus.

Notes

One: 'I Am Spartacus'

1. Kirk Douglas, *The Ragman's Son: An Autobiography* (London, Simon & Schuster, 1988), p. 304.
2. *Ibid.*, p. 305.
3. Quoted in John Baxter, *Stanley Kubrick: A Biography* (London, HarperCollins, 1998), p. 6.
4. *Ibid.*, p. 125.
5. Douglas, *The Ragman's Son*, p. 311.
6. *Ibid.*, p. 316.
7. *Ibid.*
8. Quoted in Baxter, *Stanley Kubrick*, p. 131.
9. *Ibid.*
10. Douglas, *The Ragman's Son*, p. 319.
11. John Cary, *Spectacular! The Story of Epic Film* (London, Hamlyn, 1974), p. 5.
12. *Ibid.*
13. Douglas, *The Ragman's Son*, p. 319.
14. An essay on the Internet by Duncan L. Cooper makes great play of the missing battle sequences, implying an odd conspiracy against Spartacus by Hollywood moguls.
15. George MacDonald Fraser, *The Hollywood History of the World* (London, Michael Joseph, 1988), p. 31.
16. Douglas, *The Ragman's Son*, p. 332.
17. Quoted in the 17,000 letters sent out to the Legion.
18. Quoted at www.spartacus.schoolnet.co.uk/USAmccarthy
19. *Ibid.*
20. Douglas, *The Ragman's Son*, p. 323.
21. Letter from Trumbo to Albert Maltz (12 January 1972), quoted at www.spartacus.schoolnet.co.uk
22. Quoted in Baxter, *Stanley Kubrick*, p. 124.
23. Quoting Fast from the CNN News Bulletin marking his death, 13 March 2003.
24. Douglas, *The Ragman's Son*, pp. 309–10.
25. Preface to *Spartacus Souvenir Film Brochure*, 1960, p. 1.

26. *New York Times*, 18 January 1919, quoted in Paul Bookbinder, *Weimar Germany: The Republic of the Reasonable* (Manchester, Manchester University Press, 1996), p. 32.
27. *Ibid.*, p. 33.
28. *Ibid.*, p. 231.
29. Franz Schoenberner, *Confessions of a European Intellectual* (New York, Macmillan, 1946), pp. 107–8.
30. Karl Marx and Friedrich Engels, *Selected Correspondence* (Moscow, 1955), p. 115.
31. 1861 was the year of Italian unification when the disparate states, which had not been one since the days of the Roman Empire, were forged by the political hand of Camillo Benso, Count Cavour and the red-shirted military bands under Giuseppe Garibaldi. The latter's enormous statue, hand on sword hilt, stands in the centre of Naples, through which he marched in triumph as Marx wrote. (Marx and Engels, *Selected Correspondence*, p. 115.)

Two: The Man from Thrace

1. Plutarch, *Crassus: The Fall of the Roman Republic*, trans. Rex Warner (London, Penguin, 1972), p. 122.
2. Quoted in *The Mammoth Book of Ancient Rome*, ed. John E. Lewis (London, Constable, 2003), p. 352.
3. *Ibid.*, p. 357.
4. Plutarch, *Crassus*, trans. Rex Warner, p. 122.
5. 'The Song of Taliesin', quoted in Philip and Stephanie Carr-Gomm, *The Druid Animal Oracle* (Rochester, Kent, Grange Books, 2001), p. 79.
6. Quoted in Ivan Marazov, 'Thracian Religions' in Alexander Fol and Ivan Marazov, *Thrace and the Thracians* (New York, St Martin's Press, 1977), p. 23.
7. Livy, *History of Rome* XXXIX viii–xix, quoted in Naphtali Lewis and Meyer Rheinhold, *Roman Civilization* (New York, Columbia University Press, 1990). Vol. 1, pp. 503–4.
8. Appian, *The Civil Wars*, quoted in Brent D. Shaw, *Spartacus and the Slave Wars* (Boston, Bedford/St Martins, 2001), p. 140.
9. Thucydides VII, 29, quoted in Christopher Webber, *The Thracians* (Oxford, Osprey Man-At-Arms Series, 2001), p. 3.
10. Quoted in Hughes and Forrest, *The Romans Discover Britain* (Cambridge, Cambridge University Press, 1981), p. 35.
11. There were exceptions in serious emergencies. Valerius Maximus in his *Nine Books of Memorable Deeds*, written in the first century AD, records that in the Second Punic War against Carthage, a panicky Senate, alarmed at the scale of casualties in the legions, appointed a three-man commission to buy 24,000

slaves, with an extra 270 for the cavalry (these were probably already competent horsemen).

12. Incident quoted in Adrian Goldsworthy, *The Complete Roman Army* (London, Thames & Hudson, 2003), p. 76.
13. *Sub pellibus* technically means under hides; the 'canvas' of Roman tents was made of leather.

Three: Men for Bread and Circuses

1. Tertillianus, quoted in Michael Grant, *Gladiators, the Bloody Truth* (London, Penguin, 1971), p. 16.
2. In the Greek tradition, Charun became Charon, the ferryman who rows the dead across the dark river Styx to Hades.
3. Tacitus, *Annales*, quoted in Michael Grant, *Gladiators, the Bloody Truth*, pp. 73–4.
4. George Gordon, Lord Byron, *The Dying Gladiator*.
5. Juvenal, *Satires*, 10.81.
6. Seneca, quoted in Michael Grant, *Gladiators, the Bloody Truth*, pp. 110–11.
7. Miranda Twiss, *The Most Evil Men and Women in History* (London, Michael O'Mara, 2002), p.15.
8. Tacitus, quoted in Lewis and Rheinhold, *Roman Civilization*, Vol. II, p. 42.
9. Howard Fast, *Spartacus*, 1951. [This edition New York, Simon & Schuster, 2000.]
10. Quoted in Michael Grant, *Gladiators, the Bloody Truth*, p. 93.
11. *Ibid.*
12. *Ibid.*, p. 94.
13. Juvenal would have been suitably appalled by today's Women's Singles Tennis Finals at Wimbledon!
14. The story has been (incorrectly) retold in two epic films – *The Fall of the Roman Empire* and its remake, *Gladiator*.
15. Dio Cassius, *Roman History*, quoted in Michael Grant, *Gladiators, the Bloody Truth*, pp. 95–6.

Four: Thrax

1. Plutarch, *Fall of the Roman Republic (Crassus)*, trans. Rex Warner (London, Penguin, 1972), p. 122.
2. *Spartacus* (Bryna/Universal, 1960) and *Gladiator* (Dreamworks, 2000).
3. Author's translation.
4. Quoted in Stephen Wisdom, *Gladiators 100BC–AD* (Oxford, Osprey Warrior Series, 2001), p. 15. Author's translation.
5. The worldly-wise toady as played by Peter Ustinov in the Douglas film would hardly seem to fit the bill.

6. It is unknown how much security was increased at gladiatorial schools as a whole as a direct result of Spartacus' revolt.
7. Symmachus, *Letters* 2.46, quoted in Shaw, *Spartacus and the Slave Wars*, p. 50.
8. Quoted in Sarah B. Pomeroy, *Goddesses, Whores, Wives and Slaves* (London, Pimlico, 1994), p. 201.
9. Quoted in Stephen Wisdom, *Gladiators 100BC–AD* p. 18.
10. Despite a long list of theories! Pliny the Elder recommended cutting open a hairy spider and removing two little worms inside and tying them to deerskin. Aetius advocated carrying a lion's uterus in an ivory tube!
11. Juvenal, *Satires*, trans. Stephen Wisdom, *Gladiators 100BC–AD*. p. 59.
12. *Mormylos*, as in merman and mermaid, inhabitants of the sea.
13. No actual Thracian military examples have been found which resemble the helmet worn by the thrax and it may be that the design evolved from misremembered accounts of the Thracians in battle.
14. The straight sword and tiny circular shield carried by Kirk Douglas in *Spartacus* bear little relevance. They could be considered practice weapons only.
15. Plutarch, *Fall of the Roman Republic (Crassus)*, trans. Rex Warner, p. 122.
16. *Ibid.*

Five: In the Shadow of Vesuvius

1. Plutarch, *Fall of the Roman Republic (Crassus)*, trans. Rex Warner, p. 122.
2. Appian, *The Civil Wars*, quoted in Shaw, *Spartacus and the Slave Wars*, p. 140.
3. Senator J.H. Hammond, 4 March 1858, *Congressional Record*, quoted in M.J. Cohen and John Major, *History in Quotations* (London, Cassell, 2004), p. 585.
4. Victor Hugo, 2 December 1859, quoted in Cohen and Major, *History in Quotations*, p. 587.
5. Letter from Thomas Jefferson to John Holmes, 22 April 1820, *The Writings of Thomas Jefferson*, quoted in Cohen and Major, *History in Quotations*, p. 584.
6. Harriet Martineau, *Society in America* (1837), quoted in Cohen and Major, *History in Quotations*, p. 586.
7. Harriet Beecher Stowe, *Uncle Tom's Cabin* (1852).
8. *The Confessions of Nat Turner* (1831), quoted in Cohen and Major, *History in Quotations*, p. 584.
9. In an attempt to measure this, historians Lewis and Rheinhold quote figures of Roman prisoners of war – 5,000 in the war against Macedonia in 197 BC; more than that twenty years later in Illyria; up to 80,000 killed and captured in Sardinia in the same year. An estimated 150,000 Epinotes were taken in 167 BC, 60,000 in Carthage in the wars against Hannibal and nearly half a million Gauls captured by Caesar in the nine years of his Gallic Wars. Having analysed

carefully the figures given for soldier and civilian losses in the rising of Boudicca of the Iceni in AD 60, I remain highly sceptical of Roman statistics; they rarely hold water.

10. Plutarch, *Life of Cato the Elder* xxi, quoted in Lewis and Rheinhold, *Roman Civilization*, Vol. 1, pp. 243–4.
11. Cato, *On Agriculture*, preface i.ii.x, quoted in Lewis and Rheinhold, *Roman Civilization*, Vol. 1, pp. 478–9.
12. *Ibid.*, p. 478.
13. Varro, *On Landed Estates* I iv 1–2, quoted in Lewis and Rheinhold, *Roman Civilization*, Vol. 1, p. 481–3.
14. Martial, VIII 13 quoted in Ugo Enrico Paoli *Rome, Its People, Life and Customs* (London, Longmans, 1963), p. 98.
15. All translations of both accounts are by Shaw, *Spartacus and the Slave Wars*, pp. 80–94.
16. Livy (*History of Rome*) 40.19.9–10, quoted in Shaw, *Spartacus and the Slave Wars*.
17. *Ibid.*
18. Valerius Maximus, *Words and Deeds*, quoted in Shaw, *Spartacus and the Slave Wars*, p. 105.
19. Voltaire (1694–1778) used this deadly phrase in *Candide*, in which he explains in connection with the execution of Admiral Byng on the deck of his own flagship on charges of cowardice that the 'English execute an Admiral now and again, to encourage the others'.
20. Plutarch, *Sulla*, trans. Rex Warner, p. 110.
21. Orosius, *The Slave War in Sicily*, quoted in Shaw, *Spartacus and the Slave Wars*, p. 97.
22. *Ibid.*
23. Cisalpine Gaul was northern Italy south of the Alps. For the best part of four centuries it had been occupied by Celtic tribes from the north-east.
24. The *fasces* would reappear in the early twentieth century as Benito Mussolini feebly attempted to recreate the grandeur that was Rome.
25. Florus, quoted in Shaw, *Spartacus and the Slave Wars*, p. 122.
26. *Ibid.*
27. Cicero, *Against Verres*, quoted in Shaw, *Spartacus and the Slave Wars*, p. 127.

Six: The Senate and the People of Rome

1. SPQR – senatus populus que Romani, the initials carried on legionary standards.
2. Varro, *The Latin Language* v.lxxx–lxxxii, quoted in Lewis and Rheinhold, *Roman Civilization*, Vol. 1, p. 98.
3. Plutarch, *Crassus*, trans. Rex Warner, p. 123.

4. Boot wearers. The *caliga* was an army sandal made of stout, hobnailed leather. The emperor Gaius Caesar was called Caligula (little boots).
5. Not in fact the zealots, despite the biblical version.
6. Plutarch, *Lives: numa XVII*, quoted in Antony Kamm, *The Romans* (London, Routledge, 1995), p. 9.
7. Dionysius of Halicarnassus, *Roman Antiquities IV 44*, quoted in Kamm, *The Romans*, p. 10.
8. Cicero, One of the Laws III 3 quoted in Kamm, *The Romans*, p. 10.
9. Livy, *History of Rome* X 5, 6, quoted in Kamm, *The Romans*, p. 10.
10. Philip Matyszak, *Chronicle of the Roman Republic* (London, Thames & Hudson, 2003), p. 77.
11. The English socialists of the 1880s, calling themselves Fabians, took the general's name as their own, using his slow, gradual tactics to ease socialism into the fabric of society.
12. Appian, *Civil Wars 1*, Introduction, quoted in Cohen and Major, *History in Quotations*, p. 72.
13. Valleius Paterculis, *Historiae 2.2.1*, quoted in Matyszak, *Chronicle of the Roman Republic*, p. 126.
14. Plutarch, Roman *Questions* 81, quoted in Matyszak, *Chronicle of the Roman Republic*, p. 129.
15. Tiberius Gracchus quoted in Matyszak, *Chronicle of the Roman Republic*, p. 129.
16. By passing a law which insisted the commander of the army (and therefore his subordinates, including Gaius Gracchus) had to remain in the field.
17. Shakespeare's observation on the Roman way of death in *Antony and Cleopatra*. The stoicism with which famous Romans took their own lives – or had servants do it for them – is one of the most remarkable features of both the Republic and the Empire.
18. Kamm, *The Romans*, p. 34.
19. Quoted in Matyszak, *Chronicle of the Roman Republic*, p. 165.
20. Appian, *The Civil Wars I, II* quoted in Kamm, *The Romans*, pp. 38–9.

Seven: The Lowest and the Worst

1. Plutarch, *Crassus*, trans. Rex Warner, p. 123.
2. Livy, *Summaries 97*, quoted in Shaw, *Spartacus and the Slave Wars*, p. 150.
3. Matyszak, *Enemies of Rome*, p. 105.
4. Villeius Paterculis, *History of Rome 2.30.5–6*, quoted in Shaw, *Spartacus and the Slave Wars*, p. 153.
5. Orosius, *History Against the Pagans 5.24.1–8; 18–19*, quoted in Shaw, *Spartacus and the Slave Wars*, p. 152.
6. Marx and Engels, *The Communist Manifesto*, 1858.

Notes

7. Florus, *A Synopsis of Roman History* 2.8 1–14, quoted in Shaw, *Spartacus and the Slave Wars*, p. 153–4.
8. *Ibid.*
9. Deodorus Siculus, *Library of History 38/39.21*, quoted in Shaw, *Spartacus and the Slave Wars*, p. 156.
10. Appian, *Roman History 109.5 19-20*, quoted in Shaw, *Spartacus and the Slave Wars*, p. 144.
11. Tom Holland, *Rubicon* (London, Abacus, 2004), p. 145. 'Nola was besieged yet again and looted.'
12. Plutarch, *Crassus*, trans. Rex Warner, p. 123.
13. *Ibid.*
14. Sallust, *Histories Book 3*, quoted in Shaw, *Spartacus and the Slave Wars*, p. 146.
15. *Ibid.*
16. *Ibid.*
17. *Ibid.*
18. Plutarch, *Crassus*, trans. Rex Warner, p. 123.
19. Flavius Vegetius Renatus, a writer from the fourth century AD who remained the supreme military authority until the Renaissance.
20. Plutarch, *Crassus*, trans. Rex Warner, p. 123.
21. Appian, *The Civil Wars*, 1, p. 65.
22. Plutarch, *Gaius Marius*, trans. Rex Warner, p. 40.
23. *Ibid.*
24. Sallust, *Histories* Books 3 and 4, quoted in Shaw, *Spartacus and the Slave Wars*, p. 147.
25. Quintus Horatius Flaccus (65–8 BC) who became, in effect, Poet Laureate under Augustus.
26. Another name for the Social War.
27. Sallust, *Histories* Books 3 and 4, quoted in Shaw, *Spartacus and the Slave Wars*, p. 147.
28. *Ibid.*
29. Appian, *The Civil Wars*, quoted in Shaw, *Spartacus and the Slave Wars*, p. 141.
30. *Ibid.*
31. Florus, *A Synopsis of Roman History* 2.8.1-14, quoted in Shaw, *Spartacus and the Slave Wars*, p. 154.
32. Vegetius, *Epitoma rei militaris* iii, 71.
33. Caesar, *The Conquest of Gaul* (London, Penguin Classics), vii 14.
34. Appian, *Roman History*, quoted in Shaw, *Spartacus and the Slave Wars*.
35. John Peddie, *The Roman War Machine* (Stroud, Sutton, 2004).
36. Plutarch, *Crassus*, trans. Rex Warner, p. 124.
37. *Ibid.*, p. 133.
38. *Ibid.*

Eight: Running from the Field of Battle

1. Plutarch, *Crassus*, quoted in Shaw, *Spartacus and the Slave Wars*, p. 132.
2. Sallust, *Histories* Books 3 and 4, quoted in Shaw, *Spartacus and the Slave Wars*, p. 147.
3. Orosius, *History against the Pagans 5.24.1*, quoted in Shaw, *Spartacus and the Slave Wars*, p. 151.
4. Virgil, *Georgics*, quoted in J.M. Brereton, *The Horse in War* (Newton Abbot, David & Charles 1976), p. 20.
5. I still beg to differ. Has Junkelmann paired a Norman knight with his stirrups and destrier against a Roman cavalryman?
6. In the 1960 film's final battle, Kirk Douglas looks decidedly awkward as he clashes with other horsemen. His sword is simply too short and this would have left him desperately exposed.
7. Sallust, *Histories* Books 3 and 4, quoted in Shaw, *Spartacus and the Slave Wars*, p. 148.
8. The medieval longbow as used by the Welsh and the English was a far more formidable weapon because the string was pulled back to the ear and the bow itself was 6 feet long.
9. For instance, in the Second World War, ground crews of American V-52 bombers painted their bombs with phrases like 'This one's for you, Adolf'.
10. The colour white is the most distinctive at long range and the most easily seen. It was not until the invention of long-range firepower, however, that this became a serious problem. Most units of the Austrian army in 1866 wore white tunics; they were destroyed by the field-grey Prussians in weeks.
11. A very good reconstruction was worn by Stephen Boyd in *Ben-Hur*, but his was the imaginative work of MGM's props department!
12. So, although, for instance, Thor Heyerdahl's *Kon-Tiki* proved that sailing with such a craft was *possible*, it does not prove that it ever happened.
13. Tacitus, *Annales XIII*, trans. Michael Grant (London, Penguin, 1975).
14. Plutarch, *Crassus*, quoted in Sallust, *Histories* Books 3 and 4, quoted in Shaw, *Spartacus and the Slave Wars*, p. 133.
15. Appian, *The Civil Wars*, quoted in Sallust, *Histories* Books 3 and 4, quoted in Shaw, *Spartacus and the Slave Wars*, p. 141.
16. *Ibid.*
17. Matyszak, *Enemies of Rome*, p. 110.
18. Appian, *The Civil Wars*, quoted in Shaw, *Spartacus and the Slave Wars*, p. 141.
19. Pliny, *Natural History 23.3.10–11*, quoted in Martin Goodman, *The Roman World* (London, Routledge, 1997), p. 293.
20. Plutarch, *Crassus*, quoted in Shaw, *Spartacus and the Slave Wars*, p. 124.

Notes

Nine: Marcus Licinius Crassus

1. Plutarch, *Crassus*, trans. Rex Warner, p. 144.
2. *Ibid.*, p. 144.
3. *Ibid.*
4. *Ibid.*
5. *Ibid.*
6. *Ibid.*, p. 119.
7. *Ibid.*, p. 144.
8. *Ibid.*
9. *Ibid.*
10. *Ibid.*
11. *Ibid.*
12. *Ibid.*, p. 155.
13. *Ibid.*
14. *Ibid.*, p. 116.
15. *Ibid.*
16. Holland, *Rubicon*, p. 139.
17. Plutarch, *Crassus*, trans. Rex Warner, p. 116.
18. Marcus Aemilius Lepidus was ever the 'third man' in the triumvirate of himself, Caesar and Pompey. Consul and Pontifex Maximus at various times, he eventually died a prisoner of Rome's first emperor, Augustus, in 13 BC.
19. Plutarch, *Crassus*, trans. Rex Warner, p. 121.
20. *Ibid.*, p. 122.
21. Appian, *The Civil Wars*, quoted in Shaw, *Spartacus and the Slave Wars*, p. 142.
22. Plutarch, *Crassus*, quoted in Shaw, *Spartacus and the Slave Wars*, p. 124. Shaw believes this to be a mistake on Plutarch's part. If the chronicler meant Picentia, south of Rome, that would make more geographical sense.
23. Plutarch, *Crassus*, trans. Rex Warner, p. 124.
24. *Ibid.*, p. 125.
25. Appian, *The Civil Wars*, trans. Rex Warner, p. 66.
26. Plutarch, *Crassus*, trans. Rex Warner, p. 125.
27. *Ibid.*
28. Cicero, *Against Verres 2.5.5-6*, quoted in Shaw, *Spartacus and the Slave Wars*, p. 159.
29. Florus, *A Synopsis of Roman History 2.8.1-14*, quoted in Shaw, *Spartacus and the Slave Wars*, p. 155.
30. Cicero, *Against Verres 2.5.5-6*, quoted in Shaw, *Spartacus and the Slave Wars*, p. 159.
31. *Ibid.*, pp. 159–61.
32. Plutarch, *Crassus*, trans. Rex Warner, p. 125.
33. *Ibid.*

34. Appian, *The Civil Wars*, quoted in Shaw, *Spartacus and the Slave Wars*, p. 142.
35. *Ibid.*
36. *Ibid.*

Ten: Gnaeus Pompeius Magnus

1. Plutarch, *Crassus*, trans. Rex Warner, p. 125.
2. I have raised the possibility elsewhere that Caesar and Spartacus were born in the same year. Caesar was twenty-seven when the Third Slave War began, older than Pompey and certainly old enough for a full command. He may have served with Crassus, although there is no mention of him in any ancient text. In 73 BC he became Pontifex Maximus and his military career was yet to blossom.
3. Plutarch, *Pompey*, trans. Rex Warner, p. 158.
4. *Ibid.*, p. 159.
5. *Ibid.*
6. The expression came from the legend of the Sabine Women, taken by force by respectable Romans who seemed unaccountably devoid of females in their own city. Some herdsmen grabbed a particularly gorgeous girl and claimed that they were taking her as a bride for Talasinus, a prominent Roman whose name they had just made up. The name caught on.
7. Plutarch, *Pompey*, trans. Rex Warner, p. 162.
8. Appian says one, Pliny three.
9. Marx to Engels, 27 February 1861. *Marx–Engels Collected Works Vol. 41*, quoted in Shaw, *Spartacus and the Slave Wars*, p. 15.
10. Plutarch, *Pompey*, trans. Rex Warner, p. 164.
11. *Ibid.*, p. 166.
12. *Ibid.*, p. 171.
13. *Ibid.*, p. 172.
14. *Ibid.*, p. 174.
15. Plutarch, *Crassus*, quoted in Shaw, *Spartacus and the Slave Wars*, p. 135.
16. Frontius, *Strategies 1.7.6*, quoted in Shaw, *Spartacus and the Slave Wars*, p. 157.
17. Plutarch, *Crassus*, trans. Rex Warner, p. 126.
18. Sallust, *Histories* Books 3 and 4, quoted in Shaw, *Spartacus and the Slave Wars*, p. 149.
19. Frontius, *Strategies 1.7.6*, quoted in Shaw, *Spartacus and the Slave Wars*, p. 157.
20. Plutarch, *Crassus*, trans. Rex Warner, p. 126.
21. *Ibid.*
22. Horace, *Satires*, quoted in *The Mammoth Book of Ancient Rome*, ed. John E. Lewis, p. 129.
23. Appian, *The Civil Wars*, trans. John Carter (London, Penguin, 1975), p. 67.
24. Plutarch, *Crassus*, trans. Rex Warner, p. 127.

25. Appian, *The Civil Wars*, trans. John Carter, p. 67.
26. *Ibid.*
27. Plutarch, *Crassus*, trans. Rex Warner, p. 127.
28. Florus, quoted in Matyszak, *Enemies of Rome*, p. 113.
29. Plutarch, *Crassus*, trans. Rex Warner, p. 127.
30. Appian, *The Civil Wars*, trans. John Carter, p. 67.
31. Plutarch, *Pompey*, trans. Rex Warner, p. 178.
32. Plutarch, *Crassus*, trans. Rex Warner, p. 138.
33. *Ibid.*, p. 127.
34. Aulus Gellius, *Attic Nights 5.6.20–23*, quoted in Shaw, *Spartacus and the Slave Wars*, p. 164.
35. George Riley Scott, *A History of Torture* (Twickenham, Senate Press, 1993 reprint), p. 153.
36. *Ibid.*

Eleven: The Legend of Spartacus

1. Quoted in Goldsworthy, *The Complete Roman Army*, p. 117.
2. Appian, *The Civil Wars*, trans. John Carter, p. 68.
3. Plutarch, *Crassus*, trans. Rex Warner, p. 128.
4. *Ibid.*
5. Suetonius, *Life of Augustus 3.1*, quoted in Shaw, *Spartacus and the Slave Wars*, p. 165.
6. Livy, *Summaries 96*, quoted in Shaw, *Spartacus and the Slave Wars*, p. 150.
7. Plutarch, *Caesar*, trans. Rex Warner, p. 302.
8. Plutarch, *Pompey*, trans. Rex Warner, p. 241.
9. *Ibid.*
10. Modern variations have turned this into a 'parting shot', which conveys the same rather sneaky tactic without acknowledging its origin.
11. Plutarch, *Crassus*, trans. Rex Warner, p. 148.
12. *Ibid.*, p. 154.
13. *Ibid.*, p. 155.
14. Jean-Jacques Rousseau, *Du Contrat Social*, Book 1 Chapter 1, 1762.
15. Voltaire, *Oeuvres 53* Vol. 9 of *Correspondances Générales* 461–3 (Letter No. 283, April 1769).
16. Saurin's 'Introduction to Spartacus', quoted in Shaw, *Spartacus and the Slave Wars*, p. 20.
17. Richard Harris, *A Young Dramatist's Diary: The Secret Records of R.M. Birch* (Library Chronicle, University of Pennsylvania, 25, 1959), pp. 16–17.
18. V.I. Lenin, *The State*, from *Collected Works 29* (Moscow, 1965).
19. Shaw, *Spartacus and the Slave Wars*, p. 23.
20. Matyszak, *Enemies of Rome*, p. 114.

Select Bibliography

Appian, *The Civil Wars* (trans. John Carter), London, Penguin 1996

Archibald, Z.H., *The Odrysian Kingdom of Thrace: Orpheus Unmasked*, Oxford University Press 1998

Auguet, Roland, *Cruelty and Civilization: The Roman Games*, London, Routledge 1972

Barker, Phil, *The Armies and Enemies of Imperial Rome*, Worthing, War Games Research Group 1981

Barraclough, Geoffrey (ed.), *Times History of the World Atlas*, London, Times Books 1999

Baxter, John, *Stanley Kubrick: A Biography*, London, HarperCollins 1998

Bennett, Matthew, *The Hutchinson Dictionary of Ancient and Medieval Warfare*, Oxford, Helicon 1998

Bradley, Keith R., *Slavery and Rebellion in the Roman World*, Bloomington, IN, Indiana University Press 1998

Brereton, J.M., *The Horse in War*, Newton Abbott, David & Charles 1976

Campbell, Duncan B., *Greek And Roman Artillery*, Oxford, Osprey 2003

Carey, Ernest (trans.) Dio Cassius, *Roman History*, Cambridge, MA, Harvard University Press 1925

Carman, John and Harding, Anthony, *Ancient Warfare*, Stroud, Sutton 1999

Carr-Gomm, Philip and Carr-Gomm, Stephanie, *The Druid Animal Oracle*, Rochester, Grange Books 1994

Cohen, M.J. and Major, John, *History in Quotations*, London, Cassell 2004

Cotterell, Arthur, *The Encyclopedia of Mythology*, London, Lorenz Books 1999

Cunliffe, Barry, *Rome and Her Empire*, London, BCA 1994

De Caro, Stefano (ed.), *National Archaeological Museum Of Naples*, Naples 1999

Douglas, Kirk, *The Ragman's Son: An Autobiography*, London, Simon & Schuster 1988

Drewery, Ian, *Times History of War*, London, HarperCollins 2000

Fol, Alexander and Marazov, Ivan, *Thrace and the Thracians*, New York, St Martin's Press 1977

Fraser, George MacDonald, *The Hollywood History of the World*, London, Michael Joseph 1988

Select Bibliography

Gardner, Jane and Wiedenann, Thomas, *The Roman Household: A Source Book*, London, Routledge 1991

Goldsworthy, Adrian, *Roman Warfare*, London, Cassell 2000

——, *In the Name of Rome*, London, Phoenix 2003

——, *The Complete Roman Army*, London, Thames & Hudson 2003

Goodman, Martin, *The Roman World*, London, Routledge 1997

Grant, Michael, *Gladiators: The Bloody Truth*, London, Penguin 1971

Graves, Robert, *Larousse Encyclopaedia of Mythology*, London, Paul Hamlyn 1960

Hazel, John, *Who's Who in the Roman World*, London, Routledge 2001

Holland, Tom, *Rubicon*, London, Abacus 2003

Jakobelli, Luciana, *Gladiators At Pompeii*, Rome, L'Erma Bretschneider 2003

Kamm, Antony, *The Romans*, London, Routledge 1995

Laffont, Robert, *A History of Rome and the Romans*, London, Macdonald 1962

Lewis, Jon E., *The Mammoth Book of How it Happened in Ancient Rome*, London, Robinson 2003

Lewis, Naphtali and Reinhold, Meyer, *Roman Civilization Vols 1 And 2*, New York, Columbia University Press 1990

Margulies, Dan, *Spartacus: The Illustrated Story of the Motion Picture Production*, London, Classics Illustrated 1960

Matthews, Rupert, *The Age of the Gladiators*, Wigston, Arcturus Publishing 2003

Matyszak, Philip, *Chronicle of the Roman Republic*, London, Thames & Hudson 2003

——, *The Enemies of Rome*, London, Thames & Hudson 2004

Mellersh, H.E.L., *The Hutchinson Chronology of World History: Vol 1 The Ancient and Medieval World*, Oxford, Helicon 1999

Paoli, Ugo Enrico, *Rome: Its People, Life And Customs*, London, Longmans Green & Co. 1963

Pearson, Mike Parker, *The Archaeology of Death and Burial*, Stroud, Sutton 1999

Peddie, John, *The Roman War Machine*, Stroud, Sutton 2004

Peterson, Daniel, *The Roman Legions Recreated in Colour Photographs*, Marlborough, Crowood Press 1992

Plutarch, *Fall Of The Roman Republic* (trans. Rex Warner, London), Penguin 1972

Pomeroy, Sarah, *Goddesses, Whores, Wives and Slaves*, London, Pimlico 1975

Santosuosso, Antonio, *Storming the Heavens*, London, Pimlico 2004

Scarre, Chris, *Historical Atlas of Ancient Rome*, London, Penguin 1995

Scott, George Riley, *A History Of Torture*, London, Senate Press 1995

Sekunda, Nicholas, *Caesar's Legions*, Oxford, Osprey 2000

Shaw, Brent D., *Spartacus and the Slave Wars*, Boston, Bedford/St Martin's 2001

Sifakis, Carl, *Encyclopaedia of Assassinations*, London, Headline 1993

Smart, Ted, *Times Atlas of the World*, London, Times Books 2000

Southern, Pat, *Pompey the Great*, Stroud, Tempus 2002

Select Bibliography

Twiss, Miranda, *The Most Evil Men and Women in History*, London, Michael O'Mara 2002

Webber, Christopher, *The Thracians*, Oxford, Osprey Men-at-Arms Series 2001

Whatmough, Joshua, *The Foundations of Roman Italy*, London, Methuen 1937

Williams, Derek, *Romans And Barbarians*, New York, St Martin's Press 1998

Windrow, Martin, *Warriors and Warlords: The Art of Angus McBride*, Oxford, Osprey 2002

Wisdom, Stephen, *Gladiators*, Oxford, Osprey Warrior Series 2001

Video/DVD

Spartacus Special Edition 2004 Universal
True Gladiator Atlantic Productions 2003

Periodicals

New Scientist January 2005

Index